More
What
Did They Mean
By That?

A Dictionary of
Historical and Genealogical Terms
Old and New

Paul Drake, J.D.

HERITAGE BOOKS
2023

HERITAGE BOOKS

AN IMPRINT OF HERITAGE BOOKS, INC.

Books, CDs, and more—Worldwide

For our listing of thousands of titles see our website
at
www.HeritageBooks.com

Published 2023 by
HERITAGE BOOKS, INC.
Publishing Division
5810 Ruatan Street
Berwyn Heights, MD 20740

International Standard Book Number
Paperbound: 978-0-7884-3571-3

Dedication

This effort is respectfully dedicated to those of my students and friends who asked for the meaning of some word or term, also to my friends who took the time to send to me those expressions that they thought might have a place here, and to those folks who do not know me from Shakespeare's goat, yet sent words hoping to thereby further render a tad easier the research of us all.

Heritage Books by Paul Drake:

CD: Now in Our Fourth Century: Some American Families: A Documentary and
Pictorial History of More Than Twenty Families Who Were Well Settled
in the American Colonies Before the Year 1700

Genealogy: How to Find Your Ancestors, Revised Edition
Paul Drake, J.D. and Margaret Grove Driskill

In Search of Family History: A Starting Place

Missing Pieces: How to Find Birth Parents and Adopted Children
A Search and Reunion Guidebook
Paul Drake and Beth Sherrill

More What Did They Mean by That?

Now in Our Fourth Century: Some American Families

What Did They Mean By That? A Dictionary of Historical
and Genealogical Terms, Old and New

What Did They Mean By That? A Dictionary of Historical
Terms for Genealogists: Some More Words Volume 2

What Did They Mean by That? A Dictionary of Historical Terms for Genealogists

You Ought to Write All That Down: A Guide to Organizing
and Writing Genealogical Narrative

You Ought to Write All That Down: A Guide to Organizing
and Writing Genealogical Narrative - Revised Edition

Contents

List of Illustrations vii

Acknowledgments ix

Introduction xi

Abbreviations: Censuses, genealogy, government, military, and generally.. xiii

Abbreviations of commonly seen societies, sororities, fraternities and organizations xxvii

Dictionary..1

List of Illustrations

Figure 1. An 1878 certificate for a War of 1812 "Widow's Pension" from the Bureau of Pensions (*BP*) xxiii

Figure 2. Civil War Lt. Harpster of Ohio (*Lt.*) xxiv

Figure 3. Sgt. James Messenger, 14th Ohio, Spanish-American War (*Sgt.*) xv

Figure 4. A receipt dated 1841 showing *accord and satisfaction* of a promissory note 3

Figure 5. Before birth certificates, *affiant* Minnie Schwilk swears to a birth in 1867 6

Figure 6. A "card" from the National Archives and Records Administration showing Hill Freeburn as an *artificer* in the Continental Line 12

Figure 7. A telegrapher and stationkeeper at Arlington, Ohio in 1895 (*cipher*) 30

Figure 8. 1868 *collotype* of the great-great grandmother of Mrs. Kennedy of Virginia 33

Figure 9. 1757 list of tithables by Surry County, Virginia *constable*, Lazarus Drake 38

Figure 10. Farmer Daniel Carner and his wife Mary Martin Carner dressed for the photographer in 1875 (*costs and prices in 1850, some*) 42

Figure 11. Secret *elopement* of young people in 1892 57

Figure 12. 1765 teamster pay order for a teamster's "waggoning" with two horses and wagons (*ferriage*) 65

Figure 13. 1774 order for service of summons from a court to a sheriff (*fined nisi*) 66

Figure 14. 1878 map showing sections, townships, etc., and several "forties" (*forty, a*) 70

Figure 15. "Union" schoolhouse for all grades in Upper Sandusky, Ohio (*grammar school*) 75

Figure 16. 1869 headstone revealing "Feb. 31" as a woman's date of death (*gravestone symbols and carvings*) 76

Figure 17. 1782 certificate by a *hay-weigher* as to the nineteen-ton load of a teamster 82

Figure 18. Order of a Tennessee court that a deposition be taken (*lawsuits, common*) 99

Figure 19. Attorney Boggs signs a 1783 itemized bill of sheriff's costs (*lawsuits, common*) 100

Figure 20. Union Pacific *locomotive* #23 and crew, c.1870....105

Figure 21. A mock-up of a French *locomotive* of the First World War. Photo courtesy of Mrs. Diane Peterson. 106

Figure 22. Andrew Jackson signs treason charge against a man named Hankins (*misprision of treason*) 113

Figure 23. Tennessee promissory note of 1857 (*non fecit*) 121

Figure 24. An 1870s newspaper ad showing *nostrums* and patent medicines for sale..122

Figure 25. *Nonagenarian* Henry T. Cline, 1797-1894 (*octogenarian, nonagenarian, etc.*)...................................127

Figure 26. 1793 Pennsylvania survey for a patent for 125 acres (*poleman*) 142

Figure 27. 1763 order to a sheriff by a Pennsylvania *prothonotary* in the name of George III 149

Figure 28. Union Depot *railroad hotel* 153

Figure 29. 1870 sheriff endorses an order given him, "Not in my Bailiwick" (*sheriffwicke*) 163

Figure 30. Three very pretty girls look out from a *silver gelatin print* of 1875..164

Figure 31. Early sheriff affirms that he has jailed a person by order of a court (*warrant*) 189

Acknowledgments

For everything (and there was MUCH), I do sincerely thank my fine children, Paul R., Diane Drake Haskins, and Cheryl Drake Bater, as well as Marty and Beth. I am no less grateful to Barb, Carolyn, Charlotte, Colleen, Debbie, Diane, Don, Donna, Jacqui, Jane, Margaret, Myron, Pat, Ray, Teresa, Thelma and Weynette for the much needed and appreciated assistance and encouragement here and in past years. Finally, I do so much thank Roxanne, Paul R., Craig, Leslie and James, without whom there would be no such book.

Paul Drake, J.D.
March 2005

Introduction

Every week that has come and gone across the handful of years since publication of the first volume of *What Did They Mean By That?* has brought additional questions or confusion over the words, terms or expressions of our ancestors. Just as those early terms have again come to the fore, so too have we seen a need for new sounds as a result of technology, invention, and imagination.

Among the hundreds, perhaps thousands, of such newly invented terms are the likes of "clickable," "pop-ups," "cybercitizen," "g-commerce," "generation zero," "gigabyte," "blog" and "imo." Similarly, many words heard and written daily throughout the twentieth century have gone the way of "steam tractor." Unless you are an antique collector or are lost in the 1960s, you no longer need the terms "snafu," "typewriter," "LP record," "curb feeler," "record player," "hi-fi," "sky-scraper," "dork," "groovy" and "streamliner."

Our language evolves just as sure as we come to our birthdays and anniversaries. Still, for genealogy and history buffs and for the curious, an understanding of the language of those who went before us will always be a requisite to study. It is to that end that here again we have set forth a few of the hundreds of thousands of words once used that likely will not again be needed in our headlong rush into the future.

The reader will come upon other terms of the past, and will watch and listen as new sounds come upon the scene. I would suggest that you make note of those; as here, one day your grandchildren will smile at some of what you now call "our language."

Paul Drake, J.D.

Abbreviations
Censuses, genealogy, government, military, and generally:

£-pound, English
S£-pound Sterling, English, silver
1Lt-first lieutenant
2Lt or *Lt2*-second lieutenant
a.a.r-against all risks
a.-about, age, acre, ante or aunt
als. Exon-alius execution
a.c-attested copy, account current
a.k.a-also known as
a.l.s-autographed letter signed
a.o-account of
a.w.c. or *a.w.c-admon.* or *adwwa*-
   letters of administration… or
   administration with will and/or
   codicil annexed
a-about
AASP-American Antiquarian
   Society Proceedings
A-aunt
ab-about
abb.-abbey
abbr-abbreviation
age-age
abd.-abdicated
Abp.-archbishop
abr-abridged, abridgment
abs. or *abstr*-abstract
abt-about
ac-acre
acad-academy
acc-according to
acco-account
accom-accompanied
accu-accurate
ackd-acknowledged
actg-acting
Ad.Cl-adopted child
Ad.D-adopted daughter
Ad.Gcl-adopted grandchild
Ad.S adopted son

Ad.S-apprentice
AD-Latin, *anno Domini*
Ad-adopted
AdCl-adopted child
AdD-adopted daughter
adj-adjoining, adjutant, adjourned
adjc-adjacent
adm-admission, admitted
admin., adminr –administration
admnr-administrator
admon or *adwwa.*-letters of
   administration or
   administration with will and/or
   codicil annexed
Admon-letters of administration
admr-administration
AdS-adopted son
af. or *affi*-affidavit
aft-after
AL-alien
ald-alderman
alleg-allegiance
als-alias
anc-ancestry, ancestor, or ancient
annot-annotated
ano-another
anon-anonymous
ant-antiquary, antonym
ante-ante
antiq or *ant*-antiquary, antiquities,
   antiquity, or antiquarian
AOP-American Order of Pioneers
Ap-apprentice
App. Div-appellate division
app-apprentice, approximately,
   appendix or appointed
App-Div-appellate division
appr-appraisment
apprd-apprised, appeared
approx-approximately

apptd-appointed
appx-appendix
ar. co. or *artly*-artillery company, artillery
arr-arrived
ascert-ascertain(ed)
asgd-assigned
asr-assessor
assn. or *assoc*-association
asso-associated or associate
Asst-assistant
atty-attorney
aud-auditor
au-gold
AWOL-absent without leave
B-brother
B Gen-Brigadier General
b.d-or *bdt*-birth date
B.Girl or *B.Boy*-Bound Girl or Boy
b.i.l-or *Bl*-brother-in-law
B.M-Bench Mark or British Museum
b.o.t.p-both of this parish
B.S-in court records, bill of sale
B.T-Bishop's Transcripts
B; *b*-born, birth
ba-bachelor
bach-or *batch*-bachelor
bapt-or *bap*-baptized or baptism
Bar-Bartender
B-Bail Bond
B-Black
BBoy-bound boy
B-Brother
bcer-birth certificate
BCG-Board for Certification of Genealogists
bd-bound, buried
bec-because, became
bef-before
bet.-between
BGirl-bound girl

BIA-Bureau of Indian Affairs
biog-biography
bish-bishop
Bk-barracks
bks-books
bl-bibliography
BL-brother-in-law
BLM-Bureau of Land Management
BLW-Bounty Land Warrant
bndsmn-bondsman
Bo or *Bdr*-boarder
Bp, bpt, bpl-baptized, baptism, birthplace
BP-Bureau of Pensions
br or *bro*-brother
Br-British
bro-i-l-brother-in-law
Bu-butler
bur-or *bu*-buried
C of A-coat of arms
c.–cousin or circa
c.r-church report
c.s-copy signed
C.W.O.-chief warrant officer
Cap or *Capt*-captain, captured
capv-captivity
catal-catalogue
cath-cathedral
CC-county clerk, county court, county commissioner, company commander
C-cousin
CCP-Court of Common Pleas
CDIB-certified degree of Indian blood
cem-cemetery
cen or *cens*-census
cent-century
cer or *cert*-certificate
cf-confer, conferred
CG-Certified Genealogist
ch/o-child of

Cha-chamber maid
chan-chancery
ch-child, children, church, chief, chaplain
Ch-Chinese
CH-court house
chldn-or *chn*-children
Christ-Christian
chr-or *chris*-christened
Cil-cousin-in-law
cir-circa
cir-ct- circuit court
civ-civil
CJ-county judge
Cl-child
clk.-clerk
Cmdr or *Cdr*-commander
Cmmdr-commodore
Co company
Co or *coty*-county
Coa-coachman
CO-commanding officer, colonial office
co-company
cod-codicil
Col-colonel
col-colony, colonel
coll-college, collection
com-commissioner, commander, commentary, committee, common, commoner, communicate, companion
Comdr-commodore
comm.-commissioners
comp-company
Comp-compatriot
confer-conferred
conject-conjecture
cont-continued
contr or *k/*-contract
Cook-cook
corp-corporal or corporation
corps-army corps

couns-counsellor
cous-cousin
coven or *covnt* or *cnvt*-covenant
Cpl-corporal
CPO-chief petty officer
CRA-church records archives
crim con-criminal conversation
Crnt-coronet
crspd-correspond or correspondence
CSA-Confederate States of America
csn-cousin, cousins
ct-court, citation, or county
CW-Civil War or church warden
CWT-hundredweight, 112 lbs.
d-& coh-daughter and coheiress
d-& h-daughter and heiress
d.s.p (*descessit sine prole*)-died without issue
d.s.p.m (*descessit sine prole mascula*)-died without male issue
d.s-document signed, died single
d.y-died young
DAB-Dictionary of American Biography
DA-District Attorney
da-or *dau*-daughter or day
dau-i-l-daughter-in-law
daus-daughters
DB or *D.B*-deed book
DB-Domesday Book
Dboy-drummer boy
DC-District of Columbia, deputy clerk, deputy county clerk
D-daughter
d-died, death, pence, or daughter
d'd-or decd-deceased
dea or *deac*-deacon
decessit sin prole (*dsp*)-died without issue
decis-decision

dec-or *dec'd*-deceased
degr-degree
dem-demised
dep-deputy, depot
dept-department
desc-descendant
devis-devise, devised
dil-or *d-i-l*-daughter-in-law
dio-diocese
discip-discipline
dis-discharge
dist-district
div-division, divided, divorced,
  divinity
Dla-day laborer
DL-daughter-in-law
doc or *docum*-document
do-daughter of
do-ditto
dom-domestic
Dom-domestic
dpl-place of death
dr-doctor, dram
dsct or *desc*-descendant
ds-daughters
dt-date
dto-ditto
dtr-daughter
dt's-delirium tremens
dum or *d-um*-died unmarried
Dw-dish washer
E.D-enumeration district
e.g-example given
ed-edited, edition, or editor
educ-education
E-east or eastern
emp-employee
en-engineer
Eng-England
ens-ensign
ensu-ensuing
establ-establishment
estd or *est*-estimated

est-estate, established
et vir-and husband
etc-et cetera meaning and so forth
exc-except, excellency, excepted,
  or exchange
exctx.–executrix
exec or *exor* or *exr*-executor
exox or *exx*-executrix
exs-executors
F or *f*-father, female, folio, farm
F.A-field artillery
F.B-family Bible
F.R.-full release (concluding
  parole)
f.e or *e.g.*-for example
f.m-free mulatto
f.n-free Negro
Fa.H-farm hand
Fa.L-farm laborer
fa-father
FaH-farm hand
fam-family or families
FARC-Federal Archives and
  Records Centers (NARA)
father-in-l or *f.i.l*-father-in-law
FaW-farm worker
FB-foster brother
FF-foster father
ff-pages following, foster father
FF's-first families
FGRA-Family Group Record
  Archives
FGS-Federation of Genealogical
  Societies
FHC-Family History Center
FHL-Family History Library
Fi-fireman
Fil or *f.inl* or *FL*-father-in-law
First C-first cousin
FL-father-in-law
fl-flourished
FM-foster mother
Fo.B-foster brother

xvi

Fo.S-foster son
Fo.Si, fsi-foster sister
foll-following, followed
freem-freeman or freemen
FR-Family Registry
ft-foot or fort
G.B-Great Britain
g.r-grave record
g.s-grave stone
GA-great aunt or grand aunt
gch-grandchildren
Gcl-grandchild
GD-granddaughter
Gdn al–guardian *at litem* (at law)
gdn-guardian
GEDCOM-Genealogical Data
   Communication
Gen-general
Gf-grandfather
GF-grandfather
GGF-great grandfather
GGGF, GGGM-great-great-
   grandfather or mother, etc.;
   one (1) "great" per generation
GGM-great grandmother
g-grand or great
giv-given, giving
GLC-Genealogical Library
   Catalog
GLO-General Land Office
gm-grandmother
Gn-grandnephew (or great
   nephew)
Gni-grandniece (or great niece)
God Cl-god child
godf-godfather
godm-godmother
Go-governess
GPAI-Genealogical Periodical
   Annual Index
gp-grandparent(s)
gr-grand, great, rarely "grant"
grs-or *gs*-or *GS*-grandson

Gs-grandson
Gt-Br-Great Britain
Gua or *Grdn*-guardian
GU-great uncle
H.Gi-hired girl
H.H-hired hand
H.Maid-housemaid
H.Si-half sister
Hb-half brother
hdqrs-headquarters
He-herder
HEIC-Honourable East India
   Company
her-heraldry
Hh-hired hand
h-husband, heir, or heiress
hims-himself
hist-historian
Hist-History
Hk-housekeeper
HM-His or Her Majesty or hired
   man
HMS-Her (or His) Majesty's
   Service or Ship
Hon dis-honorably discharged
hon-honorable
honor-honorary
Hsb-husband
Hsv-house servant
hund-hundred
Hw-household worker
i.e.-against all risks
ibid-ibidem, same reference as last
   above written
Id-same reference as the
   immediately preceding "ibid"
IGI-International Genealogical
   Index
ign-ignorant
I-inmate
illus-illustrated
imp-importation or imported
In-American Indian

inc-incorporated, incomplete
incl-included or inclusive
IND.S.C-Indian Survivors' Certificates
Ind-Indian(s)
*Ind-T-*or *Ind-Ter-*Indian Territory
Ind-W.C-Indian Widow's Certificate
inf-infant or infantry
info-information
inhab.-inhabitant
inh-inherited
Inm-Inmate
inq-inquest or inquiry
ins-insert
inst-institute or institution
int-an interest or interred
inv or *invt* –inventory
ISBN–International Standard Book Number
JAG– Judge Advocate General
JA-Judge Advocate
JNH-Journal of Negro History
Jp-Japanese
JP-Justice of the Peace
Jr-Junior
jud-or *judic*-judicial
junr-junior
jur-"jurat," a certification that a document was acknowledged or written by the person whose signature appears
k.-killed
kn-known
K.B.-King's Bench
K.C.-King's Counsel
Knt-or *KT*-knight
l.e-local elder in a church
l.p-said to be a local preacher
la, La or *labr*-laborer
Lat-Latin
Lau-launderer
LBC-Letter Book Copy

lb-pound
LC-Library of Congress
LCpl-lance corporal
ld-land
ldr-leader
LDS-Chuch of Jesus Christ of Latter-day Saints
Li or *liv*-lived, living
lib-library
lic-license
lieut-lieutenant
liv abt-lived about
l-license or lodger
ll-lines
L-lodger
lnd-land
LS-Latin, *locus siglii* (location of seal)
Lt Cmdr or *Lt. Cdr*-lieutenant commander
Lt Col-lieutenant colonel
Lt Gen-lieutenant general
ltd-limited
Lt-lieutenant
m.bn-marriage banns
m.h.-meeting house
m.i-monument inscription
m.o.-mustered out
m/1, m/2, etc-married first, married second, etc.
mag-magistrate
Maid-maid
Maj Gen-major general
Maj-an officer, a military major
Man or *Mgr*-manager
mat-maternal
Mat-matron
MB-minute book
MCC-Microfilm Card Catalog
MCD-Municipal Civil District
MCt-municipal court
MD-Doctor of Medicine
md-married

mem-member
ment-mentioned
messrs-plural of mister
Mex-S.C-Mexican Survivors'
Certificates
Mex-S.O-Mexican Survivor's
Originals
Mex-W.C-Mexican Widows'
Certificate
MGH-Middle High German
MG-Minister of the Gospel
MIA-missing in action
mil or *milit*-military
mi-mile, miles
M-in-l, MIL or *ML*-mother-in-law
min-minister
MLG-Middle Low German
MLW-military land warrant
mm or *mmo*- membership,
memorial, memoir
MM-Monthly Meeting of Society
of Friends (Quakers)
m-month, male, mother; rarely:
married, marriage
M-Mother
mo-month or mother
mors-death
*mov-*or *mvd*-moved
MQ-Mayflower Quarterly
Mr.-Mister
Mrs.-Mistress
ms-a woman, usually divorced or
who prefers an identity other
than Miss or Mrs.
MSgt-master sergeant
Mss, ms-manuscript(s)
mtg-meeting or mortgage
Mu-mulatto
my/d-my daughter
my/s-my son
n.d-no date
N.E-New England, North East
n.-nephew

n.p-no place
N.W-North West
n.x.n-no Christian name
NA-Native American or National
Archives
NARA- National Archives and
Records Administration
nam-named
NA-naturalized
NARS-National Archives and
Record Service
nat-Latin, *natus*, birth, son,
offspring
NEHGR-New England Historic
Genealogical Register
NEH-National Endowment for the
Humanities
neph-i-l-nephew-in-law
neph-nephew
nfi-no further information
nfk-nothing further known
NHPRC-National Historical
Publications and Records
Commission
Ni-niece
nmed-named
NMI-no middle initial
nm-name
NMN-no middle name
N-negro, north, or nephew
not-noted
NP-notary public
nr-none or not recorded,
naturalized
NS-New Style date (after 1752) or
Nova Scotia
NUCMC-National Union Catalog
of Manuscript Collections
nunc-nuncupative
Nu-nurse
NWC-Navy Widow's Certificate
NW-Terr-North West Territory
O or *Ofcr*-officer

O.B-order book
o.c-only child
O.E-Old England, Old English
o.p and *o.o.p*-out of print
o.t.p-of this parish
obit or *obit*-obituary
ob-obit
offor and *offic*-official
OM-organized militia
o-oath, officer
ord-ordained, ordinance, order and
 ordinary
org-organization
orig-origin, original
OS-Old Style date (before 1752)
Ot-all others
p.a-power of attorney
P.M., p.m.-Post Meridian, Prime
 Minister, afternoon, post
 mortem, after death, and police
 magistrate
P.O-post office
p.r-parish record
P.R-parish register
Pa and *P/N* –partner and
 partnership
Pa or *Prtn*-partner
pam-pamphlet
PA-naturalization application
 pending
par-parentage, parents
par-parish, parent, parents
pat pend-patent pending
pat-patent, patented, paternal
pat-patient
pchd-purchased
peo-people
PE-presiding elder
Perhundred, phundred-a
 hundredweight
Pers prop-personal property
petitn-pet-petition
petr-petitioner

PFC-private first class
Phys, ph-physician
PJP-Probate Judge of the Peace(?)
PLB-Poor Law Board
plt-plantiff
PO1-petty officer first class
PO2-petty officer second class
PO3-petty officer third class
POA-power of attorney
POE-port of entry
PO-petty officer
Por-porter
p-page or pence
PPA-per power of attorney
P-patient
pp-pages
preced-preceding
Pri-principal
prob-probable
prop-property
pro-probate
propr-proprietor(s)
PRO-Public Record Office
 (London)
provis-provision
Pr-prisoner
pr-proved, proven, probate, and
 prisoner
Prv and *Pvt*-Private
ptf-plaintiff
pt-point or port or pint
public records
pub-public, published, publisher,
 or publication
Pu-pupil
pvt-private
pymt-payment
q-Latin *quarto*, a book in which every
 sheet twice doubled makes four
 leaves, an oversize book
Q.B.-Queen's Bench
Q.C.-Queen's Counsel
R Admrl-rear admiral
R.C-Roman Catholic

rat-rated
rcdr-recorder
rcpt-receipt
RD-release of dower
rec-record
Reg-Gen-registrar general
reg-register or regulation
rel-relative
ren-renunciation
repl-replaced or replacement
rep-report, representative, or
  reprint(ed)
repud-repudiated
re-regarding
res-research, residence or resides
ret-retired
Rev War-American Revolution
Rev-reverend
RG-Registered Genealogist
Rgstr-registrar
rinq-relinquished
RIP-Latin, *requiescat in pace*, rest
  in peace
Rom-Roman
RR, rr-railroad
R-range or river
r-rector, river or road
R-roomer
S, s-son or shilling
S.E-southeast
s.p.l-Latin, *sine prole legitima*,
  without legitimate offspring
s.p.m-Latin, *sine prole mascula*,
  without male offspring
s.p.-Latin, *sine prole*, without
  offspring
s/o-son of
sal-saleslady
s-and h-son and heir
sa-sailor
SASE-self-addressed stamped
  envelope
SA-step-aunt

SBL-stepbrother-in-law
Sb-step Brother
scl-step child
SDA-Seventh Day Adventists
sd-said, a legal term
Sd-step-daughter
Se or *Svt*-servant
sec-second, secretary, section,
  sector or security
serg-sergeant
serv-service or servant
se-servant
sett-settlers or settler
sev-several
SFL-stepfather-in-law
Sf-stepfather
Sgt1-first sergeant
Sgt-sergeant
sil or *sl*-son-in-law
SiL-sister-in-law
sin-Latin, *sine*, without
si-sister
sis-sister
SL-son-in-law
SML-stepmother-in-law
Sm-stepmother
soc-society or societies
SO-survivors' originals
spr-sponsor
srnms-surnames
sr-senior
SS or *ss*-Latin, *silicet*, abbreviated
  in almost all legal documents,
  meaning "in particular" or
  "specifically" or "namely"
SSgt-staff sergeant
SSiL-stepsister-in-law
Ssi-stepsister
SSL-stepson-in-law
S-son
Ss-stepson
St-saint
sup-superior

supt- or *Su*-superintendant
surg-surgeon
sw-swear or sworn to
syl-syllabus
t.p.w.-title page wanting
t.p-title page
ten-tenant
terr-territory
test-testament
TIB-Temple Index Bureau
   (records)
tn-town or township
top-topographical
Tp-township
transcr-transcription
transl-translation
treas-treasurer
TRIB-Temple Records Index
   Bureau
tr-troop, translated, or translation
TSgt-technical (tech.) sergeant
T-township
TVA-Tennessee Valley Authority
twn-town
twp-township
U.K-United Kingdom
unasgd-unassigned
unc-uncle
unk-unknown
unm-unmarried
unorg-unorganized
USCG-U.S. Coast Guard
USCT-U.S. Colored Troops
USMC-U.S. Marine Corps
USN-U.S. Navy
USS-U.S. ship
USWPA-U.S. Works Progress
   Administration
U-uncle
V Admrl-vice admiral
v.a-Latin, *vixit annos*, he lived ?
   years
V.L-Vulgar Latin

v.r-vital records
v.s-vital statistics
var-various, variant, variation
VIP-Very Important Person
Vis or *Visc*-viscount, viscountess
vit-vital
Vi-visitor
viz-Latin, *videlicet*, namely
vols-volunteers, volumes
vs-versus
w or *W*-wife, will, west
W.B-Will Book
W.D-or *W-Dept*-War Department
w.d-will dated
W.O-warrant officer
w.p-will probated, will proved
W.S-writer to thesignator
w/o-wife of
wag-wagoner
Wai-waitress
Ward, *Wa*-ward
Wa-warden
wd-widow, ward
wf/o-wife of
Wh or *W*-white
wit-witness
wk(s)-week(s)
Wkm-workman
WPA-Works Progress Administration
wtn-witness
Wt-waiter
ww/o-widow of
wwr-widower
ww-widow
X-a mark made by a person
   instead of a signature
xch-exchange
Xn-Christian
Xnty or *Xty*-Christianity
Xped-Christened
Xt-Christ
yd-graveyard
yr or *y*-year

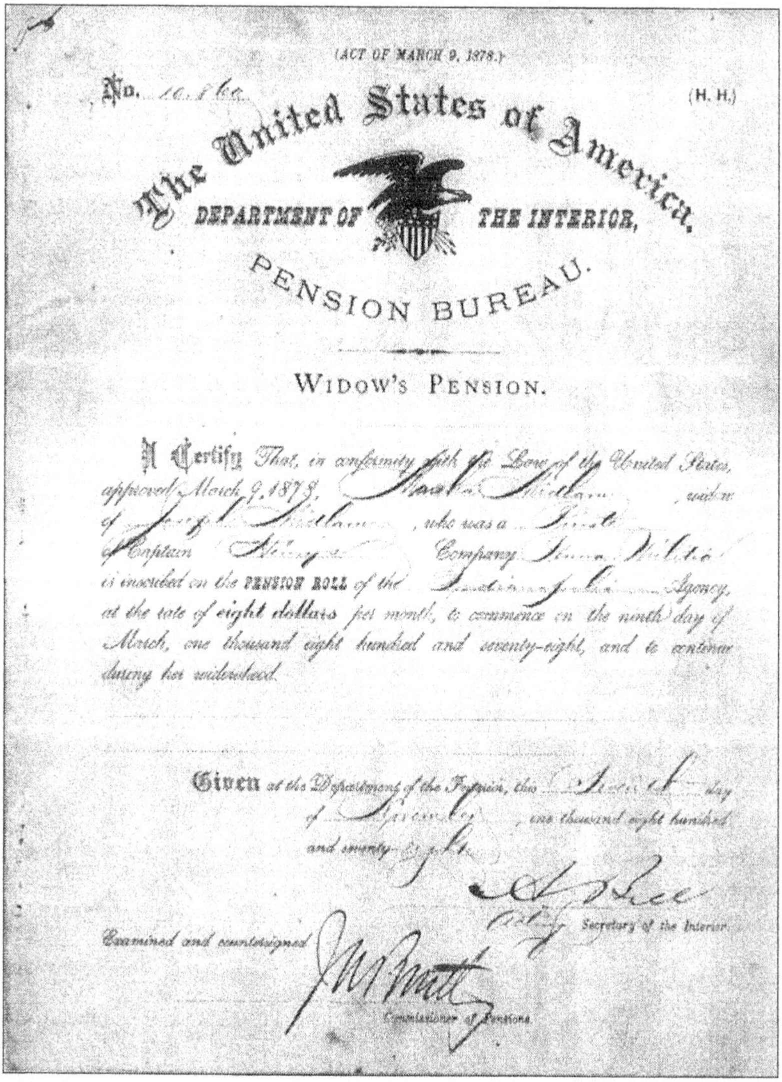

(ACT OF MARCH 9, 1878.)

No. 10,8[illegible] (H. H.)

The United States of America,

DEPARTMENT OF THE INTERIOR,

PENSION BUREAU.

WIDOW'S PENSION.

I Certify That, in conformity with the Law of the United States, approved March 9, 1878, [illegible], widow of [illegible], who was a [illegible] of Captain [illegible] Company [illegible] is inscribed on the PENSION ROLL of the [illegible] Agency, at the rate of eight dollars per month, to commence on the ninth day of March, one thousand eight hundred and seventy-eight, and to continue during her widowhood.

Given at the Department of the Interior, this [illegible] day of [illegible], one thousand eight hundred and seventy-eight.

[illegible] Secretary of the Interior.

Examined and countersigned

Commissioner of Pensions.

Figure 1. An 1878 certificate for a War of 1812 "Widow's Pension" from the Bureau of Pensions. See abbreviations: ***BP***.

Figure 2. Civil War Lt. Harpster of Ohio.
See abbreviations: *Lt.*

Figure 3. Sgt. James Messenger, 14th Ohio,
Spanish-American War. See abbreviations: *Sgt.*

Abbreviations of commonly seen societies, sororities, fraternities and organizations:

AF&AM-Ancient Free and Accepted Masons
AL-American Legion
ALOH-American Legion of Honor
AOF-Ancient Order Of Foresters
AOH-Ancient Order Of Hibernians
AOKMC-Ancient Order Of Knights of Mystic Chain
AOP-American Order of Pioneers
AOUW-Ancient Order Of United Workmen
APG-Association of Professional Genealogists
APG-Association of Professional Genealogists
APG-Association of Professional Genealogists
APJI-Association for Protection of Jewish Immigrants
APJI-Association for Protection of Jewish Immigrants
APJI-Association for Protection of Jewish Immigrants
App. Div-Appellate division
ASG-American Society of Genealogists
ASG-American Society of Genealogists
AUM-Ancient Order of Mysteries (Masonic Order)
BPOE-Benevolent and Protective Order of Elks
BPOEW-Benevolent and Protective Order of Elks of the World
CAR-National Society, Children of the American Revolution

CBKA-Commander Benevolent Knights Association
CCTAS-Crusaders-Catholic Total Abstinence Society
CDA-Colonial Dames of America
CK of A-Catholic Knights of America
COOF-Catholic Order of Foresters
CSA-Confederate States Army
CTAS-Catholic Total Abstinence Society
DAC-National Society of the Daughters of the American Colonists
DAR (ASDAR)-(American Society) Daughters of American Revolution
DCG-Descendants of Colonial Governors
DFPA-Daughters of Founders and Patriots of America
DR-Daughter of the Revolution, Diocesan Registry
DVR-Society of the Descendants of Washington's Army at Valley Forge
EBA-Emerald Beneficial Association
F&AM-Free and Accepted Masons
FAA-Free and Accepted Americans
FASG-Fellow American Society of Genealogists
FFT – First Families of Tennessee
FFV-First Families of Virginia (and so with all states)
FOE-Fraternal Order of Eagles

GALSTPTR-German American
Legion of St. Peter
GAR-Grand Army of the Republic
GAR-Grand Army of the Republic
GLAUM-Grand Lodge Ancient
Order of Mysteries (Masonic
Order)
GSW 1812-General Society of the
War of 1812
GUOOF-Grand United Order of
Odd Fellows
HAS-Huguenot Society of
America
IHSV-Red Cross of Constantine
IOI-Independent Order of
Immaculates
IOKP-Independent Order of
Knights of Pythias
IOOF-Independent Order of Odd
Fellows
IORM-Improved Order of
Redmen
ISH-Independent Sons of Honor
IWW-Industrial Workers of the
World
JAOUW-Junior Order-Ancient
Order of United Workmen
JOUAM-Junior Order-Order of
United American Mechanics
K of FM (*KFM*)-Knights of
Father Matthew
K of H-Knights of Honor
K of L-Knights of Loyola
K of M-Knights of Malta
(Masonic)
K of SJ-Knights of St. John
K of STP-Knights of St. Patrick
K of STW-Knights of St.
Wenceslas
K of TE-Knights of Tennessee
KC, K of C-Knights of Columbus
KGE-Knights of Golden Eagle
KGL-Knight Grand Legion

KHC-Knights of Holy Cross
KKK-Knights of Klu-Klux Klan
KMC-Knights of the Mystic Chain
KM-Knights Militant
KOTM-Knights of Macabees
KPC-Knights of Peter Claver
KP-Knights of Pythias
KSC-Knights of St. Columbkille
KSF-Knights of Sherwood Forest
KSL-Knights of St. Lawrence
KSTG (*KG*)-Knights of St. George
KSTI-Knights of St. Ignatius
KSTJ-Knights of St. Joseph
KSTM-Knights of St. Martin
KSTP-Knights of St. Paul
KSTP-Knights of St. Peter
KSTT-Knights of St. Thomas
KT (*K of T*)-Knights of Tabor
KT-Knights Templars (Masonic)
KWM-Knights of Wise Men
LAOH-Ladies Ancient Order of
Hibernians
LK of A-Loyal Knights of
America
LOM-Loyal Order of the
M.O.O.S.E (MOOSE)
MOKHSJ-Religious and Military
Order of Knights of the Holy
Sepulchre of Jerusalem
MOLLUS-Military Order of the
Loyal Legion of the U.S.
MRA-Royal Arcanum
MWA-Modern Woodmen of
America
NEHGS-New England Historic
Genealogical Society
NGS-National Genealogical
Society
NOK-New Order Knights (KKK)
NSCDA-National Society of the
Colonial Dames of America

NSDAR-National Society, Daughters of the American Revolution
OA-Order of the Arrow
OCR-Order of the Confederate Rose
OES-Order of the Eastern Star
OUAM-Order of United American Mechanics
PM-Patriarchs Militant (Independent Order of Odd Fellows)
POSA-Patriotic Order of the Sons of America
RAM-Royal Arch Masons
RK-Roman Knights
RO-AUM-Rosicrucian Order (Masonic)
RSTV-Rite of St. Vaclara
RSTV-Rite of St. Vita
S of R-Sons of the Revolution
SAR (ASSAR)-Sons of the American Revolution
SAR, NSSAR-National Society of Sons of the American Revolution

SBCL-Saint Bonifazius Catholic Union
SBL-Society B. Lafayette
Scottish Rite (Masonic Order)
SCV-National Society of Sons of Confederate Veterans
SNA-AUM-Shrine of North America (Masonic)
SUV-National Society of Sons of Union Veterans
SUV-Sons of Union Veterans
SV-Sons of Veterans
TH-Temple of Honor-Independent Order of Odd Fellows
UCV-United Confederate Veterans
UDC-United Daughters of the Confederacy
UDC-United Daughters of the Confederacy
VFW-Veterans of Foreign Wars
VFW-Veterans of Foreign Wars
WOW-Woodmen of the World
WRHS-Western Reserve Historical Society

Dictionary

A

a conciliis: of counsel, e.g., "When Viola found the record of a lawsuit with the name of her ancestor associated with the words 'a consiliis,' she knew that the ancestor was an attorney in the case, but not the principal counsel."

a forty: See *forty, a.*

ab intestato: the corollary to *ex testamento;* actions arising from or property descending by virtue of a death *intestate* (q.v., *What Did They Mean By That?*), e.g., "When a tract of land descends to one by virtue of the rules of descent and distribution applicable to intestate death, that person is said to have become the owner ab intestato." Also see *ex testamento.*

abandonment, abandon: to abandon any object or right with the intention to not again take up, claim, or resume that interest, e.g., "As a result of activities or inaction by an owner of a patent or grant that were legally considered abandonment, such patents or grants were declared forfeited and were no longer the property of the original patentee."

abettor, aider and abettor: One who encourages, instigates, or induces another to commit a crime, yet does not himself participate otherwise, e.g., "Though he had not actually participated in—aided—in the crime in a legal sense, T. Ray was found guilty of being an abettor since he had planned and suggested over and over that Brown would not get caught if he stole the pig."

absolution: a term of Canon Law, meaning that clergy acted to absolve a penitent person of his or her sins, e.g., "Early Catholic records, both here and in the Old Countries reveal many acts of absolution."

absolve, to be absolved: to be set free or released of a debt or obligation by a court or other law-making body, or by one who has suffered injury or loss at the hands of another, e.g., "The seventeenth-century court found that Hunt had not been a party to the obligations that arose, and so absolved Hunt of liability."

abuse: had several early meanings, and usually meaning the use of a person or thing in an inappropriate or wasting way, and it was not a word of common parlance as now, e.g. "In 1703 John Drake was brought before the court for 'abusing' Anne West, he likely having made inappropriate gestures or actions or words suggesting intimacy"; "In civil law, the word *abuse* is defined as to consume, injure, diminish in value, such as drinking the wine of another person without his permission."

abut, adjoin, adjacent: early, usually found in deed descriptions, e.g., "Every early judge, surveyor, clerk, J.P., magistrate, and lawyer knew that 'abut' meant touching end-to-end, 'adjoin' meant the sidelines touched, and 'adjacent' meant nearby yet not touching." Also see *coterminous* and see *contiguous*.

accessory, after the fact, during the fact, before the fact: in early criminal law, distinguished from an aider or abettor since an abettor must be on the ground or incite, command, actively encourage or cajole another to commit a crime, while accessories help plan, encourage and incite, during the commission of the crime, knowingly stand silently by and make no effort to discourage the criminal, and after the crime remain silent or assist the criminal in his flight or by assisting in hiding such as stolen property, e.g., "The accessory Moore helped plan the crime, stood silently a block away and said nothing as Thomas accepted the stolen property, then provided Ray with a means to get away and hide."

accomplice: one who knowingly and actively assists a criminal in a crime, e.g., "When Ray helped Moore in breaking into the house, he became an accomplice." Also see *accessory* and see *abettor.*

accord, accord and satisfaction: a satisfaction of a debt, obligation, or a an agreed settling of an injury or loss, whether written or oral, by which a party accused or charged and a person so charged or accused agree that the matter is settled and no further legal action may be taken, e.g., "An accord in early records reveals that the parties settled the matter, debt or difference to the satisfaction of both."

account, action of: a very early action at law against one who had a duty to set forth an account of income and disbursement, yet refused to do so, e.g., "The Texas court found Virginia in contempt and jailed her until she responded to the action of account filed in order to learn where the child's funds had been spent."

accusation: See *information* and see *indictment.*

accuse, to be accused, accusal: as now in common parlance, but in the law, the act of bringing, or lodging before a court or magistrate, a formal criminal charge against another person; to be formally accused of a crime, e.g., "The researcher must be aware that the accusations and statements of blame by such as newspapers or citizens at large do not constitute an accusal in the law."

action of account: See *account, action of.*

action, cause of: See *cause of action.*

ad quod damnum: Latin "to what damage"; an early writ of chancery, the same ordering the sheriff to determine damages to named parties as a result of the proposed (sometimes past) actions of another person, e.g., "Order Book 11, p. 498 of Augusta County (1768) reveals that Samuel Todd was the subject of a writ ad quod damnum before building a water mill on his land on Whistle Creek."

...howing *accord and satisfaction* of a promissory note.

ad sectum: at the (law)suit of; a Latin term of the law meaning that the stated result was the product of a law suit, e.g., "When seeking *execution* (q.v.), Evan told the court that the money to be paid was ad sectum from Haskins vs. Jones."

ademption: means the extinction or revocation of a will provision by the actions of the testator during his lifetime, e.g., "Though Thomas had bequeathed the slaves to Evan, the fact that he had sold or given away most of those before he died revealed an intentional ademption."

adjacent: See *abut.*

adjoin: See *abut.*

adjournment sine die: See *sine die.*

Administration of Justice Act: See *Coercive Acts, etc.*

administrators' bonds: See *probate bonds.*

admitted to record: admitted to the record, meaning the court is ordering that the clerk make a permanent record of the document, proceeding or record of testimony, e.g., "Courts' orders often reveal the judge directing his clerk that facts, testimony, deeds, and his decisions be admitted to record."

adoptee, adoptive child: a child who by public or private placement has become the child of other than both its birth parents. Also see *adoption, system, etc.*

adoption triad: see *adoption, system, etc.*

adoption, system, common terms of: a creature of statute only and unknown to the *Common Law* (q.v., *What Did They Mean By That?*); court ordered placements, orders of apprenticeships, and assignments of children to churches or the public charge have existed for centuries before adoption as we know it, e.g., "Since the first formal adoption in Massachusetts in 1910, the terms, adoptee, adoptive mother and father, birth mother and father, adoption agency, private and public adoption, closed files, open files, social workers and agencies all have been introduced, those being related to of the adoption triad."

adoptive parent: a parent who is such by virtue of a formal adoption. Also see *adoption, system, etc.*

adultery: See *fornication.*

adulthood: See *full age.*

adventure: early, meant a risky or hazardous undertaking, usually of a business nature, in which the result turned on the unknown factors of the future, e.g., "The early writings are replete with references to the Virginia adventure of settlers, investors, or entrepreneurs."

adverse possession, hold adverse to another: common in early times, especially on this continent; to move on to and remain for years on the real estate of another with no permission legal or otherwise for doing so, and intending to so remain adverse to the owner and thereby earn title to that land, e.g., "Though it was frequently said that a settler held title by adverse possession, very few of such cases actually resulted in ownership by the intruder being recognized."

affiant: one who makes and acknowledges (swears to) an affidavit, e.g., "Affiant Minnie Schwilk swore to the fact that a woman known to her was born in 1867."

affirm, affirmation: a formal document and act affirming that an *affidavit* (q.v., *What Did They Mean By That?*) of another person is true; the act of Quakers and others whose religious beliefs prohibit the swearing of oaths to such as documents, to truth or as witnesses, e.g., "It is customary for a witness to affirm an affidavit filed with a court in the course of a lawsuit"; "In November of 1782 Ethelrod Ruff was wrongfully held in contempt by a North Carolina court for refusing to do other than affirm that he would tell the truth."

affray: a fight between two or more persons, e.g., "Fights, if not at the level of *mayhem* (q.v., *What Did They Mean By That?*) and greater than 'disturbing the peace' were often placed in courts' records as affrays."

after acquired title: the rule that if a deed or other instrument of transfer failed to convey the title intended and expected, and then the grantor gains what should have been conveyed, his/her new acquisition will inure to the benefit of the original grantee, e.g., "In earlier times when heirs were sometimes not known to have existed, when one appeared and conveyed a partial interest he should have received earlier, he is transferring after acquired title."

after term: See *out of term, etc.*

agreement, memorandum of: See *memorandum of agreement.*

ague-chill: cold stage of an intermittent fever, e.g., "The period during illness and high fever when the victim feels cold and chilled."

aid, aid and abet: See *abettor.*

albumen negatives: an early (1848/9–1865+) method of creating photographic likenesses, e.g., "Enormously popular and rendering feasible the production of many copies, albumen negatives of the mid-nineteenth century were well known to Brady and were followed by the *salt paper prints* (q.v.)."

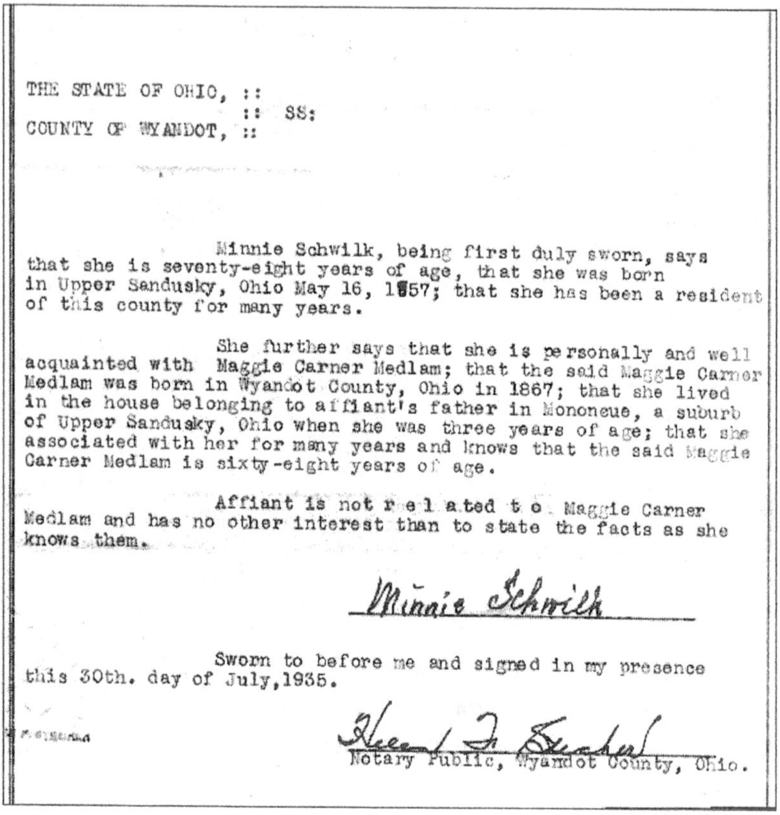

THE STATE OF OHIO, ::
                                :: SS:
COUNTY OF WYANDOT, ::

Minnie Schwilk, being first duly sworn, says that she is seventy-eight years of age, that she was born in Upper Sandusky, Ohio May 16, 1857; that she has been a resident of this county for many years.

She further says that she is personally and well acquainted with Maggie Carner Medlam; that the said Maggie Carner Medlam was born in Wyandot County, Ohio in 1867; that she lived in the house belonging to affiant's father in Mononeue, a suburb of Upper Sandusky, Ohio when she was three years of age; that she associated with her for many years and knows that the said Maggie Carner Medlam is sixty-eight years of age.

Affiant is not related to Maggie Carner Medlam and has no other interest than to state the facts as she knows them.

Minnie Schwilk

Sworn to before me and signed in my presence this 30th. day of July, 1935.

Notary Public, Wyandot County, Ohio.

Figure 5. Before birth certificates, *affiant* Minnie Schwilk swears to a birth in 1867.

alderman: a very general term meaning a judicial or administrative officer, e.g., "The genealogist must be wary of the term alderman, since the meaning and duties may vary greatly from colony to colony, state to state and even from county to county."

Aldermen's Courts: See *state court web sites.*

aleatory contract: a contract or agreement in which the parties, no matter how many, are bound at the occurrence of an event that is not certain to happen, e.g., "Since the frontier was ever westward advancing, and it was not certain that any person would return home after going there, or even be heard of again, aleatory contracts depending upon the return of a certain person were not uncommon."

alias dictus: usually abbreviated "alias" or "also known as," e.g., "Our ancestors shortened Latin legal terms whenever it did not affect the meaning, and it was easier to write 'alias' than to write 'alius dictus,' though both have the same meaning." Also see *alius.*

alibi: unlike common usage now in which reasons or explanations are commonly so called, early and in the law meaning that a person was elsewhere at the specific moment of the crime, e.g., "The fact that Jacqui was ill at the time of the crime could not be used as an alibi, though the fact that she was in the hospital on that day very well could be."

alienation fees: very early Maryland colony term, and meaning a fee, usually equal to the rents for one year on the tract to be conveyed, and paid whenever there was a transfer by gift or sale, or a conveyance of all or part of a tract of land by anyone to anyone, e.g., "Alienation fees were transfer taxes recorded and payable to the Lord Proprietor, such fees having been required from the earliest days of Lord Baltimore's grant until about the middle of the seventh decade of the eighteenth century." Also see *fiefdom.*

alienation: unlike commonly now, in the law of real estate meaning to transfer or convey all of one's rights in land, e.g., "When the 1780 Sussex County court found that Parker had alienated himself from the forty-seven acres, the court was not referring to his feelings about the tract."

aliter: Latin for otherwise, e.g., "The court order found that the prior court ruling was aliter as to the new decision, meaning the two rulings were at variance."

alius, alias: early, alius was the preferred spelling; a very common second order of court or warrant issued when the first identical such writ was unsatisfied or otherwise did not accomplish what was intended, e.g., "To name but a few, you may find alius executions, alius execution writs, alius subpoenas, alius summons, alias tax order warrants or summons, or 'aliuses' of any writ."

all and singular: a common legal expression meaning without exception, e.g., "When attorney Mikaila represented to the court that Allison owned all and singular the personal effects of her mother, it meant that nothing was excepted or excluded from what she had."

all fours: usually a term meaning that two arguments or sets of facts are for all legal purposes identical, e.g., "When Martha Diane represented that the facts and ruling in Brittany's lawsuit were on all fours with those in Bethany's case of a few years before, all knew that the prior ruling would surely come into play in the decision of this case."

allegations: See ***lawsuits, common, procedural steps.***

alms-boxes: See ***Boxing Day.***

amblotic: having the chemical or physical properties capable of causing abortion, e.g., "Though it had failed to do so, Deb took her mother's advice and took several tablespoonfuls of kerosene and quinine as an amblotic."

ambra, amber: an ancient term of measure of such as grain and meaning four bushels, e.g., "There are several notations of ambras of apples in seventeenth-century New England store ledgers."

ameliorate, ameliorations, ameliorative waste: to better, add to, or improve, usually land, property of another, e.g., "The court recognized the ameliorations of Bruce, and declared that those became the property of his landlord when the lease expired."

amerce and fine: fines for monor crimes imposed arbitrarily and at the discretion of a court; a fine or other penalty for commission of a misdemeanor, e.g., "As early as 1655 New England records reveal amercers and amerces, meaning those imposing penalties for minor offenses and those who commit such."

American Indians, lending firearms to: See ***peaces (pieces), lending of, to Indians.***

American Indians, Native Americans, some diseases and medicines of: in addition to the magic and pleas to spirits for relief from illnesses of every sort, conjunctivitis was common due to life in a smoke-filled tepee, structure or cave; the outdoor life resulted in widespread neuralgia, arthritis, and rheumatism; likely digestive problems were common from periods of plenty and other times of near starvation; for ***fevers***, they administered rest, purges, diuresis, and liquids; the Plains and Great Lakes Indians were generous with phlebotomies; emesis was common for all intestinal dysfunctions; coryza brought smartweed in several forms, as did bronchitis, pleurisy and lung infections, with some tribes performing incisions and draining; asthma was treated with the plant Lobelia syphilitaca; cupping was widely used for chest pains of many sorts; holly, horsemint, Virginia poke, and Irish morning glory were variously used for heart disease, including angina; ***decoctions*** (q.v.) of sumac, juniper berries, magnolia, sarsaparilla, wintergreen and yellow root were common diuretics; narcotics from their areas and intoxicants made from grains were most common; hysteria and such as epilepsy were treated with loud sounds as in their dancing; and their treatments of dislocations, fractures, wounds and retained placentas was said to be better than those administered by eighteenth-century whites." Also see Gordon, *Aesculapius Comes To The Colonies*, 1949, generally, and see ***homeopathic medicine*** in *What Did They Mean By That?*

American plague, yellow fever: See ***calenture*** in *What Did They Mean By That?*

American Revolution, rations in 1775: See ***rations for soldiers, etc.***

Anadama bread: a bread of the Northeast made of corn and wheat flower, yeast, and allowed to raise, e.g., "Anadama bread is said to have been named for an early woman who made fine bread, however there seems to be little proof of that fact."

anaphrodisia, dyspareunia: sexual frigidity for any reason in either sex, dyspareunia usually referring to women; inability to have sexual intercourse, e.g., "Though divorces were very difficult to obtain, even very early anaphrodisia was sometimes a basis for granting such."

ancient writings: a term of evidence, often improperly used by genealogists, and meaning a writing more than thirty years old that has been kept in an official depository or office of government, e.g., "Loreda suggested to her audience that 'ancient writings' were more than simply 'old.'"

anew: See ***de novo.***

Anglo-Irish: the name given those people from the area in and near Dublin known as the English Pale, it being populated with a mixture of Irish and English descendants from those officers and administrators etc., who moved there at the time of Henry I and after, e.g., "Mr. Fulton has suggested that although the mixture of people was similar, the Scots who moved to Ireland (***Scots-Irish***, q.v., *What Did They Mean By That?*) arrived there long after the English who did so, and so resisted assimilation till the seventeenth century and even to now."

Angostura bitters: from plants akin to the ginger family, a warm, sweet spice is traditionally found in Indian cooking, and found in a wide variety of curries, rice dishes, and Indian-style desserts, e.g., "Angostura

bitters was used as an ingredient of the 1860 Drake's Plantation Bitters."
Also see *bitters*.

answer: see *lawsuits, common, procedural steps.*

anthrax: an acute infectious disease caused by spore-forming bacteria. Thought to be severe carbuncles and also known as violent carbuncles, splenic fever, dread fever, malignant pustule, charbon, wool sorters' disease, and carbuncle fever, e.g., "The feared anthrax was often quickly transferred from the highly susceptible cattle and livestock to humans."

antimacassar, animacassers: clothes or upholstered thin pads, and sometimes padded covers for the arms of chairs, e.g., "Melanie had and used antimacassars with every upholstered chair in her home."

antinomian: an apparent contradiction arising when two laws or regulations or a law and a powerful custom do or seem to contradict each other, e.g., "The 1675 court noted that the fact that there was freedom of religion and the law requiring attendance at the Anglican Church was an antinomian."

apparent heir: one whose inheritance is established and settled in the law, presuming only that he/she outlives the person from whom the inheritance will distribute, e.g., "Ms. Jane had a life estate, Beth had the **remainder** (q.v.), however Beth died before Jane, so Beth's interest passed to her heirs."

appeal bond: See *lawsuits, common, procedural steps.*

Appellate Courts: See *state court web sites.*

appendicitis, Bilious colic, Flatulent colic (wind colic), painters' colic, bellyaches: not diagnosed until 1812, severe intestinal pain was called variously by these names and likely took a terrible toll in the colonies. (Painters' colic also may have been lead poisoning.) e.g., "For severe colic in adults, Dr. Ritcheson administered *decoction* (q.v.) of yam-root, tincture of opium or lobelia, laudanum, extract of smart-weed and catnip tea."

appertaining: having to do with, in association with, connected to or involved with, e.g., "Many deeds recited that land and buildings and 'all gardens, grounds and other structures appertaining thereto' were included in the conveyance."

apportion, opportionment: to distribute proportionally, e.g., "The court ordered the apportionment in accordance with the rules of intestate distribution."

apron and necktie party: a social event for the young adults of the nineteenth century in Pennsylvania and New York and perhaps elsewhere, e.g., "Each of the guests brought a necktie and an apron of the same color, all were placed in a box, each man drew a tie and each lady an apron, the person with the same color and fabric as that you drew was your companion for the evening."

aptha: See **thrush** in *What Did They Mean By That?*

aqua vitae: brandy; any strong alcoholic drink other than beers and ales; brandy, a ration of which was regularly given soldiers and navy men; also called "burning water," e.g., "It was thought by virtually all that aqua vitae if taken in modest quantity before battle would strengthen the resolve and courage of the combatants."

arbor, brush: See **brush arbor.**

ardent spirits: synonym for "distilled spirits"; distilled liquors, e.g., "The court decided that beer and ale are not ardent or spirituous liquors."

array: an ancient term meaning those pieces of equipment and that apparel worn and carried by a man prepared for armed combat; the order in which appear the entirety of a list of jurors subpoenaed or otherwise ordered to appear and be questioned as to their competency to serve as jurors, e.g., "Concerning the assault planned for the third day, Longstreet wrote that he told Lee that the '...15,000 men who could carry that position have never been arrayed for battle'"; "Though it sounds as though they are to be armed for battle, an array was and remains but a list of prospective jurors."

art of cropping and farming: a term revealing those skills to be taught to an apprentice who was to learn planting, growing, and generally dealing with such as corn, wheat, tobacco, rice, cotton, or other crops, e.g., "In November of 1783 Philip Newton was bound to Shadrack Stevens to learn the 'art and mistery of cropping and farming.'"

article, articles: of which there are many incidents in the law; any separate and distinct portion from any two or more provisions of a written instrument, e.g., "Among others to be found in the law, there are articles of agreement, articles of association, of incorporation or of partnership, Articles of Confederation, articles of faith, articles of impeachment, articles of religion, articles of clergy, articles of the navy, articles of the peace, and articles of war"; "The first paragraph that bequeathed furniture in the 1756 Thomas Drake will was entitled 'Article Three.'"

artificer: a person enlisted in the army whose tasks included general mechanics, repair and building as needed by the army, e.g., "Hill Freeburn was an artificer in the Pennsylvania Continental Line."

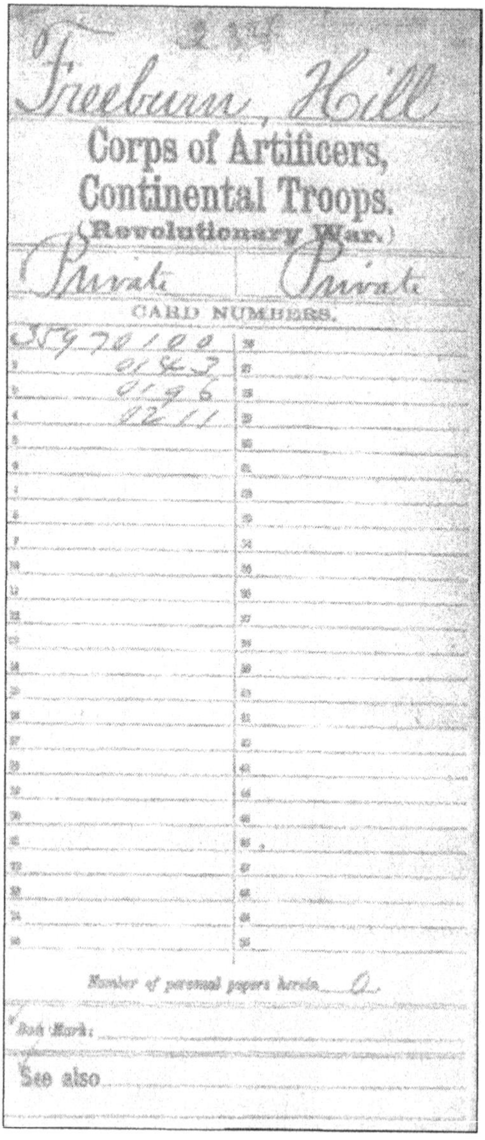
Freeburn, Hill
Corps of Artificers,
Continental Troops.
(Revolutionary War.)

Private | Private

CARD NUMBERS.

35970100
0183
0196
0211

Number of personal papers herein 0

Book Mark:

See also

Figure 6. A "card" from the
National Archives and Records Administration
showing Hill Freeburn as an ***artificer*** in the Continental Line.

assault and battery: a very common expression, "assault" meaning threatening words or actions, usually causing fear for the assaulted, and "battery" meaning a physical touching or unlawful restraint of one's free actions, e.g., "When he alleged that he was assaulted, he was not stating that he had been struck or even touched."

assign, assignment, assignor, assignee: a transfer of some—any— rights in any property or claim to an assignee, quite usually made with some formality and acknowledged by the assignor, e.g., "In early times, as now, assignments by colonials of accounts receivable to another person for collection in England or elsewhere were common."

assistance, writs of: See ***writs of assistance.***

assumpsit: a promise, either oral or in writing, to pay or do or forbear to do specific acts, e.g., "Early records reveal myriad lawsuits in assumpsit, either 'special' where the agreement was in writing, or 'general,' where the duty to pay or otherwise act arises from the law."

at bar: a case being before a court or being argued, e.g., "When Attorney Drake Bater told his secretary that his case was at bar, she knew it was being argued or presented at the moment or would be so imminently."

at the courthouse door: See ***courthouse door, etc.***

attachment: a court order usually directing that a sheriff or other officer of the court or county secure or take into possession some person, property or money which is or may be subject to an action of court in a specific case, e.g., "A write or attachment directed Lazarus to take into possession and hold the entirety of the property of the Jones family." Also see ***lawsuits, common, procedural steps.***

attest: to bear witness to; to affirm that some statement or fact is true; to execute a document as a witness that another person did or affirmed some act or belief, e.g., "Parker attested to the fact that William Hunt had admitted liability in the lawsuit."

attorneys at law, early legislation concerning: in 1644 the Virginia Council ruled that greedy or ill-prepared lawyers would be prohibited from further practice, e.g., "The law stated that many attorneys 'have more intended their own profit and their immediate Luck than the good and benefit of their clients....,' and so such 'Mercenarye' men would be disbarred."

attractive nuisance: an early doctrine of law that brings liability to a person, particularly a landowner, who maintains a condition on his property that would bring harm to unknowing children, e.g., "In the early days of oil exploration, many were the lawsuits holding liable the owners of drilling machines and pumping units for injuries that children sustained by viewing such as something on which to play." Also see *nuisance*.

autopsy: an examination of a corpse to determine the medical cause of death, even early by *physitions* (q.v., *What Did They Mean By That?*) or one with training in medicine, e.g., "The medical examiner determined that the man died of massive loss of blood from a head wound, following which the coroner after examining all the details ruled that the death was murder."

aver, averment: to state, declare or assert, e.g., "An averment in a lawsuit is a statement of a fact pertinent to that case."

Avowant, avow: one who has avowed, as opposed to having "sworn," to the truth of some matter or statement, e.g., "Weynette suspected that Mitchell was a Quaker when she found that he had been referred to as an 'avowant' in a lawsuit."

Awakening, the Great: See *Great Awakening*.

B

bacon, flitches of: See *smokeloft*.

bad blood: early and today, a Southern Appalachian expression often referring to syphilis; long-lasting anger and hostility between families or clans, e.g., "Dr. Don mentioned that his back country patients often labeled syphilis or other sexually transmitted diseases as 'bad blood'"; "The Swaffords and the Tolletts of Tennessee north of Chattanooga have held 'bad blood' since before the twentieth century."

bailiee, bailment, bailor: the giving over of personal property to another person to hold or secure for the giver or for some other person, e.g., "When Evan left his horse at the *livery stable* (q.v.) overnight, his action was that of bailment, he was a bailor, and the livery keeper was a bailee."

bakers' meats: pastries, usually sweet, e.g., "Dorothy and Vera often made *springerles* (q.v., *What Did They Mean By That?*) and oatmeal cookies for the holidays, those serving as a large part of the bakers' meats to be enjoyed."

bald, mountain bald: those areas that have limited vegetation and no trees, and which appear frequently on the peaks of the Appalachian mountains, e.g., "Thelma explained that 'Roan Mountain Bald,' 'Andrews' Bald' and 'Gregory's Bald' are but three of the many Smoky Mountain balds, the last mentioned known by botanists worldwide for the beautiful 'flame azaleas' that grow there."

ball-hooting: sliding a log down a hillside, e.g., "The term 'ball-hooting' was and remains well known to those in the timber business."

bandore: a stringed instrument that is plucked, e.g., "Because of the similarity, Richard referred to his grandfather's bandore as a banjo."

bankruptcy courts: See *state court web sites.*

banns, banns of matrimony: the ancient public notice of an impending marriage given in order that those who objected might come forward, e.g., "In the early Virginia colony the church required that banns of a marriage be read before the congregation on three consecutive Sundays."

bar, the: the totality of lawyers and judges having jurisdiction or practicing in a given judicial or geographical area; the actual bar across a courtroom separating the court, lawyers and others participating in the action from the spectators or general public, e.g., "When the court referred to the bar of Surry County, he was speaking of all the judges and attorneys who regularly practiced there"; "The ancient expression 'bench and bar' meant the judges and those having permission or authority to practice before that court." Also see *at bar.*

bardery: and ancient term, obsolete since the end of the nineteenth century; to induce with words and gifts a naïve woman to engage in illicit sexual relationships, and usually synonymous with seduction, e.g., "In 1895, as a result of his being so indiscreet as to the extent of their sexual relationship, Melanie sued Jacob, charged him with bardery, and won handily, though the whole affair was extremely embarrassing for her."

barrators, barretors: one who incites violence or induces others to quarrel or file lawsuits. See *felons, barrators, and rioters.*

bastardy bonds: See *bonds, surety, etc.*

bath, baths, bathe: now defined as immersion, however early also as with cloths, towels, or in closed spaces such as in steam rooms. For centuries, baths were thought by many to be of no value in healing or as cures, and were even considered harmful by many, however by the last decades of the nineteenth century that attitude changed rather abruptly and baths became common, either with bathtubs, "stand-up" baths or otherwise, e.g., "Baths of many sorts were administered, including those listed in 1882 by Dr. Pierce, namely, cold, cool, temperate, tepid, warm, hot and very hot, as well as hot air, steam, Russian, Turkish, vapor, electric, sea, shower, sponge, douche, foot, sitz, head, medicated, alkaline, acid, iodine, and sulphur."

bats: See *hoes, etc.*

battaeux, battoe, batto, battoes: a long, heavy, narrow boat for transportation of men and supplies in rivers especially; two bateaux of the French and Indian War period are said to have measured 32 feet in length by four feet across the beam, e.g., "In 1775 Washington wrote, '...Fishing in Battoes...(is)...Prejudicial to the men's Health....'"

battery, assault and: See **assault and battery.**

battery, galvanic: See **galvanic battery.**

battle array: See **array.**

bawdyhouse, brothel, whorehouse, house of ill fame, cat-house, sporting house, hoo-hah house: ancient expressions meaning places where unlawful sexual activities take place, usually in exchange for money or something of value, e.g., "The well known bawdyhouses known as the 'Burning Stump' at Kenton and 'Gracies' in Marion operated for decades during the years 1890 -1950."

be drawn, ordered that indentures: a common expression of early courts in concluding that a certain child or minor should be apprenticed to or placed in the care of other than its parents, e.g., "By court order, myriad early children were placed in the care and keeping of those who had chosen so to act, and the words commonly used to reveal that the court, rather than private parties, had so decided were, 'It is ordered that indentures be drawn.'"

beam and balance: a scale for weighing any objects, e.g., "The inventory revealed three beams and balances." Also see **steelyard** in *What Did They Mean By That?*

beating the bounds, bounce the bounds, riding the marches (Scotland): the ancient practice of processioning (known as early as Edward I [1346] and often called perambulating) most often the parish boundaries, also at times the boundaries of tracts of land for either public or private purposes, and accompanied by celebration and attended by many, e.g., "While it is written that 'beating the bounds' was known to have taken place in the American colonies, no records have been found by this writer."

bed ropes: the rope strung between the rails and usually from headboard to footboard, the same serving to suspend the **ticking bag** (q.v.) or other mattress material, "As were most, Allison's bed ropes were of strong hemp."

bees: See **honeybees.**

beetle: a heavy mallet, e.g., "The 1677 Essex County, Virginia inventory of one Hollingshead reveal the presence of tongs and a beetle, likely used in the metal work required on his plantation."

beginning tree: almost universally found in any description of land other than **town lots** (q.v., *What Did They Mean By That?*), and meaning the beginning point in the survey of the tract, e.g., "In the earliest times roads and paths changed course frequently, hence a conspicuous tree, even though it be at a road side, often was the beginning point of land surveys."

behoof, behoove: in behalf or to the advantage of, e.g., "Myriad early deeds speak of the grantor conveying the interests 'to the use and behoof' of the grantee."

bench and bar: See *bar*.

bench warrant: a warrant or order for the arrest of a person or the seizure of property issued by a judge peremptorily and on his own motion and often literally from his seat during a trial, "When Judge Haskins learned that Ray was hidden at a neighbor's house, she at once issued a bench warrant for his arrest."

bench, King's Bench, Queen's Bench, King's Counsel, Queen's Counsel: the courts of law in the English legal system, our judges still yet referred to as "the bench" (as opposed to those "chancellors in equity"), all of whom represented the power of the sovereign or Crown, e.g., "The judges and lawyers (attorneys) in the American colonies who were appointed or later elected to the King's Bench or as King's Counsel were the best trained of any who sought the job and had no small measure of political influence." Also see ***chancellor*** and ***chancery, courts of*** in *What Did They Mean By That?*

benefit of his labor, he/she might have: an expression meaning that one might receive the payment for his labor directly; a very common early expression for courts' orders allowing minors to be paid for their work and efforts, though those persons yet be under age, e.g., "In January of 1697 the Surry court ruled that though he be not yet of age, a young man named Barham should 'have the benefit of his labor.'"

besom: a very early term meaning a broom (Johnson, 1755) of any size, e.g., "Early colonial and British records and writings often refer to besoms."

betrothed, intended wife: the act of promising marriage to a woman, thought sometimes by a woman to a man, e.g., "When the judge said that in his opinion Drue was betrothed to Sarah, he meant that he recognized Drue's promise to marry her."

between terms: See ***out of term, etc.***

bilious colic: See ***appendicitis***.

biliousness: jaundice or unusual yellow or yellow/green skin tone, e.g., "In 1858 Dr. Drake diagnosed the liver disease of Mrs. Glover by reason of her biliousness."

bill of appraisement: a formal statement concerning an appraisal of any personal property, especially in administrations of estates, e.g., "Interestingly, the 1864 Alabama bill of appraisement of the estate of the wealthy John A. J. Whitehurst included in part '...Hire of Slave Henry till 25th December 1863, 24.00; Sale personalty...1863, 2,349.83...Total in Confederate Money, $3253.49...1 By amt. CS Bond March 24th 1864, $1000.00,' etc."

bill, due bill: a debt or account due and payable or to be paid at a future time certain to happen or a date that is ascertainable, quite usually written, e.g., "John Sugar of Virginia was sued for his failure to pay a bill in 1694/95"; "It was not unusual for a court to direct that a bill from an estate was to be accepted by a creditor until such later time as funds were available from such as a tobacco crop growing at the date of a death or from unpaid debts owed to the decedent."

bill: (legal) in the law a list or a statement of facts or details; in commercial law, a statement of indebtedness or contract particulars, e.g., "Such terms as 'bill of exceptions,' 'bill of evidence,' 'bill of attainder,' 'bill of foreclosure,' 'bill of review,' 'supplemental bill,' etc., all refer to general lists or itemizations of specific facts or data having to do with the matter mentioned"; "Commerce has devised such as bills of sale, bills receivable, bills of credit, bills of lading, and many more, all stating facts concerning a bargain or exchange transaction."

bills, order to take: See *taking bills, order for.*

billy club: origin may be lost; a cudgeon or club carried by policemen, e.g., "Upon being asked, the chief stated that he had no idea of the origin of the expression 'billy club,' even though he had carried one throughout his early years as a policeman."

bind of fodder: a quantity of corn stalks with the leaves still attached and tied together by the use of one of the stalks wrapped around the bind and tied, e.g., "Dalton recalled that in South central Tennessee a shock of corn would produce about four or five binds of fodder."

birth parent: the natural parent of a child. See *adoption, system, etc.*

birth whites: See *white leg.*

bitters: Since 1824 a highly favored base or additive for alcoholic drinks or wines, "For centuries bitters, including orange, peach, and after 1824 the favored Angostura, have been used and consumed for the pleasant taste imparted to wines and other drinks by adding those products of herbs and fruits, as well as for the supposed medicinal value of such."

black arts: See *wizard* and see *witch.*

Black Codes, Jim Crow laws: a general term referring to the many Civil War Southern legislative and executive acts and orders concerning slavery, e.g., "The rules prohibiting Blacks from moving freely in public places were the most restrictive of the Black Codes." Also see ***Jim Crow laws*** in *What Did They Mean By That?*

black dog: recurrent bouts of depression, e.g., "Churchill, Goethe, and Martin Luther all were said to have been afflicted by black dog."

black fever: perhaps no longer known, but probably any of the diseases that carried a fever and caused the tongue to darken, e.g., "Dr. Ritcheson treated black fever with 'flowers of sulfur' and quinine."

black mariah, black maria: a wagon with bars on all side and used for moving prisoners, e.g., "Not unlike the stocks and pillories, it was the intention of the law-givers that prisoners be placed at public ridicule by being visible to all through the bars of the black mariahs."

black pox: probably ***smallpox*** (q.v., *What Did They Mean By That?*), e.g., "An 1828 Boston paper recited symptoms likely revealing smallpox and diagnosed the ailment as 'black pox.'"

black vomit: See ***yellow fever*** in *What Did They Mean By That?*

blackberries: See ***whortleberries.***

bladder: as now, an organ; early, any sore blister or seeping swelling of any mucous gland, e.g., "Edith told her sister that her baby had a throat bladder and she was in fear of serious consequences, even death."

bleares, narrow bleares, fine bleares: unknown, but likely a woven fabric, e.g., "On 31 January, 1664, William Glanfield acknowledged before the court that in trans-oceanic carriage, Mr. Rowland Place of Virginia had lost through water damage, among other personal property, 'Narrow Bleares' amounting to £4,2S and £1,14S in another lot of 'fine Bleares.'"

blenhorrea: See ***gonorrhea*** in *What Did They Mean By That?*

blind tiger, bootlegger, jointist: a place where liquor is sold without a license or permission of government, e.g., "During the decades of the 1940s and 1950s there was a blind tiger on East Mark St. in Marion." Also see ***bootlegger, etc.*** in *What Did They Mean By That?*

blood-letting: the settlement means or results of a feud or extreme difference that resulted in physical combat, e.g., "While political parties label deep differences that lead to quick, dramatic changes as blood-letting, in early times the term meant to draw blood from an inflicted person for the supposed medical efficacy of such actions." Also see ***cup, cupping*** in *What Did They Mean By That?*

blue laws: See ***Sabbath-breaking, etc.***

boarder: one who makes a contract to be supplied with regular meals by another person or buisness, e.g., "Whether or not a man also needed a bed or place of sleep, he was known as a boarder."

boatswain's book: a log kept by a boatswain concerning his activities and duties. See *boatswain* in *What Did They Mean By That?*

bodily assault: See *assault and battery.*

boelling mill: See *bolting mill.*

bolting cloth: See *bolting, etc.*

bolting mill, bolling mill, boling mill: A mill also offering sifting as a service, usually driven by water, where grain is both ground and bolted, e.g., "There was a very early bolting mill across Town Creek in Edgecombe County, and it was there that the Drakes had their meal ground, sifted, and bagged."

bolting, bolted: screening in order to sort grades of flour and meal and to remove the debris before sale; cloth of varying weaves (called bolting cloth), often made of silk, served as the filters or screens for bolting, e.g., "Bolting with three sizes of weaved cloth was common, those three providing two or three grades of flour, high quality, middlings (sometimes called shorts), and bran." Also see *flour, meal.*

bombo-toddy: a favorite drink of the early colonies, e.g., "Todd made bombo-toddies from water, sugar, rum, and nutmeg, and served those at room temperature or warm."

bona fugitiva: See *waif, waifs.*

bond servant: See *bond maid, bondman* in *What Did They Mean By That?*

bonds, supersedeas: See *supersedeas, etc.*

bonds, surety, etc.: generally, obligations of many sorts in writing or sworn before courts or other officers qualified to administer oaths that guarantee the court or another party known as an obligee, that money will be paid or duties performed by the person bonded, and should that person fail to so pay or act, the bond will be forfeited and the obligor required to pay over the required sums or do as promised to the obligee or to the court as the case may be, e.g., "In most marriage bonds the courts accepted as sufficient security either the word and reputations of those posting it or pledges of real estate or other assets by those obligors." Also see *probate bonds.*

bone shave, spinal inflammation: sciatica, e.g., "In 1886 Dr. Weaver of Buffalo wrote that the treatment for spinal inflammation—sciatica—should be sexual abstinence, mild and gradually increasing electrical current, and decreasing 'intellectual activity.'" Also see *lumbago* in *What Did They Mean By That?*

boodle, boodling: obsolete; money paid as bribery; corrupt actions by an elected or public official, usually for money or other thing of value, e.g., "The Georgia lawyer Tom was well known to be a boodler, even by his clients."

boon: somewhat like now, a gift or grant, e.g., "When referring to a grant of land, Griffith noted in the ledger that he had gained a boon."

boot hose tops: largely forgotten, yet appearing often in early colonial records, including in Essex and the Tidewater counties of Virginia; probably an expensive decoration attached to the breeches and of that length permitting such to be pulled down over the tops of high boots, e.g., "Pepys referred to a boot hose top as an '...old-fashioned ornament for the legs, that is to say, a particular addition to breeches.'"

Boston Massacre: 5 March 1770; a principle reason given by colonists for the American Revolution, e.g., "Fighting between Bostonians and British soldiers had been frequent, then came the Boston Massacre in March of 1770, and though the writers are not agreed, it is certain that several people were killed."

Boston Port Act: See *Coercive Acts, etc.*

bound out: a non-specific common early term meaning that one person has placed another, usually a child, in a position of servitude to still a third person, e.g., "As a boy, Jesper Gransum was bound out to Richard Parker."

bounder: a mark, rock, cairn, blaze, tree, post, pin, or other identifier of a point or corner in a land description; also, an early term for one who was common, rowdy as a practice, coarse, crude, kept low class company, or was slovenly; one whose actions were beneath the minimum standards of conduct expected from a "proper," "well-bred," or "high class" person, e.g., "The corner slippery elm in Drake's line was called a bounder in the surveyor's drawing"; "Tom's habit of frequenting the saloons at the docks, of keeping the company of low class and unkempt women, and of failing to maintain a clean appearance led Charlene and her mother to say that he surely was a bounder." Also q.v., *What Did They Mean By That?*, and herein *rounder.*

bounty: lands or money as rewards for military service; sums of money or other property of value as rewards or pay for services performed that are out of the ordinary course of the calling of the one so performing; money paid for the capture or killing of pests, e.g., "The payment or compensation for providing passage across the sea and into one of the colonies was quantities of land varying from one-fourth acre in parts of New England to 180 acres in colonial Georgia"; "Bounties paid for the capture of wanted criminals are and were well known"; "Bounty land was provided to those who served in our wars down to and including the twentieth century"; "To collect from the county in early Virginia the bounty for wolves, it was necessary to provide the scalp or both ears as evidence of the kill." Also see *patents* and see *indentured servants* and also see *land grants*.

bounty jumpers: those who having been paid a bounty for enlistment or reenlistment in the military, unlawfully absent themselves, and again enlist or reenlist at another location in order to again be paid the bounty, e.g., "Before modern identification methods, many were the bounty jumpers in all wars."

bouts: forty strands of thread used when weaving. See *warping bars, etc.*

Boxing Day, St. Stephens Day: December 26, named for the first Christian martyr and celebrated in the UK and early here, on which day since the Middle Ages alms-boxes have been placed in and about churches in which parishioners placed money to be given to the parish poor, e.g., "The early American colonies left records of churches observing Boxing Days."

brand, stock: See *stock mark, stock brand, etc.*

brandlet: a large trivet, e.g., "Though often not listed by size, Mikaila noted that it is likely that many of the common trivets listed in estates, in fact, were brandlets."

branny tetter: See *eczema*.

breach of the Sabbath: any failure to attend services, pay levies, or otherwise fail to observe the regimen and protocol of the Church of England, e.g., "In early Surry County Richard Parker and George Lee were fined 10S each for failing to attend church without good reason." Also see *disguised in drink*.

breast of the court, in the: being within the memory, discretion or conscience of the judge; the facts and rulings existing during a trial or term of court that may be changed as the trial or term continues, e.g., "Once the case ends and the matter reduced to permanent record all facts within the breast of the court cease to exist and are incorporated within the final order."

brethren: a term relating to religion and usually referring to those persons united in some certain religious beliefs or doctrine; in *early* wills, either brothers or sisters, and not restricted to the male gender, e.g., "Baptist preacher Alexander spoke of all members of his congregation and faith as brethren"; "The provision in the Brunson will that directed that all personal property go to "my brethren" was ruled to include his sisters, as well."

bring suit: See *lawsuit, suit, etc.*

britches, leather: See *leather britches.*

broken debts: a debt, uncollectible except by legal process or an obligation that a debtor stated he would not pay and then did not, e.g., "What we now know as a 'bad debt' also was known as 'broken' in Virginia and the Carolinas by 1650 and later."

bronze John, brown John, calenture (q.v., *What Did They Mean By That?)* yellow fever, e.g., "The probable origin of the term 'bronze John' was the color of the skin and eyes of those with the dreaded *yellow fever* (q.v., *What Did They Mean By That?*)."

brothel: See *bawdyhouse, etc.*

brueing (brewing) tub: a large vessel or container, usually of fired clay (crockery) in which beverages of any sort were mixed and otherwise handled, e.g., "No small number of early colonial inventories refer to brueing tubs."

brush arbor: those scant, usually temporary, wooden frameworks covered with brush, grass, or other vegetation, the purpose being to shelter itinerant preachers from the hot summer sun, especially in the South, e.g., "Ms. H. noted that the absence of church buildings or meeting houses for the use of wandering or circuit preachers often gave rise to the need that the local men build brush arbors for the traveling preachers."

bulies, sloos: unknown; probably a fruit, and the terms appeared with some frequency in the seventeenth-century American colonies, e.g., "It was written that. 'Wyne of wylde Plums, bulies and sloos' were often made and also flavored with cinnamon and sugar." Also see *Hypocras, etc.*

burden, burthen: usually given in tons; that weight of load of which a boat or ship was capable of carrying, e.g., "By the mid-eighteenth century, the Blackwater, Nottoway and Nansemond rivers were being used as waterways for ships of up to '100 tons burden' moving to and from Albemarle Sound." Also see *staves.*

Burgess: somewhat unlike in English law, in towns here, and since the earliest times, the executive officer or a board of such officers of a town or village and having the same duties as a mayor, manager or town council in larger communities, e.g., "Asa Sherwood was a Burgess in Newtown in the late eighteenth century." See *Burgesses, character of.*

Burgesses, character of: the requirements of the office of Burgess in 1654 in Virginia were said to be of twenty-one years and "known of integrity and good conversation," e.g., "In fact, those elected to the House of Burgesses were almost without exception men of wealth, property and of high standing in the community and among their peers."

Burgesses, electors of: as it seems, and note that only tax payers voted, in addition to the other requirements, e.g., "The early Virginia law established 'all ***housekeepers*** (q.v.), whether freeholders, leaseholders, or otherwise tenants shall be only capable to elect burgesses' by a majority of those who had the rights to vote."

burning water: boiling or very hot water. See ***elsater wine.***

bursten: hernia or rupture, e.g., "Since there was no procedure by which bursten might be alleviated, early people suffered mightily from it." Also see ***death, causes of in 1720.***

butolier: obsolete; probably a bottler of drinks or juices, "The term 'butolier' appears now and then, at least in the cities of the South, and usually associated with sales of strong drinks."

butt: a liquid measure of 108 gallons, e.g., "Many early American colonial records and inventories mention butts of liquids, especially wine and rum."

butter churn: See ***churn, butter.***

butter pans: See ***set pans, etc.***

buttery: great buttery: a room or place in a cool part of the house where, as Johnson says, "provisions are laid up," e.g., "The word buttery quite usually appears in the context of a home of more affluent early people."

butts and bounds: See ***metes and bounds*** in *What Did They Mean By That?*

by the report of common fame: See ***common fame, etc.***

C

cabbage, to cabbage onto something: very early, meaning to steal items of but slight value, such as cuttings from a tailor's work (Johnson 1802), e.g., "The expression 'he cabbaged onto it' arises from the early definition of 'cabbage,' meaning to pilfer inconsequential items."

cachexy: anemia, malnutrition, e.g., "Many early physicians administered warm milk and tea as a first medication for cachexy." Also see ***marasmus.***

cadowe: rough woolen cloth (see *stuff, What Did They Mean By That?*) or fabric, e.g., "Numerous references to cadowe may be found in the early colonies in association with apparel or coats."

café: a small business serving usually only food, but occasionally also beer and liquor, but without lodging or facilities for horses, e.g., "The *sticky buns* (q.v.) served by the Virginia Café in Bristol were enjoyed by all for decades."

call the shots: one in command or in charge; derived from the fact that on a military rifle range one man is assigned to shout out the placement of each shot when fired by a shooter, and his call is quite nearly final, e.g., "As Paul shot bull's-eye after bull's-eye, the man shouted that there was no point in calling the shots, since all were in the center of the target"; "Gene was the superintendent of the manufacturing line and so called the shots every day."

camisole: a woman's, usually lace-trimmed underwaist; a short light garment worn by ladies when dressed in negligee or without a bra; a strait jacket for lunatics or criminals condemned to the guillotine, e.g., "The elegant Mrs. D. told that she hardly ever wore a bra and preferred a camisole."

Cape Cod turkey: fish, usually cod, so called since not long after the first settlement of New England wild turkeys had become scarce, e.g., "Cape Cod turkey was baked, as was wild turkey, with bread or cornmeal dressing, potatoes, carrots, and a butter gravy, the term arising, if the story is true, it was only in the Northeast, since wild turkeys were common in the South, even to our day."

capias: Latin, "you shall take," or simply "do this," and meaning a general order to an officer of the court or a member of the executive branch, and directing that officer to take into his custody some individual—"take his body," e.g., "A *bench warrant* (q.v.) is one of the writs sometimes known as a 'capias.'"

capitation tax: a poll or head tax. Also see *head tax* and see *poll* in *What Did They Mean By That?*

caput: quite unlike now, the head or life of a person; the governmental head of a county, e.g., "While now the word 'caput' signifies 'gone,' 'finished,' 'obliterated,' 'vanished,' the word meant something quite different in the early law."

carbuncle fever: See **anthrax.**

cardamom, cardemon: a warm, sweet spice and seasoning early brought to the colonies from the Far East, including India, and especially favored in lamb dishes and curries, e.g., "While somewhat rare, cardemon occasionally appears in inventories of merchants in the larger cities, particularly Boston and New York."

carnal abuse; sexual acts by a man involving the female genitalia, yet not including penetration (known as carnal knowledge), e.g., "Whether or not physical acts attended the words, the early courts found men guilty of 'abuse' where sexual advances and suggestions of intercourse were advanced, especially toward young girls." Also see *abuse.*

cart path: a trail or early path through the forest that was wide enough and with few enough hazards that a draught animal (horse, mule, donkey, or oxen) pulling a cart could pass through, e.g., "By 1700 there were many cart paths throughout the colonies." Also see *common path.*

cask, tobacco: See *tobacco roller, etc.*

castigatory: See *cucking stool* and see *ducking stool* in *What Did They Mean By That?*

casualties, by war, of the U.S.: See **war dead of the U.S.**

catamenia: difficulty or irregularity in menstruation, e.g., "Several patients at the Toledo Lunatic Asylum in 1872 were said to be there as a result of 'menstrual flux' also then known as catamania."

catarrh, catarrhal (q.v., *What Did They Mean By That?*): any moderate or severe discharge from the nose and mouth, e.g., "What Jane declared to be 'catarrhal draining' by her teenage son was likely an allergy."

caul: an ancient term nearly synonymous with *snood* (q.v., *What Did They Mean By That?*); a net for a woman's hair placed on the back of a hat; sometimes the thin membrane or film which forms on the lining of the throat and mouth, e.g., "While Donna referred to the hair net on her hat as a caul, Marty referred to hers as a snood"; "Martha Diane told that the presence of caul often brought fear of diphtheria, scarlet fever, and tuberculosis."

cause of action: the exercise of one's *right of action* (q.v.); a concept of the law and meaning that time or place where events come together, usually coincidentally, such that one party is damaged or put at disadvantage in some fashion, even remote, for which the law may award damages or order actions or forbearance taken to the benefit of or remedy for the damaged person, e.g., "When Paul could not see and then slipped on ice that had been in place for hours at the store, the court found that his complaint stating those facts constituted a cause of action against that station."

cause, for: See *for cause.*

cavalry sword: See *horseman's sword, etc.*

caveat, withdrawn caveat: A landowner knowing or suspecting that a survey or even a patent to another person included some of his land could file a caveat to protest against such infringement, thus gaining an investigation of the matter; a withdrawn caveat meant that the caveator no longer believed the survey crossed his boundary lines, that an elder caveat revealed his to be in error, or the matter had been settled, e.g., "When Haskins file a completed survey for his grant, Drake filed a caveat revealing that 10 acres of the Haskins survey was located on Drake's land."

censuses of the states, odd years. See *odd years, censuses etc.*

cephalitis: See *phrenitis, etc.*

certificate for land: See *land certificate.*

cestui que trust: usually pronounced "set-ee-kuh-trust"; Latin for that person who has the right to assets, property or money in the hands of and being under the control of another person—a trustee, e.g., "The court ruled that the provision that Mikaila should have the funds when she was eighteen constituted a trust, and that she was the cestui que trust."

chain carrier: See *poleman.*

chair, wain scott: See *wain scott.*

chair: as now, and a sedan chair or any other small, very light buggy or carriage for one personal, e.g., "A 1782 Connecticut newspaper referred to a light buggy for hire as a 'chair.'"

chaldron, chaldern, chalder: usually 1.5 tons of coal, e.g., "The coal miners who emigrated from Wales to Pennsylvania and there again worked in the mines were accustomed to referring to coal by chaldrons, though their American employers were not."

chancellor: the judge of a court of chancery, e.g., "While in early law there was a sharp division between courts of law and those of equity, today in most states those two courts are not separated nor are those distinguishable, and judges act in either capacity—judge or chancellor—based upon the nature of the claim and remedy sought in the *cause of action* (q.v.)."

chancery courts: See *state court web sites* and see *chancellor.*

chandler: as in *What Did They Mean By That?*, a candle maker; also one who deals, sells, or trades in supplies, trinkets, *gee-gaws* (see *What Did They Mean By That?*), and merchandise of all sorts; the title occasionally given to that person who was responsible for the furniture of a ship (q.v., *ships furniture*), e.g., "Though he did not live aboard or sail with the ship, *Rose and John* out of Boston, Martin was the very able London chandler to that vessel."

charbon: See *anthrax*.

cheap shot, a: a term of derision; one of many terms of the early American colonies, derived from our use of firearms, meaning that a person has been critical of or sarcastic to another, which words brought emotional harm/hurt to another person, yet cost the speaker nothing and was rude, e.g., "When one man said to a wounded veteran who sought cheaper prescriptions, 'You didn't have to go to Vietnam, you know?' a bystander angrily said 'That was a cheap shot!!'"

cheese, a: as now; also any prepared food shaped as to appear like a wheel of cheese, e.g., "*Housekeeping in Old Virginia*, 1889, speaking of preparing *souse* (q.v.) from hogs, noted that 'one head and a dozen ears will make a good-sized cheese.'" Also see *wheel of cheese*.

cheese, wheel of: See *wheel of cheese*.

chiefs, Indian: See *great men, greate men*.

chickpeas: a small brown pea-like seed from the garbanzo plant and called an herb by Johnson (1755); brought to the American Colonies by Southern Europeans and from Latin America and used widely in salads and in cooking, e.g., "As now, early settlers of the South and Southwest routinely added chickpeas to soups, stews, and mixed such with vegetables in such as sallets." See *sallet* in *What Did They Mean By That?*

chilblain, a swelling from cold of fingers, ears, toes, nose and ears, e.g., "Many early mothers mistakenly treated chilblains by applying snow or ice."

child of ease: an expression from very early colonial times, meaning a child born to position, wealth and affluence, e.g., "In his writing he used Thelma as an example of a child of ease, she having been born in 1754 to great wealth and likely not expected to ever be called upon to perform menial or common labor."

child, to lay a: See *lay a child*.

childbed fever: infection and high fever in a new mother shortly after giving birth, e.g., "Maggie had nine children and was said to have suffered childbed fever after every one."

chinquapins, chinkapins: probably from the Algonquin language; a seed, much like chestnuts, from a shrub-like tree, and introduced to the early settlers by the American Indians, e.g., "As boys, Tyler and Ryan would gather chinquapins from the woods, then roast those and carry such in their pockets for snacks while working or walking long distances."

chlorosis, **green sickness:** anemia in teenage girls from iron deficiency causing a yellow/green complexion, e.g., "For chlorosis Dr. Drake apparently administered rust in cooked cereal."

chops: quite unlike now, the mouth of a harbor, e.g., "Early writings often refer to ships at or 'entering the chops.'"

chose in action: a personal right, usually to compensation, that has not been reduced to a formal claim or a judgment, but which right the claimant may pursue by action at law, e.g., "A right of James to file a mechanics lien and later to sue on that right to gain his pay for the work done is known as a *chose in action,* since he has not yet proceeded to reduce that right to a formal claim or a judgment in order that he collect that money." See *lien, mechanics, tax, etc.*

church warden: a caretaker and lesser officer of the church appointed by the parish priest, e.g., "Quan reminded all that Johnson (1802) had defined church wardens, such as those in early Virginia, as 'officers appointed yearly to look to the church, church yard and such things as belong to the church; and to observe the behavior of the parishioners.'"

cilice: See *hair sifter.*

cipher: early and now, the ability to use and know numbers and calculate in basic ways; writing in unintelligible words or phrases; in telegraphy, a message that is unintelligible, e.g., "Telegrapher Drue at 'AC Tower' thought it humorous that while he had been taught to cipher well in his earliest schooling, he used the same term to describe nonsense messages received."

circuit courts: See *state court web sites.*

city courts: See *state court web sites.*

claim, liquidated: See *liquidated claim.*

Claims, Courts of: that court and all its branches established in 1855 and having jurisdiction over all claims against the U.S. that arise from government contracts or claims arising from acts of Congress or actions of members of the Executive branch, e.g., "When the U.S. Postal Department failed to reimburse the Arlington postmaster for his travel, he filed a claim and then a lawsuit in the Court of Claims."

clamp: a varying quantity or measure of bricks not yet fired (Johnson, 1802), e.g., "Early inventories occasionally list clamps of bricks, indicating that the owner or someone there had knowledge of making and firing bricks of clay." Also see *clamps* in *What Did They Mean By That?*

...er and stationkeeper at Arlington, Ohio in 1895. See *cipher*.

clan, clansmen: as in Ireland, Wales and Scotland, meaning literally "children" and "children of," e.g., "The ancient expression 'gathering of the clan' indicated that the children and descendants of an ancient family had come together to celebrate and commune."

clap: See *gonorrhea* in *What Did They Mean By That?*

clapper: See *cowbell, etc.*

clean hands: a maxim of the law requiring that if one seeks equity though an action in the courts then that person must not be guilty of or responsible for any illegality or impropriety of his own in that matter, e.g., "When Cliff sued the estate for money for his advice, the court found that in violation of the clean acts doctrine, he had fraudulently represented to the decedent that he had special knowledge of the matter which he did not have."

clear from ground leaves or seconds: a common expression of those who bought, sold or otherwise dealt in tobacco, describing the quality and purity of the bulk tobacco being exchanged, e.g., "Many early records of the tobacco producing colonies mention the sale or purchase of 'tobacco clear from ground leaves or seconds and in good caske (barrel).'"

clear title: not an expression of the law; a generality meaning a complete or full title; that state of title to land such that the entirety of the rights for which the buyer bargained and purchased is given over to that person; title to land free and clear of encumbrances of any sort, e.g., "The agreement was that when he received the purchase money John would deliver clear title to Fred."

clerk's certificate: See **land certificate.**

close: as now; early, a tract of land enclosed by a fence; later, a tract, whether fenced or not, and surrounding and a part of one's residence, e.g., "When the court order referred to Owen Griffith's close, it meant his small kitchen garden tract around which had been erected a *snake fence* (q.v., *What Did They Mean By That?*)."

coach: a railroad train car; a general term meaning a covered carriage, usually box-shaped, e.g., "The beautiful phaeton was listed for tax purposes simply as 'coach.'"

coalscuttle: a wide-mouthed, handled bucket, usually of sturdy galvanized metal and used to carry coal from storage to a place near the fireplace or stove, e.g., "Maggie kept the coalscuttle behind the heating stove in the middle room of their home."

cock of hay: in early New England, a small pile of hay, usually covered in winter, e.g., "Early Connecticut records reveal a criminal who 'secreted himself in a cock of hay.'"

cockler, cockles: one who hunts, gathers and markets cockles, those, a small, hard-shelled, sand burrowing, shore line creature, similar to a clam, e.g., "While cockles as gathered in Britain and France for millennia are unknown on our east coasts, similar food bivalves were gathered by Indians and early settlers on the northwest coast of America and the west coast of Canada."

cocotte: a women who occasionally engages as a prostitute; one who charges for incidental sex, e.g., "The early New York reports reveal a case where a loose woman was referred to as a cocotte when it was revealed that she was paid for sexual favors."

coddle, caudle: See *mollycoddle.*

codicil: an addition or correction of a will by the testator, executed and witnessed. See *codicil* in *What Did They Mean By That?*

Coercive Acts (Intolerable Acts): in part as punishment for the *Boston Tea Party* (q.v., *What Did They Mean By That?*) and also to deter further hostile activities by American colonists, e.g., "Britain passed *The Boston Port Act*, 31 March 1774, thereby closing Boston Harbor to all shipping except for coasters carrying necessary supplies; the *customs service was moved* to Salem and Marblehead; *The Massachusetts Bay Regulating Act* 20 May 1774 replaced the General Assembly with a *Mandamus Council* at Marblehead nominated by Governor (General) Gage; the *governor was given the power to appoint and dismiss any law officers;* there were to be no *town meetings* (q.v., *What Did They Mean By That?*) without royal assent; and there would be *no election of juries by freeholders.* Following that was the *Administration of Justice Act* 20 May 1774 (called by us, *The Murder Act*) empowering the governor to remove trials to another colony or to Britain; and *The Quartering Act* 2 June 1774 that broadened the *Quartering Act of 1765* (q.v.)."

coffee mill, coffee grinder: usually a small wooden box, approximately 8"x8"x8", containing a grinding mechanism, and closable on all sides, with an opening in the top for placing coffee beans into the machine, and another port on a side close to the bottom, through which ground coffee could be removed, e.g., "Early coffee mills are very popular as collectibles now."

cohort: unlike now, a small, usually formally organized troop or group of fighting men, e.g., "When Richard referred to his cohorts, he was speaking of his militia comrades in arms."

Figure 8. 1868 *collotype* of the great-great grandmother
of Mrs. Kennedy of Virginia.

cohosh, black or ***blue:*** black snakeroot; widely prescribed as having value for "uterine difficulties"; one of the ***emmenogogues*** (q.v.) frequently given as a ***nervine*** (q.v.), e.g., "Drs. Drake and Pierce prescribed black cohosh for women experiencing unwanted pregnancies, menstrual pain or difficult menstrual periods, and also believed it efficacious for nervousness in either men or women."

collateral lines: those ancestral family members to whom one is related by affinity, and not by consanguinity, e.g., "Mikaila and Allison were first cousins and so were related through consanguinity, however their husbands were related for affinity."

collodion, wet and dry plates: popular from the period 1855 to the twentieth century, innovations in photography after "daguerreotypes" (could not be reproduced) and "collotypes" (that revealed any defect in the print paper), allowed shorter exposure times and multiple copies to be made, e.g., "We must be grateful to Mathew Brady and Alexander Gardner, and their students, for the wonderful wet plate collodion images they created of the Civil War and the early 'West.'" Also see ***ambrotype*** and ***tintype*** in *What Did They Mean By That?*

collotypes: See ***collodion, wet, etc.***

colonial government, natures of: of the thirteen original colonies, there were "charter," "royal" and "proprietary" forms of governments, those more recently referred to by historians as "corporation" and "provincial" forms, e.g., "Charter colonies were Massachusetts, Rhode Island, and Connecticut, the royal colonies were Maryland, Pennsylvania, and Delaware, and those known as proprietary colonies were Virginia, both Carolinas, New Hampshire, Vermont, New Jersey and Georgia." (Author's note: for more information, the reader is advised to "search" those governmental categories on the Internet.)

colostrum: the first milk produce by a women in late pregnancy and the first few days after birth, high in nutrients. Was said to reveal an unhealthy state of breast milk, e.g., "Though scarcely understood, early colonists, knowing of the importance to all animals, including a child, of the very first milk from a mother, it was thought that when an infant was not doing well, the mother's colostrum might be 'in an unhealthy state.'"

commingle, confusion of goods: to place together, e.g., "When two farmers each place their grain in an elevator, thus mixing it with all other, and yet are free to take a quantity equal to what they placed there, they have 'commingled' their grain resulting in a 'confusion' of that commodity."

commission, commissions of administration: a writing or document properly executed by which a government empowers a person or persons to perform specific acts or to have specific authority for a stated period, e.g., "In 1727 Virginia commissioned Col. William Byrd to establish a Northern dividing line between Virginia and North Carolina"; "Commissions of administration directing that a certain named person should preside over an estate were very common, early as now." Also see *dedimas potestatum, etc.*

commissioned officer: in the U.S. armed forces, those men above the rank of Ensign and commissioned as officers by the authority of the President, by which they rank above all non-commissioned personnel, e.g., "Sergeants and petty officers are not commissioned, though they have substantial jurisdiction and control over personnel of all ranks lesser than their own."

committing authority: any judicial officer with the authority to issue arrest warrants for those believed to have committed crimes including breaches of the peace, misdemeanors, and felonies, e.g., "The *police magistrate* (q.v.) was one of the officers of the community that also had committing authority in Marion County."

commodities: movable wares, goods, and personal property used as movable stock in trade or in commerce, e.g., "While many items we buy were chattels and many times commodities, money, whether paper or coin arguably is not."

common fame, by a report of: so well known to a community or a substantial group of the citizenry that a court will presume its truth, subject, however, to proof otherwise, e.g., "In 1695 when Anne was charged with having delivered a bastard child fathered by a man named Curle, the court ruled that her fornication with him was 'known by common fame.'"

common inn: an establishment open to the general public, regardless of station in life, that provided the needs of a traveler and his journey, including overnight lodging, food, usually spirituous liquors, and care and food for his horse or other draft animals, e.g., "The well-known common inn known as *Crab Orchard Inn* was established in 1796 in Crab Orchard, Tennessee, that being the first town to be reached by those traveling west through Crab Orchard Gap." Also see *inn* in *What Did They Mean By That?*

common path: a path for people afoot or on horseback or with a narrow cart, and open to the public, e.g., "There are many common paths identified in the early colonies."

common school: a public school, as opposed to a private school, e.g., "With the coming of the common schools in the eighteenth and nineteenth centuries, education to some extent was open even to the very poor."

Commonwealth Courts: See *state court web sites.*

community property: all property gained by a husband or wife during their marriage becomes community property, except any property intended by either party to be his or her own, e.g., "Because she did not intend to be the sole owner of her furniture, when Diane bought a couch and four chairs, those became community property, even though Todd knew or cared nothing of the purchase."

compilation: a composition, in writing or electronically gathered together and made up of the intellectual products or writings of other persons, e.g., "His book having to do with how famous people died was a compilation of the records and data of many other writers and sources."

complainant: See *lawsuits, common, etc.*

confession of judgment: That state of a legal dispute when a defendant formally states and confesses that he is, in fact, obligated as claimed by the plaintiff, and agrees to pay the amount claimed in that suit or an agreed different sum, that agreement then reduced to a judgment in the case, e.g., "When the loan company sued Cody for $11,000.00, Cody agreed that he would confess judgment for $7,800.00 in exchange for a dismissal of the law suit with *prejudice* (q.v.)."

confusion of goods: See *commingle, etc.*

consensual marriage: an oral marriage; a marriage by present agreement of the parties, and without further ceremony or license, e.g., "Because of the frequent absence of those who might perform a ceremony, and since licenses to marry often were not required on the early frontier, many were the consensual marriages that now confound genealogists."

conservator: a guardian or protector, e.g., "The term conservator often was used when assets were to be protected for the benefit of minors or others legally incompetent to appropriately manage or dispose of the same, e.g., "When his father died and left the three-year-old boy a substantial amount of money, the court ordered that the mother continue having the care and nurture of the youth, however a conservator was appointed to manage the assets."

consideration: as now; in law, that sum or thing having real or perceived value that is promised or given over in exchange for the acts, forbearance, or promises of the other party, e.g., "The consideration paid and promised to Drake for the use of Parker's tillable land for two years was $250.00 per year and a promise to also pay one-third over the value of the crops that might be raised there."

consortium: as now, the rights to the companionship, assistance, and affection of one spouse with the other, e.g., "Though not desirous of so acting, she submitted to his sexual desires as a part of her duties of consortium."

constable: now, an officer of a city, town, village or other municipal entity; early, a public civil officer with reduced powers similar to those of a sheriff, and charged with keeping the peace in his district, e.g., "In 1754, Lazarus Drake and two other men were appointed constables in Surry County."

constipation: See *costiveness*.

constitutional county courts: See *state court web sites*.

constuprate: to rape or sexually assault or abuse any girl or woman, e.g., "In the 1860 New York case of Koening vs. Nott, Nott was found guilty of violation and constupration of Jane Koening."

contempt of court: any act or words that might, may, or are intended to diminish the respect to be paid to a court, or to obstruct justice or hinder any judicial proceeding, e.g., "In his courtroom a judge has great authority to prevent the disruption of justice in any way, and on myriad occasions such judges have peremptorily fined or imprisoned any who have obstructed or violated the dignity of such proceedings."

contiguous: somewhat unlike now, early, near to, but not touching; neighboring, but not adjoining another designated location or object; now, similar yet perhaps touching, e.g., "The early statement that the Hunt land was contiguous to that of Griffith may or may not reveal that those tracts shared any common boundary or point of contact." Also see *abut, etc.*

Contracts, aleatory: See *aleatory contracts*.

contumacy: a failure to appear before a court or other duly authorized tribunal after being ordered to do so; occasionally, a failure to perform or obey an order by a court, e.g., "Johnson failed to appear after being served an order of the court that the sheriff had served upon him, so the court found that his conduct was contumacious and fined him."

convent: a voluntary group of nuns, friars or monks, usually having a superior member, e.g., "The nineteenth-century Tennessee lawsuit of Sacred Heart Academy vs. Karsch further defined a convent as a reclusive body of people that was one society or organization."

conversation: as now; one's manner of living; intercourse of the wife or husband of another person, e.g., "A nineteenth-century Illinois case spoke of conversation as in 'chaste life and conversation'"; "In both Massachusetts and Delaware nineteenth-century courts referred to criminal conversation when awarding damages for harm done by men in seducing the wives of other men."

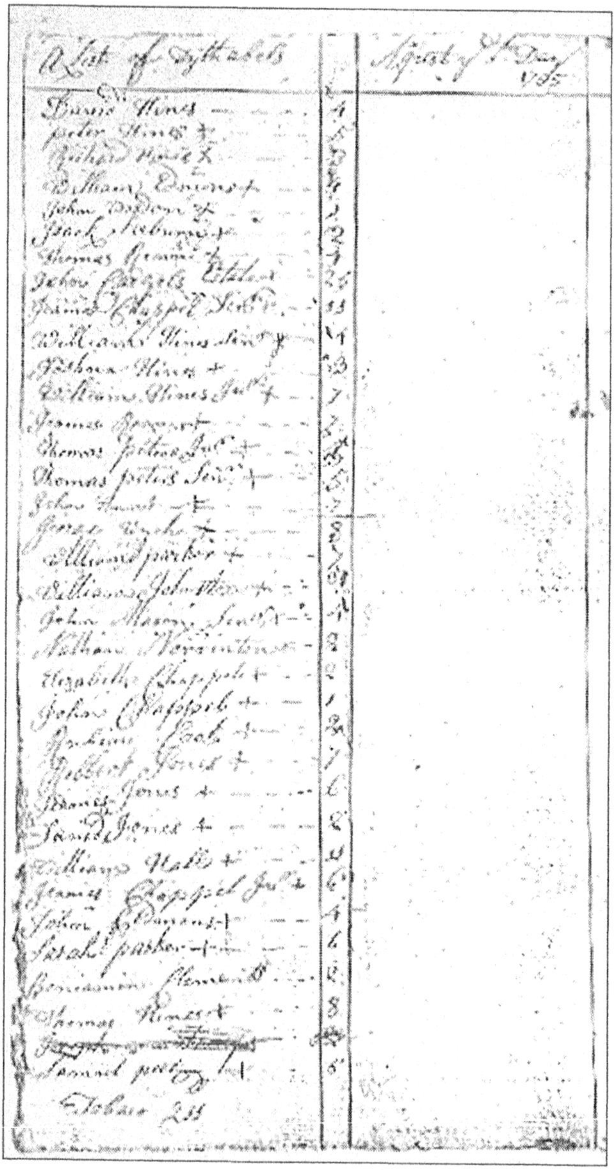

Figure 9. 1757 list of tithables by Surry County, Virginia *constable*, Lazarus Drake.

conveyance: any act of transfer of an interest in land, and also the document accomplishing such a transfer, e.g., "The warranty deed Drake executed, and the fact that he did so, both were properly called a conveyance."

copyhold, copyhold tenure; virtually unknown in the American colonies, a tenancy by a usually unwritten agreement by which a tenant was admitted to use of the lands of a landlord, e.g., "The earliest records of Maryland reveal discussions of the need for copyholds, though not one seems to have been accomplished."

corn, bread: See *grindin' of, etc.*

corn oysters: as with *plum pudding* (q.v.), corn oysters contain no oysters, but rather are flour and egg batter, plus whole corn rolled into round and flat shapes and fried, e.g., "The children were soon tired of corn oysters, but by February and March there was little else remaining of the crops of the prior year."

corned beef: as with *corn oysters* (q.v.) and *plum pudding* (q.v.), and to the surprise of many of us now, corned beef contains no corn and early settlers often made it from the meat of worn-out or broken-down oxen that had been used to pull the plows, e.g., "Three-to-six-pound slabs of lean beef were placed in salt pickling and pepper."

coroner's inquest: See *coroner* in *What Did They Mean By That?*

corporal oath: synonymous with "solemn oath"; an oath made or spoken when the oath giver has his or her hand on a Bible, e.g., "The Kentucky case wherein the court spoke of a corporal oath referred simply to the 'swearing in' quite usually required of all trial witnesses."

corporal punishment: any punishment consisting of physical force or restraint, e.g., "Early courts in Colorado, as well as California, ruled that just as was whipping, the use of stocks and pillories was corporal punishment and so was prohibited."

corporeal property: as opposed to incorporeal property; any property that may be sensed—touched, seen, heard, felt or smelled—is corporeal, e.g., "Though he had every right to receive the money from the wheat crop, that money and his rights to it were incorporeal, while the crop itself was corporeal."

corruption, corrupted: any infection or rotting of the flesh, e.g., "Many are the comments concerning the corruptions caused by diseases or injuries."

corsair: a pirate, e.g., "Blackbeard was likely the most well-known of the eighteenth-century corsairs."

corum nobis: a common writ since the earliest times; a writ filed in the same court alleging an error of fact not appearing in the record of a prior case, and seeking to reverse, overturn, or modify some judgment previously rendered by that same court, e.g., "An early Missouri court ruled that a writ of corum nobis should issue where a judgment had been rendered against a married woman without notice of the lawsuit or knowledge of it having been given her husband."

co-signer: a guarantor; quite nearly slang now and used very generally to mean anyone who agrees to pay or share in a debt, regardless of the conditions, if the principal does not does not do so as agreed, e.g., "Henry co-signed for Evan, and when he left town the mortgage company collected from Henry." Also see **guarantor** and see **surety**.

cosmopathic: healing as a result of supernatural, preternatural, or cosmic forces, e.g., "In nineteenth-century Massachusetts, Zimmerman was charged with fraudulent practices as a physition by utilizing what he labeled as cosmopathic medicine."

costiveness: constipation, e.g., "After the Civil War Dr. Walker believed that whole wheat breads and cakes, frequent glasses of water, and ripe fruits were helpful in cases of constipation, and also believed that severe uterine problems might result if the problem was not relieved."

costs and prices in 1850, some: following are some typical retail prices for common needs during the year 1850, by which with a multiplier of 40-45 prices in 2000 may be compared. It also is interesting that *Dr. William K. Drake* (central Ohio) taught school and made an entry in 1849 revealing that he charged $1.50 per student (two 66 day terms = 2.75 cents ea. per day); 50 cents for a daybook (bound notebook 100 pg.; $1.25 for a front "quarter of beef"; 35 cents for 10 pounds "beef"; 39 cents a lb. for 5 pounds tallow; 23/4 per lb. for 42 pounds flour; 17 cents for 10 pounds lard; 80 cents for 10 pounds sausage; 1 cent per lb. for 14 pounds spare ribs; 66 cents for 14.25 pounds ham; 62.5 cents for 5 pounds butter; $1.00 for a bu. dried apples; 10 cents per gallon for 5 gal. vinegar; $1.19 for 28 pounds of pork; $1.00 for a bu. of potatoes 1.00; 1.00 for having a pair of pants made; $1.50 for having a linen coat made; $1.99 for 2 prs of drawers; $1.50 room and board for one week; $3.00 for wood and candles for 3 months for a boarder; ; $1.00 per week room and board "and washing done" @ 4-5 cents per item; 3-5 cents per item of clothes laundered; $1.00 per week room and board "and washing done" @ 4-5 cents per item; $1.25 for having a horse shod; $3.00 for house call at night, $1.00 daytime; $3.00 for obstetrics; $20.00 for a colt; $1.00 for leather for a pr. of shoes, and $1.00 to have those made; 37.5 cents for a tin bucket; 1.12^{1/2}$ for a leather vest; $5.00 for an overcoat; $1.00 for 2 shirts; $1.00 for 2 prs. Trousers; 62.5 cents a day for raking and binding; 50 cents a day for hoeing corn; 50 cents a day for reaping and the same for raking; 50 cents a day for hauling grain (teamster); $1.00 per day for threshing (theses rates equal 4 to 6 cents per hour for such farm work); 1 cent per bd foot for 375 linear ft. lumber (1"x1'). Also see *costs and prices in 1900, some.*

costs and prices in 1900, some: following are some typical retail prices for common needs during the year 1900, by which with a multiplier of 30-32 prices in 2000 may be compared; 50 cents for a solid steel shovel with wooden handle; 45 cents for a mattock (handle 5 cents); 20 cents for a steel and wooden handled garden rake; $1.65 for a 40" 8 rib table umbrella; $1.10 for a high quality 22" hand saw; 45 cents for a 1 lb. nail hammer; 85 cents for a 3 bladed, higher quality penknife; $4.75 for an all wool cassimere man's suit; $1.25-1.55 for a pr. of ladies high quality button shoes; $1.30 for a pr. of high quality ladies' kidskin slippers; $1.00 for 3 of men's white shirts; 75 cents for the best cotton man's dress shirt; 47 cents for a worsted cotton man's sweater; $1.75 for "heavy" Australian wool, ribbed collar, man's sweater; 19 cents for a heavy, silk, men's Windsor necktie; 47 to 58 cents for an extra fine ladies' percale, full sleeved blouse; $1.95-2.50 for a fine, taffeta lined, wool ladies' full skirt; $5.50-6.35 for a fine serge & mohair, silk lined ladies suit; $125.00 for a ebony upright, ivory keyed piano; $6.25 for a high quality breech loading, single barrel shotgun; $12.95 for a single action Army Colt's 12.5" barrel revolver; $10.94 for a Winchester 1873; $13.00 for a Winchester 94; 60 cents (6 for $3.48) for fine hip-rest, oak dining chairs; $2.00 for a fine, leather seated, armed, heavy oak rocker; 80 cents for a child's oak high chair with adjustable table; $4.40 for an elegant 5 leg Oak dining table with leaves to 10'; $4.10 for quarter-sawn oak turned leg, ball and claw foot parlor table; 11.75 for oak pigeonholed, side-by-side secretary-bookcase with mirror; $16.00 for oak 3 piece bedroom suit bed, dresser and commode; $10.00 for iron and brass trimmed bed; $11.30 for large armchair, platform rocker, large sofa, & 2 side chairs; $7.50 for 6' 10" quarter-sawn oak hall and tree seat with mirror & umbrella stand; $9.95 for English Wetherby porcelain 100 pc. Dinner set (s&h free!); $2.75 for 36 pcs. of cut glass tumblers and stemware; $3.35 for elegant Gone-With-The-Wind lamp; 75 cents for swivel, wall bracket, kitchen lamp with reflector; $7.50 for fine baby carriage with umbrella and rubber tires; $35.90 for a FINE, gold-stripped Ohio buggy, with top, full curtains, & robe. Also see *costs and prices in 1850, some.*

Figure 10. Farmer Daniel Carner and his wife
Mary Martin Carner dressed for the photographer in 1875.
See *costs and prices in 1850, some*.

coterminous: a property line sharing the same termination points with another adjoining line; sharing a common boundary for its entire length, e.g., "Drake's north line was identical to the south line of Weaver, hence the surveyor wrote that the lines were coterminous." Also see *abut, etc.* and see *contiguous.*

counter-claim: See *lawsuits, common, procedural steps.*

counter-complainanant: See *lawsuits, common, etc.*

county courts: See *state court web sites.*

courser: a well trained and groomed, highly bred and fine horse used for pulling sleighs or fine light carriages, e.g., "In 'The Night Before Christmas' Moore described Santa's beautiful reindeer team by saying 'More rapid than eagles his coursers they came...'"

court of chancery: See *chancellor.*

court of claims: See *claims, court of.*

court of law: See *chancellor.*

court of ordinary: See *ordinary, court of.*

court of private land claims: See *private land.*

court recess: See *out of term, etc.*

court, general: See *general court.*

courthouse door, at the: an expression meaning that billboard or other place designated for posting public notices and court or sheriff ordered sales, e.g., "The sale was advertised to take place at the courthouse door at noon on Saturday, July 16, 1764."

courts of appeals: See *state court web sites.*

courts of claims: See *state court web sites.*

courts of special appeals: See *state court web sites.*

courts, Ecclesiastical: See *Ecclesiastical courts.*

courts, names of: See *state court web sites.*

courts' minutes: See *minutes, etc.*

courts' orders: See *minutes, etc.*

covenant: an enforceable promise, whether express or implied, and usually in a contract or a deed, e.g., "Drake sued on the deed covenant of peaceable possession and was held to be entitled to compensation because the man who sold him the land grossly disturbed Drake's family by building a new saw mill within twenty feet of the boundary between the two properties."

covin, covinous: a secret agreement or arrangement between two or more people to bring harm or to defraud another person, e.g., "Several early cases in New England and New York have described reprehensible conduct by a defendant as covinous."

coxalgia: perhaps now indeterminable, Pierce (1882) called it "disease of the hip joints" associated with drainage, extreme weakness of the hip joint, and a shrinkage of that leg, e.g., "Shortly after the Civil War Dr. Rhu treated coxalgia with exercise and a homemade prosthetic device which stretched apart Mr. Haskins' knee and hip joints."

cracks, trotting cracks: well bred trotters and pacers (horses), e.g., "Horse racing having been very popular in the nineteenth century, Currier and Ives published a colorful depiction of a trotter, **sulky** (q.v., *What Did They Mean By That?*) and driver moving rapidly over a race course, that print entitled 'Trotting Cracks at the Forge.'"

cramp colic: See **appendicitis.**

cream boat; a bowl lipped for pouring and used to hold cream at the dining table, e.g., "What today we would call a creamer or cream bowl was also known as a cream boat." Also see **slop bowl.**

creditor: See **debtor, etc.**

cretinism: a condition of mental disability that is accompanied by a physical disability, e.g., "Ed's male child was born with severe cretinism; an extremely low IQ and a near total inability to maintain his balance."

crib: a flat, usually padded, bed-like piece of furniture upon which prostitutes plied their trade, e.g., "Promontory, Utah, as did many other towns of the old West, had cribs aplenty occupied by the whores who followed the railroad."

criminal bonds: See **bonds, surety, etc.**

criminal courts: See **state court web sites.**

crockery: any dish, bowls, or container made of clay and baked, e.g., "Early inventories are replete with items such as 'crocks,' 'crock pots,' 'crock jugs' and 'crock bowls.'"

crook: as now; a pothook for use in a fireplace, e.g., "The inventory of utensils in the Hines estate revealed three crooks." Also see **crook** in *What Did They Mean By That?*

cropper, sharecropper: one who works the land of another without compensation, yet receives a percentage or pre-established amount of the proceeds from the crop, e.g., "As 'poor as a sharecropper with a short-handled hoe' was commonly said, since it was almost impossible to support a family and increase one's wealth with only the customary percentages agreeable to early landowners."

cross-complainant: See **lawsuits, common, etc.**

cross-complaint: See **lawsuits, common, procedural steps.**

cross-petition: See *lawsuits, common, etc.*

croup: a very common inflammation of the throat of children throughout the centuries, e.g., "Few were the children of the early years who did not suffer from croup."

cruiser, timber: See *timber cruiser.*

cubebs: much like galingale, a favorite spice from Africa and known since ancient times, and having a pungent, acrid, slightly bitter and persistent flavor that also has been favored for centuries in treating gonorrhea, e.g., "We likely would say that cubebs taste like strong peppers, and such were boiled, the oil skimmed off, saved, and used as seasoning or administered for the medicinal value." Also see *hippocras, yprocras.*

cucking stool, tumbrel, castigatory, trebucket: see *What Did They Mean By That?*, **ducking stool**, a stool to which a person—usually a woman—was tied and then ducked in water as punishment, e.g., "In an early Pennsylvania case the term was used when a woman sued to prevent the use of such."

culpa: an ancient term used commonly and meaning neglect, fault, blame, e.g., "Mea culpa is the most common use of culpa and means 'I am at fault.'"

cum testamento annexo: Latin; literally, with a will annexed, e.g., "'Administrator cum testamento annexo' is a very common early expression revealing that the court has ordered an administration and has made a will by the decedent that was not legally complete in some fashion (improper witnesses or impossible terms, etc.) a part of that administration."

cunning witt and judgment: An American expression of the seventeenth and eighteenth centuries meaning to seriously consider and ponder some issue in question, e.g., "In 1664 a court charged a jury of inquest that they should use their 'cunning witt and judgment' in investigation into the mysterious death of Robert Whitell."

currency, uncertainty of: See *uncertainty of currency.*

currency: any coinage or paper money that circulates and is authorized by a government in power at the place of issue, e.g., "Proclamation money was legitimate eighteenth-century currency, since it was widely used and approved by the legislature of the North Carolina Colony." See *proclamation money* in *What Did They Mean By That?*

curtesy: an estate similar to a widow's rights in land belonging to her husband, e.g., "Curtesy was the right of a husband to a life estate in any real property held in fee or in fee tail by his deceased wife during their marriage, provided only that there had been living children of the couple who otherwise would have inherited that property." See *entailment, etc.* in *What Did They Mean By That?*

cut nails, square nails: synonymous; a nail cut from a piece of flat iron of varying thickness and tapered on two sides; a successor to *forged nails* tapered on all sides and made by blacksmiths, and a predecessor to *wire nails* that are round for the full length and cut from lengths of wire, cut nails were invented about 1785, and commonly available by about 1815, e.g., "Melanie knew that structures could be approximately dated by the nails used, since virtually all furniture and wooden structures made between 1820 and 1890 contained cut nails."

cutling: very early; meaning probably unremembered; perhaps; a superlative in matter of cleanliness, as in "cut cleanly with a very sharp knife," e.g., "Charlene recalled that her mother on occasion referred to some person, especially a well-groomed child, as 'clean as a cutling.'"

cuts, draw cuts: to draw lots, or cuts of paper of varying lengths, to decide a winner in some dispute or difference, as in flipping a coin, e.g., "A seventeenth-century Charles City court accepted as a means of settlement an agreement by the parties that they would draw cuts one time."

cutteau knife: a heavy single-bladed knife, used to cut many materials and as a weapon, and occasionally issued to Maryland troops during the American Revolution, e.g., "The common soldier of the 1776 Fourth Independent Company of Maryland State Troops was issued or carried a musket, cartouche box, and, when available, a cutteau knife also was issued."

D

damages: money or other thing of value paid to or demanded by one who has suffered harm or loss at the hands of another, e.g., "Mrs. Sherrill demanded $1240.00 as the damage she incurred when her landlord failed to keep the roof in repair at her leased store space."

damnify: to have suffered damages from some outside force or person. See *damnified* in *What Did They Mean By That?*

daw: an American crow, or sometimes a raven, arising from the sound made by those birds, and seemingly thought to be a variation to the ravens and crows of Britain, e.g., "There are many early American references to daws, especially by those untrained in bird identification."

dawdle: very early term, meaning to move ahead haltingly, very leisurely, lazily, or with uncertainty, e.g., "The word dawdle used to describe a lazy worker appears very early in English and American writings and literature."

day fever, daytime fever: See *diary fever.*

de bonis non (d.b.n. administratis): Latin, meaning an administration of the assets, property or rights not administered during a previous probate proceeding, e.g., "When Attorney Looney found that the estate had been closed after which a tract of land had been discovered belonging to the decedent, he was required to seek an administration de bonis non."

de facto: Latin, literally "of fact"; in fact, in truth, actually so, as distinguished from *de jure* (q.v.), e.g., "Though he had never been appointed or authorized to be a trustee and attend to her affairs when ill, he was de facto such."

de jure: Latin, legally so, by reason of the law of the matter, legitimate, e.g., "While Scott was the named trustee and thus had the authority to handle her financial affairs, yet had stood by while Margaret did so, he was the trustee de jure, while Margaret was the trustee de facto." Also see *de facto.*

de novo: Latin, literally "of new"; to start afresh, to commence again from the beginning, e.g., "The judge ordered a trial de novo, meaning that the matter was to be litigated as though it never had been before."

de: from the Latin, meaning by, from, out of, in respect to, concerning, e.g., "The many surnames containing the prefix or the foreword 'de,' such as *DeAngelo*, mean of that line, family or that father."

deacon: unlike now, an assistant to the parish priest or bishop or an employee of the church who had responsibilities in congregational activities, e.g., "The term *deacon* when found in seventeenth- and early eighteenth-century Virginia and Carolina records reveals the person had duties that were other than those of the preacher, pastor or priest."

dead as a door nail: a nail when clinched over in order that it not work loose is called a *dead nail* since it can not move, so, that condition became a metaphor for a dead person, e.g., "Though forgotten by most now, dead nails were employed in the making of doors and gates, and the long life, rigidity, and immovability of such jointure reminded early folks of the dead."

dead weight: referring to the fact that a heavy inanimate object is as difficult for a person to lift off the ground as would be a dead body, e.g., "Drake commented that the crate of castings was dead weight if ever there was such."

deadened, deaden trees: to kill trees on a tract of land, usually by girdling, e.g., "It is said that James McCormick deadened the trees on forty acres in 1832; an enormous task." See **girdle, girdling** in *What Did They Mean By That?*

death bell: See *passing bell, mourning, etc.*

death pall: See *veil over her face.*

death rattle: the gurgling sound often heard at the moment of death resulting from the loss of the capacity to swallow in the death process, e.g., "In the back seat, Hank Williams was heard by the driver of his Cadillac to make the death rattle." Also see *veil over her face.*

death veil: See *veil over her face.*

death, causes of in 1720: From the "Historical Register" of 1720, the following causes of death were set forth with the numbers of those who had died of those causes during the year from December 15, 1719 through December 13, 1720, total males, 12,713, females 12,741, total 25,454, e.g., "Causes of death; Abortive 132; Aged 2317; Ague 15; Apoplexy 82; Asthma 86; Bedridden 3; Bleeding 4; Bloody Flux 11; Broken leg 2; Bruised 3; Burnt 3; Bursten (q.v.), 6; Cancer 64; Canker 20; Childbed 260; Chin-cough (whooping cough) 10 ; Cholick (colic) 98; Chrisoms 56; Consumption 3054; Convulsion 6787; Diabetes 5; Dropsy 1021; Drown'd 66; Evil 24; Excessive drinking 18; Executed 20; Fever 3910; Fistula 12; Flux 11; Found dead 21; French Pox 108; Frighted 1; Gangrene 5; Gout 30; Gravel 15; Grief 12; Griping in the guts (gripping) 731; Head Mould Shot (near the same as horseshoe head), 66; Hooping cough 33; Horseshoe head (near the same as head mould shot), 46; Imposthume (q.v.), 47; Infants 14; Inflammation 6; Jaundice 107; Kill'd accidently 47; Kill'd by falls 13; Kill'd with a sword 3; Lethargy 6; Liver-grown (q.v.), 1; Looseness 45; Lunatick 44; Measles 213; Mortification 184; Murder'd 4; Overlaid 69 (q.v.); Pain in the head 3; Pain in the ass 6; Pain in the stomach 1; Palsy 40; Planet struck 1; Plurisy (pleurisy) 32; Purples 16; Quinsy 7; Rash 10; Rheumatism 22; Rickets 84; Rising of the lights; Rupture 20; Scalded 1; Scaldhead 2; Scarlet fever 3; Scurvey (scurvy) 1; Shot 1; Smallpox 1440; Smother'd 4; Sores and ulcers 32; Spleen 6; Spotted fever 66; St. Anthony's Fire (q.v.), 8; Stabb'd 1; Stillborn 562; Stone 59; Stop in stomach 125; Strangury 10; Suddenly 119; Suffocated 3; Surfeit 8; Teeth 1817; Thrusa (Thrush) 80; Tissick 455 (q.v.); Twisting of the Guts 77; Tympany 9; Vomiting 21; Water in the Head 110; White swelling 1; Worms 75."

death-bed will: See *nuncupative will* in *What Did They Mean By That?*

debtor, creditor, obligor, obligee: common and ancient terms describing the parties to a debt or obligation, e.g., "In virtually all promissory notes, mortgages, most contracts, and deeds of trust, the names of the debtor (the obligor) and the creditor (the obligee) will be spelled out." Also see *promissory note.*

debtors, passports required of: See *passports, debtors*

decoction: the boiling of any generally insoluble chemical plant thought to have medicinal or curative value, e.g., "Maggie prepared a tonic for her children by steeping rhubarb leaves with grape leaves and administering the liquid by the spoonful."

dedimas potestatum, dedimus, didimas: a commission to do some act or perform some duty in behalf of some element of government, e.g., "In Virginia in September of 1699 a dedimas potestatum issued from the council for 'constables, headboroughs, coroners, escheators, and Indian interpreters' to administer and hear oaths of allegiance to the Crown."

defendant: See *lawsuits, common, etc.*

defile: to dishonor or corrupt the chastity of a woman, a family or a sacred or patriotic symbol, e.g., "When Jack told that Pat's wife was a common street walker, he had not only defiled that wife but their family as well"; "To burn the American flag is to defile it and our nation." Also see *abuse.*

defunct: a Scottish term early brought here, and somewhat unlike now, means a dead or deceased person, e.g., "A early Maine lawsuit required that the judge define 'defunct,' and he ruled it to be synonymous with 'dead.'"

demise: to lease or create an interest in land for a specific or determinable number of years, e.g., "The expression 'lease, let and demise' is very frequently found in leases, even to now." Also see *lett and farme sett,* and see *let*; see *devise* and also see *lease* in *What Did They Mean By That?*

demurrer, to demur: See *lawsuits, common, procedural steps.*

denizen, denization: a person who is a citizen of one country yet has privileges to remain in a country other than that of his citizenship, "Myron suggested that a denizen legally is between an alien and a citizen, and denization here is not unlike having a 'green card.'"

depression, severe: See *black dog.*

deserted land: an expression of the law of land patents meaning that a tract awarded by a colony or an authority to an individual had not been planted and seated within three years after the patent date, e.g., "It is likely that the patent in Isle of Wight County to John Drake was labeled 'deserted' before 1692." Also see *seating, etc.* in *What Did They Mean By That?*

determinable: may end or cease, usually at the happening of some event, "When Lazarus conveyed the tract to William 'so long as he farms the land,' a determinable fee was created, and that conveyance would end when and if William no longer engaged in farming on that tract."

detournement: theft by a servant of property of his/her master, usually cash, bills of exchange, personal property, or stock in trade, e.g., "A category of embezzlement, however in detournement the embezzler was a servant, bound or otherwise."

devil, instigation of: See *instigation of the devil.*

devise: See *legacy*, and see *first devisee*, and in *What Did They Mean By That?* see *devise* and also there see *bequeath.*

devolve, devolved: early common expression describing the passing of title to property from a dying person to one who was alive, e.g., "When Beth wrote in 1790 that her father's medallions had devolved from her mother to James, all knew that the mother passed those when she was dying or had died."

dew lap: See *stock mark, stock brand, etc.*

dialect: in the American colonies, any of the several established variations in spelling, usage and pronunciation of words of the English language, e.g., "We have at least seven recognizable dialects in the U.S.; New England, Delaware/Maryland, Southern Tidewater, Appalachian Highlands, Cajun, that of the north central states influenced by the Scandinavians, and that rapidly developing variation in the SW as a result of the Latin influences."

diary fever, day fever, daytime fever, twenty-four hour fever: an unexplained fever lasting but one day, probably the same as "twenty-four-hour cold," e.g., "A diagnosis of diary fever was frequently given by mothers and grandmothers, those likely being one or more of any number of viral infections."

diphtheria: feared affliction and very often fatal, characterized by severe swelling and blisters in the throat, putrid discharges from that area, very high fevers, intense thirst, and a change in tongue color from pink to dark red, dusky gray and even near black, e.g., "One child having already died from diphtheria, when baby Alice contracted a severe sore and swollen throat Diane feared that the horrible disease had struck yet again."

dipsomania: one possessed with an irresistible desire for alcohol or other drugs, e.g., "The 1896 ledger of the Toledo Insane Asylum noted at least two patients who suffered from dipsomania."

disavow: to repudiate acts, usually done by a master or employer concerning purchases, debts, or obligations incurred in his name by a servant or employee; the actions of one who upon coming of age, denies any obligations undertaken by him while yet a minor, e.g., "The court ruled that Glynda could disavow a debt she had incurred for a cow she had purchased when she was 17."

disfranchise, disenfranchise: the former spelling is preferred in the law, the latter in common parlance perhaps; the removal or deprivation of one's rights to vote and otherwise participate in the rights and privileges of one's country of citizenship, e.g., "The story 'Man Without A Country' vividly describes the life of a person who had been disfranchised."

disguised in drink: one who is drunk, e.g., "A Surry Grand Jury of 1698/99 made a presentment that charged William Hunt with being drunk since he had so appeared 'disguised in drink' at church on *Whitsunday* (q.v.)." Also see *presentment.*

disinherison: as distinguished from *disinheritance* (q.v.), any provision in a will that deprived one from inheriting who otherwise would have done so by law, e.g., "An early Louisiana held that the will provision of disinherison of the son was not self-enacting and evidence of estrangement beyond that was required for that will provision to be effective."

disinheritance: as distinguished from *disinherison* (q.v.), any act by which someone that would otherwise by law inherit is deprived of the right to do so, e.g., "The affidavit filed with the clerk of the court declaring that James wanted none of his assets to go to his son, if proper legally, constituted a disinheritance."

disparagement: marriage of partners unequal by reason of race, station, or class, e.g., "An early North Carolina court held that a marriage without disparagement was a union of two people of equal class or rank."

distemper: early, unlike the common meaning now, any illness, usually of a more serious nature; before there were any preventatives, Johnson wrote of smallpox, "a distemper of great malignity," e.g., "Reports and daybooks of physicians, letters, and newspapers very often refer to someone suffering from a distemper, yet rabies was not what was meant."

distilled liquor: See *liquor, distilled, etc.*

distress, levy of distress, distress warrant: distress being a noun, a levy of distress is the taking of personal property out of the hands of a debtor and making it or its value available to a creditor or the government, e.g., "After the 1797 court found that Martin was delinquent in his tax payment for the third time, a distress warrant was issued ordering the sheriff to seize Martin's livestock."

distributive share: that share, no matter the percentage, sum, or quantity of an intestate estate received by any heir, e.g., "The court ruled that Mr. Haskins would receive as his distributive share 5.75% of the assets of the estate after all expenses and costs were paid."

District Attorney: See *lawsuits, common, procedural steps.*

dividend, divident: a portion or any fraction of property or tract of land, usually associated with an estate or the division of such, e.g., "An early Delaware case referred to the ownership of one of the parties as 'half of a dividend of 600 acres,' and in 1669 Christopher Holland conveyed to William Morris 'half of my divident.'"

divorce courts: See *state court web sites.*

dock fever: See *yellow fever* in *What Did They Mean By That?*

dockets, judgment: See *judgment dockets.*

doed koeks, mourning cookies: as in "dead cookies"; funeral cookies for those visiting in mourning, e.g., "Most early *Pennsylvania Dutch* (q.v., *What Did They Mean By That?*) women saw to it that visiting mourners and funeral attendees had doed koeks, those often bearing the initials of the deceased."

domestic relations courts municipal courts: See *state court web sites.*

door nail, dead as a: See *dead as a door nail.*

dope, dope of: as now; very early, likely at times synonymous with boring, a waste of time, or uneventful, e.g., "In 1882, Allison wrote that her church social event the prior day 'was a dope of an evening.'"

doulas, dowlas: coarse linen *stuff* (q.v., *What Did They Mean By That?*), used for children's, servant's and slave's work clothes, "Mikaila insisted that her children's doulas play clothes be worn when they went out to play."

dowable: meaning that some property or asset may be subject to the dower rights of some person, e.g., "When Cheryl bought the land from Diane she was aware that should Diane's husband die before Diane, unless she also signed the deed, the land then would be dowable."

dowlas shirt, lockram shirt, French fall: e.g., "Items, as these, appeared in a Virginia inventory of the seventeenth century, dowlas and lockram meaning made of coarse linen, and a French fall meaning a hair piece for a lady."

drafts: unlike now, a simple game of drinkers, usually beer, ale, and such taken, often as toasts, in large swills in concert with companions, a tavern pastime for men, e.g., "Shakespeare labeled 'drafts' as swilling."

dram, dram-shop, drinking shop; a dram is a single drink of an alcoholic beverage; businesses where alcoholic beverages are sold, served and consumed on the premises, e.g., "In 1963 Paul owned a small dram-shop called "Boston Rocker."

Draper Manuscripts: Lyman Copeland Draper (1815-1891) was the librarian of the State of Wisconsin. At his death he left boxes of letters that were later organized by topic by the successor librarian (R. Thwaites) and staff and put into scrapbooks (or something similar). There are nearly five hundred volumes (or scrapbooks). Draper would take an interest in a person or subject and try to find out everything he possibly could through personal interviews, newspapers, etc. The Wisconsin Historical Society is still working on this collection and is unable to anticipate when it will be completed. The collection is quite eclectic and extremely interesting. Anyone who was seriously researching any family on the western Virginia frontier should make an effort to examine these manuscripts.

draw cuts: See ***cuts, draw cuts.***

drayage: those charges for hauling any goods in any vehicle with wheels, e.g., "In 1885 the drayage for transporting fifty bales of hay from Marion to Green Camp, a distance of six miles, was $2.50."

dread fever: See ***anthrax.***

dredge: early, unlike now, a drag or net for oyster hunting and recovery, e.g., "The early records of coastal states referring to a person owning a dredge quite usually meant that he was an oysterman."

dressed to the nines: origin probably lost; a superlative, e.g., "Mary Elizabeth suggested that the expression 'dressed to the nines' arose from the nine beautifully dressed muses of Greek mythology."

drift: See ***sounder.***

drills, militia: See ***meets, meets of the, etc.***

drinking shop: See ***dram, etc.***

dropsy of the brain: probably usually those persons diagnosed with dropsy of the brain were suffering from encephalitis, e.g., "For dropsy of the brain, in 1886 Dr. Pierce prescribed alkaline baths, diuretics, and digitalis."

dropsy of the lungs: probably congestive heart problem, since pneumonia was well known to all, e.g., "When old Jacob was said to have died of dropsy of the lungs at age eighty-one it is thought that he suffered from heart disease and the result was congestive heart failure."

drummer: a traveling salesperson who sells and supplies goods or merchandise to merchants at wholesale prices; one who shouts, gestures, carries signs or "sandwich boards," or otherwise generates business by his physical activities, usually for pay, e.g., "Though he thought *manufacturer's representative* to be a more dignified term, Lou was a drummer in every sense"; "On her first day of business, Beth hired a drummer to stand on the street in front of her millinery shop." Also see *sandwich board.*

due bill: See *bill, due bill.*

due course, in: See *in course, etc.*

Duke of York's Laws: 1665; a body of law for the control and operation of government in the New York Colony, e.g., "The early colonial reports frequently refer to a ruling or effect of the Duke of York's Laws."

Dutch wheel: a sort of spinning wheel, so called from its wide use by early Pennsylvania Dutch women, e.g., "Callie had both a *walking wheel* (q.v., *What Did They Mean By That?*) and a Dutch wheel that she used for most of her life."

dwelling, dwelling house, dwelling-place: dwelling is different from domicile; one's residence considered by him or her as rather permanent and the abode of the family, e.g., "Even though John's domicile was in Tennessee, his dwelling-place throughout much of the year was in Virginia." See *legal residence,* and see *domicile* in *What Did They Mean By That?*

dyers: those who were trained in dying fabrics (stuffs), e.g., "Many of the *stuffs* (q.v., *What Did They Mean By That?*) were taken to dyers in order that those be colored chemically or through the use of herbs and dyes from such as tree bark, roots, and sap."

dying declaration: statements made by one who is at life's end and knows of that imminency of his death or who was responsible or involved in the actions leading to that end, e.g., "Contrary to popular belief, a dying declaration has nothing to do with the estate of the person whose death is at hand and, instead, has to do with how the injury occurred and who may be involved."

dyscrasy: Pierce states "abnormal body condition," e.g., "Records of the ailments that led to patients suffering discrasy likely may not now be interpreted in order that the disease be further understood."

dysmenorrhea: painful menstruation.

dyspareunia: See *anaphrodisia* in *What Did They Mean By That?*

dysury: difficulty in urinating, e.g., "Dysury likely was disease of the prostate, the *stone* (q.v., *What Did They Mean By That?*), or a venereal disease, e.g., "It is thought that the diagnosis that of dysury that was so very painful for Daniel was a prostate cancer from which he died in 1909."

E

earthwork: See *glasee, etc.*

eating-house: a restaurant where no beer or liquor are served, e.g., "Though he could have gained a license to sell spirituous *liquors* (q.v.), the very devout Carroll chose not to do so."

Ecclesiastical courts: Those early courts having jurisdiction here over doctrinal matters of the Episcopal and Anglican Church congregations here, as well as the conduct and business of church officers, e.g., "In the nineteenth century, courts in both Georgia and Delaware discussed ecclesiastical courts and duties of those, and set forth the hierarchy of those as with the church in England as: Archdeacon's Court, Arches Court, Consistory Court, Court of the Archdeacon, Court of Peculiars, Prerogative Court, Court of Delegates, Court of Convocation, Court of Audience, and Court of Faculties."

Ecclesiastical law: in this country the ancient law of the church was modified and tempered to a substantial measure, e.g., "In the nineteenth century an Ohio court had reason to describe this body of rules as limited mostly to affairs, discipline, doctrine and worship."

eclampsy: epilepsy; convulsions suffered during labor, e.g., "Diagnoses of eclampsy that were not followed by further symptoms of epilepsy likely are not now interpretable."

ecstacy: probably catalepsy; a disease in the course of which the patient was said to suffer loss of reason, e.g., "Which of the now known mental illnesses was known as ecstacy usually can not be known."

eczema infantile: See *eczema.*

eczema: any of the many eruptions or other causes of skin or scalp itch or flaking were so labeled, those including scabies, branny tetter (dandruff), pityriasis, humid tetter, salt-rheum, running scall, heat eruption, lichen (papular rash, tooth rash, plus numerous other lichen differing in the nature of the symptoms), impetigo, gutta rosaccea (rosy drop), eczema infantile, psoriasis, pityriasis rubra, pityriasis negra, e.g., "From the Civil War until after 1880 Dr. Pierce treated all eczemas with bloodroot boiled in vinegar, followed by glycerin mixed with oxalic acid, and direct application of boiled walnut leaves, and scabies, being viewed as caused by insects and filthy lifestyles required the above and also cleanliness."

egg stand: as now; a small container, often of pewter or porcelain when found in inventories of the upper class, and down into which a baked or boiled egg was placed, served, the egg thereby eaten with a spoon, e.g., "Inventories of the seventeenth and eighteenth centuries occasionally reveal egg stands, those being almost never seen except in the homes of the very affluent."

ejectment: an ancient action at law to remove a person from one's land and recover any damages done by that person, e.g., "Ejectment actions were many in colonial America, especially for landlords who needed to recover possession of lands from tenants whose term had expired or whose conduct otherwise warranted removal, and for removing squatters on frontier tracts."

elopement, elope: today's common usage but also, the departure of a married woman from her home and husband with the intention to live with or be in the romantic company of another man, which departure was required to be to a place or situation that rendered her out of the control of that husband.

elseter wine: obsolete, and apparently used as a flavoring; only once found mentioned in records of the New York colony in the seventeenth century, e.g., "To make elseter wine, 'bynd sugar candy in a linnen cloth, or mix hony diligently clarified with burning water, in a vessell well stopt, & when thou wilt use it, wringe out a linnen cloth dipt in this liquor, into the...' wine."

emblement: as seen in many early leases and deeds, those crops that are harvested annually and which have been planted, tended or otherwise cultivated by someone, e.g., "While such as cotton, wheat, and vegetables are emblements, walnuts or wild cherries growing on trees on a property are not."

emetics: compounds that induced vomiting and evacuation of the stomach; vomiting was induced for any number of ills and to cause that reaction emetics were used, e.g., "In 1886, as emetics, Dr. Pierce recommended mustard, copper sulphate, zinc sulphate, mercuric sulphate, ipecac, lobella ('indian tobacco'), and boneset." Also see *emmenagogues*.

emmenagogues: herbs or chemical mixtures that were used to induce miscarriage—abortion, e.g., "Of the several concoctions that sometimes ended unwanted pregnancies, Donna knew that pennyroyal, tansy, ergot, life-root (called 'female regulator'), motherwort and smartweed sometimes were effective."

ELOPED

Will Drake and Miss Ida Roberts Steal a March

On the Parents of the Young Lady—He has but One Leg and One Arm.

The elopement of Miss Ida Roberts and Will Drake Saturday night is the chief topic of conversation about the city today.

"Billy" is the one armed and one legged bicycle rider, and telegraph operator, the bride is the youngest daughter of councilman Thomas Roberts, of north Prospect street.

They were married by Squire McKinley about 10:15 Saturday night and it is supposed they left on C. & E. train three for Mr. Drake's former home.

The strange part of the affair is, that Mr. Drake has for some time past, been devoting his attention to Miss May, the older sister of Ida, and everyone looked for a marriage from that direction, but it is very evident that this seeming devotion to one was only a blind to hide the real affection for the other.

The affair has created no end of gossip and is a startling surprise to the parents and many friends of the contracting parties. Mr. Drake has charge of the operators' tower in the Erie yards and has hosts of friends.

Figure 11. Secret *elopement* of young people in 1892.

emolument: the stipend, profits, fees, salary or monetary rewards from an any office; any perquisite, e.g., "As constable appointed by the county, Lazarus drew as emoluments a salary, was provided a horse, and was reimbursed for any expenses he incurred as a result of performing his duties."

empiric: one who practices medicine or surgery or both with no formal education or training, e.g., "It is suspected that Dr. W. K. Drake 'read medicine' with another physician, hence was not referred to as an empiric." See *read medicine and law.*

encephalitis: See *sleeping sickness.*

English Pale: See *Anglo-Irish.*

enroll: to register or admit to a record or list, e.g., "In early records one will often find that a court has ordered a document enrolled, meaning simply that the clerk or other officer so ordered was to copy or transcribe that writing into a register or record of his court, e.g., "Kentucky Judge Tom Clark ordered that the will of Daniel Matheny be enrolled in the record of 'Wills and Administrations.'"

enteric fever: See *typhus.*

enteritus: said to have been "inflation of the bowels"; probably not interpretable from old records, e.g., "Thought by him to be caused from exposure to the cold, indigestible foods, 'acrid substances' and fatigue, in 1882 Dr. Pierce prescribed senna, sage and ginger tea and 10 drops of opium every 4 hours."

entertain, to: as now; in colonial times, to lure to and maintain the servant or child of another and to do so illegally or without right, e.g., "In 1696 a Charles City court found that a landowner had entertained a neighbor's woman servant for 88 days, and ordered that the entertainor pay to the woman deprived of that service the sum of fined 5280 pounds tobacco (60 pounds per day, about $100-$120 in the money of 2005)."

enure: usually inure.

environmental courts: See *state court web sites.*

Epiphany: the twelfth day of Christmas, January 5th, e.g., "The ancient observance of Epiphany occasionally was celebrated with a sumptuous meal in the very early Deep South and New England colonies."

equity judge: See *master, master in chancery,* and in *What Did They Mean By That?* see *chancellor* and there also see *chancery court.*

ergot: very early, a part of the harnessing of a horse; later and now, one of the *emmenagogues* (q.v.), e.g., "Dr. Pierce prescribed two to five drachms of ergot to encourage menstruation or spontaneous abortion."

escheat: a reversion of the title to land back to the state or colony, such being common when there was no heir to which land could descend and in patents, grants and transfers that contained or bore conditions of improvement, e.g., "For reasons not yet known, John Drake's patent land tract escheated to the Virginia colony in 1692."

escheators: "An ancient county wide office, in England limited to one term of one year to avoid chicanery, the duties of whom were to keep an accounting of any land or personal property within the county that might escheat to the Crown for such as failure to seat and break land to the plow." Also see *headboroughs* and see *dedimus potestatum.*

estoppel: that state of evidence where one is prohibited from asserting a contrary position, no matter the truth, by reason of past contrary actions or words, e.g., "Glover was estopped from saying that Davis owed him for the horse, since on many prior occasions Glover had told their acquaintances that Davis had paid him 'far more than enough for any horse.'"

evidence, genealogical: every word, monument, memento, artifact, writing, anecdote, or record that in any way whatever tends to establish any lineage, and it varies not in kind but only in quality, e.g., "Bill knew that if he was to be thorough he was required to consider every bit of evidence, pro or con, having to do with his lineage as he researched his family history."

ewer: a large container, usually made of crockery and later of metal, and used to hold water for use at the *washstand* (q.v., *What Did They Mean By That?*), e.g., "The 1862 Bater inventory entry listed a 'basin, ewer, and toilet cover.'"

ex officio, services or activities: duties, obligations, and responsibilities arising from an office, but not expressed in the definitions of that office, e.g., "In May of 1782 Sheriff Myron Wilson informed the trustees that his duties ex officio included instructing the constables in procedures of arrest."

ex parte: very common early and now, by, for, or from one party only, e.g., "A lawsuit or court order reciting, especially in the heading, the term 'ex parte,' such as in 'Ex parte the infant child of John Brown' means that the relief or action sought in that petition or complaint is in behalf and for that child."

ex tempore: arising from the passage of time; without pre preparation, e.g., "It was said that the sheriff's duty to go to the aid of the citizens increased ex tempore."

ex testamento: the corollary of *ab intestato* (q.v.); arising from or growing out of the terms, legal force, or actions resulting from the terms of a will, e.g., "The term 'ex testamento' was often employed in courts' orders or entries that spoke of property or actions that were transferred, inherited or requirements of a testate death."

excepting: reserving to the transferor or testator; to withhold from a conveyance or by the terms of a will; early and now, common words of deeds, wills and other instruments of land transfer, e.g., "When Lazarus signed the deed transferring the 120 acres and including the words 'reserving and excepting the cemetery thereon,' he was being redundant."

exchange broker: very common early; a person of another nation who acts, negotiates, buys, sells or manages sums of money or debits and credits for another person, e.g., "Many were the planters and colonial businessmen who had ongoing business relationships with exchange brokers in Britain and on the Continent."

exchequer, exchequar: a term of Norman France origin, describing an office that virtually disappeared in the American colonies at the end of the Revolution; a court of record in Britain; that department of the kingdom that collected, accounted for, and maintained those sums of money that came to the Crown of England (or other countries), e.g., "The great Prime Minister Winston Churchill had been Chancellor of the Exchequer in the early decades of the twentieth century."

executed, execution: as now; legally, already completed or performed; carried to the intended effect or purpose; having been accomplished; proceeding in putting into effect a judgment, e.g., "The records reveal myriad uses of the word 'executed' in revealing the signing and completing of a will, deed, or agreement"; "Garnishment, sale of assets, and attachments are but three of the proceedings in aid of execution of judgments."

execution, alius: See *alius dictus.*

executors' bonds: See *probate bonds.*

exit cert., exit certificate: a written certification by a town father that the bearer had not been ordered or warned out of a New England community or town, e.g., "Undesirables were occasionally *warned out* (q.v., *What Did They Mean By That?*) of a community in early New England and elsewhere, hence it was that upstanding citizens often carried an 'exit certificate,' lest they be thought of as criminals, debtors, or malcontents upon arriving at another community."

external taxes, internal taxes: in genealogy, those taxes levied or assessed at the times and places of export from one nation or place to another; those taxes levied or placed internal to the place of destination, either at the ports of arrival or afterwards and before reaching the consumer or market, e.g., "The *Townshend duties* (q.v.) were 'external,' while the taxes upon such as shoes, fabric and tobacco made, manufactured or grown within the colony were 'internal.'"

extra-dotal property or *assets:* dowry property a woman brings to the marriage that remains her own to do with as she pleases, e.g., "In early Louisiana, extra-dotal property was also called 'paraphernal property.'" Also see *paraphernalia.*

F

fabrick: obsolete, a building or edifice, e.g., "Defined by Johnson, citing Wooten, the then common word 'fabrick,' meaning a structure or building, seems to have disappeared from common usage here by or before the nineteenth century."

fabrics and stuffs, different: perhaps the widest variety of fabrics and stuffs to be found in inventories of the American colonies can be viewed at *Inventory of Thomas Phenix, merchant, Charles County, Maryland Inventories, 1791-1797,* pp. 383-393, taken 10 May, 1796, recorded 12 May 1796. (Author's note; an astounding list of fabrics now largely unknown to researchers.)

faggot: as now; early, a bundle of anything, e.g., "An 1800 Charles City inventory spoke of '2 faggots of *nail rods* (q.v.).'" Also see *fagot* in *What Did They Mean By That?*

faire days, public days: See *court days* in *What Did They Mean By That?*

Fair-play men: from 1769, a three-man extra-legal tribunal in what was to be Lycoming County in Pennsylvania that was given jurisdiction by the community of their peers to settle land boundary questions, e.g., "The Fair-play men and their panel of three came about as a result of land that had been granted to men for service in the French and Indian War, the title to which was in dispute since it was thought that the Indians had ceded it, yet the boundaries and locations of their cessions may or may not have included such lands."

faker: somewhat unlike now, a petty thief or swindler, e.g., "A Nebraska court, when sentencing a charlatan swindler of naïve citizens, used the then common term 'faker' to describe the man."

falconry: a method of sport hunting practiced for thousands of years, early reserved to only those of high station, e.g., "In early Britain, the most rapid and grand falcons were reserved to royalty, the preferred gyrfalcons and peregrine falcons being those most beautiful and finest of the hunters."

falsify: somewhat contrary to its apparent meaning, a term describing proof of falsehood or representation, e.g., "The verb, 'falsify' was used commonly and particularly by nineteenth-century Georgia and California judges in describing judgments, verdicts, and allegations of error to the courts of appeal."

family Courts: See *state court web sites.*

family hotel, ostery: an inn or hotel designed and catering to patrons who would remain in residence for long periods or permanently; a hotel or inn (probably housing a brewery) for the poor with only the most meager of accommodations, e.g., "The 1880 Hotel was built as a family hotel, however it was not successful"; "Translating Boccaccio's *de Cameron,* he mentioned 'an honest meane man, who kept a poore Inne or Ostery for travellers, where they might have some slender entertainement for their money (sic).'" Also see *railroad hotel.*

fancy woman: a mistress, e.g., "It was said that Lincoln's law partner in Illinois had a fancy woman." Also see *fancy man* in *What Did They Mean By That?*

far-fetched: bring something from a great distance; a metaphor for calling up an idea from deep in one's imagination, e.g., "Todd's reaction to Evan's perpetual motion idea was that it was far-fetched indeed."

feast: somewhat unlike now, Johnson (1802), quoting Hayward, says "to delight, to pamper" and "to entertain," e.g., "The 1847 diary of Allison Roberts of the wealthy Roberts family mentioned that a friend had called and 'we feasted her and then we had a nice dinner with wine.'"

febrifuge: any medication thought to be effective in reducing or subduing acute and severe fevers, e.g., "For acute fevers, Dr. Drake prescribed a steeped mixture of the flowers, roots, and stems of the poisonous aconite, known to country people as friar's cap, helmet flower, monk's hood, mousebane or wolfsbane."

Federal courts, information as to: at this writing there are ninety-four courts within the Federal court system, all of which keep records critical to complete genealogical research. To investigate those you should search the Internet with the words *U.S. Federal Court System Primer* or *Federal Court System: U.S. of America.* Also see *state court web sites.*

fell swoop: an ancient expression of *falconry* (q.v.); a superlative; to capture, seize, attack, accomplish, conquer, or subdue with one swift and powerful action; from the early term 'fell,' meaning to dive, and swoop; the act of a bird of prey in capturing prey, e.g., "It was said that by her decisive business movements, Bethany took over the local trade, caused the competition to fall far behind, and gained much satisfaction, all in one fell swoop."

felons, barrators, and rioters: e.g., "The oath taken by a Virginia sheriff in 1652 required that, among his many other duties, he would swear to prevent the mischief and evil-doings of felons, barrators, and rioters."

felony: either Federal or state, a serious crime usually punishable by a fine or incarceration in a state penitentiary or both; in the early English colonies, punishable by forfeiture of property up to all of one's assets of any kind, and also capital punishment or incarceration in the state penitentiary, e.g., "It is said that there are no minor felonies and many result in loss of civil rights even after the penalty is served and paid. Then too in early Virginia and most other English colonies, upon conviction men lost all, and their families were destitute, often for life."

feme covert: a married woman, e.g., "A July 1775 North Carolina affidavit recited that "...Martha Hackney, a feme covert, was privately examined..." Also see *feme, etc.* in *What Did They Mean By That?*

ferriage: tolls or fares fixed by government for transportation by ferry of property, animals and people, e.g., "In 1809 the legislature determined that the fare to ferry a man and a horse across the Ohio River should be thirty cents"; "In Virginia immediately before the Revolution, one county court determined that ferriage across James River should be: man & horse, 1S; cart and 2 horses, 4S; empty cart, 3S; loaded wagon, 6S; and for ea.; horse 6d; horse and chair, 2S, foot man (man on foot), 6d; and the rule also prescribed that jurymen, judges and those going to and from general muster were exempt from fees."

ferrous oxide, medicinal value of: See *iron rust.*

fetus: See *in ventre sa mere.*

feud: See *bad blood.*

fiefdom: a term of the feudal system, perhaps only seen within what is now the U.S. in the form of the king's grants to George Calvert (Lord Baltimore) of what we know as Maryland, e.g., "Baltimore held his grant in theory forever, with annual sums based upon its profits due to the Crown, that land being held very much like a lease which he could subdivide and pass on to others also for whatever term, as he chose, those new 'owners' also owing rents and profits to Baltimore and permitted to pass their holdings to their descendants or to any buyer."

field: a tract of land that is or has recently been cultivated, e.g., "In the law a field differs from a meadow by definition, the latter being open land, not cultivated."

filiation: the relationship of a parent and child, e.g., "The courts early decided that the term filiation included both legitimate and illegitimate children."

fine bleares: See *bleares, narrow bleares, etc.*

fined nisi: pay a fine subject to conditions; shorthand in courts' orders or minutes revealing that a defendant or a person in contempt was fined subject to conditions, e.g., "A North Carolina court order reveals that in November of 1783 several men were 'fined nici' (sic) for non attendance as jurors who had been served with summons."

fire devils: burning scraps or embers cast into the air by intense winds created by great fires, those causing an ignition where such fall to the ground, e.g., "The newspapers spoke of the 'many terrible fire devils' created by the *Great Chicago Fire of 1871.*"

firearms, lending of, to American Indians: See *peaces (pieces), lending of, to Indians.*

firebote, fencebot, cartbot, plowbot, etc.: compensations for damages or as allowances by those for whom one works or performs services such as carting, burning, maintaining fences, plowing, etc., e.g., "Though it is written that bots appear in records of the American colonies, this writer has not found such references."

fireplace dinner as the name reveals, a New England meal made entirely at the fireplace, and usually consisting of corned beef, chicken or fish, onions, rutabagas, turnips, parsnips, and often precooked beets, e.g., "Particularly on rainy nights, Rebecca would make fireplace dinner for the family, after which they all would remain by the fire to chat."

first devisee (second devisee, etc.): that person who stands first in line to inherit land by will, e.g., "Though she had years before moved away and so knew nothing of it, Jane was first devisee to the land of her grandparents, and had to be found before the estate could be closed." Also see *first heir, etc.*

first heir (second heir, etc.): that person who stands first in line to succeed to land when an existing life estate is extinguished by death or by law, e.g., "In 1723 the Connecticut court ruled that of the three brothers and two sisters surviving, the first heir was the eldest son, Jacob and the second heir was the son, Abraham who was born after both his sisters."

fish kettle: as now, a large, deep, metal kettle for cooking whole fish, e.g., "Miss Weynette had two fine fish kettles for which she paid a whopping $2.50 each in 1820."

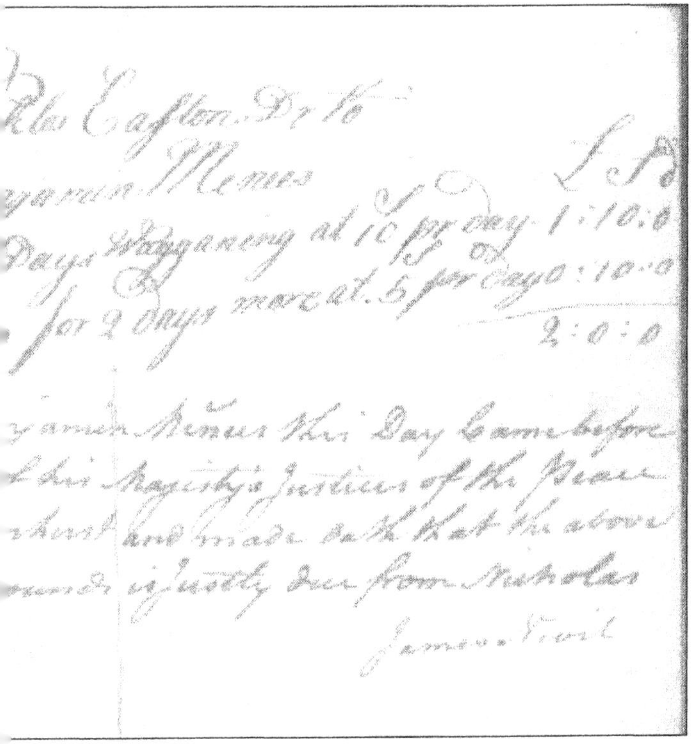

...las Easton Dr to
...jamin Menes £ s d
...Days Waggoning at 10s per day 1:10:0
... for 2 Days mare at. 5s per Day 0:10:0
2:0:0

...jamin Menes this Day Came before
...l his Majesty's Justices of the Peace
...ehurst and made oath that the above
...ounds is justly due from Nicholas
James Nevil

mster’s “waggoning” with two horses and wagons. See ***ferriage***.

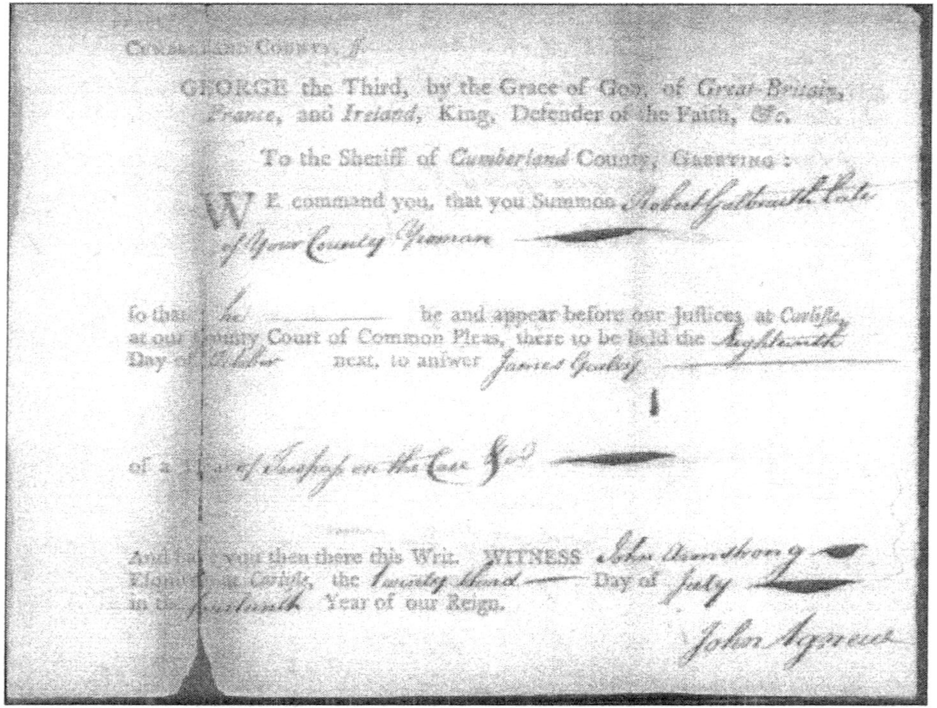
Cumberland County, ss.

GEORGE the Third, by the Grace of God, of *Great-Britain, France,* and *Ireland,* King, Defender of the Faith, &c.

To the Sheriff of *Cumberland* County, Greeting:

WE command you, that you Summon *Robert Galbraith Late of your County Yeoman*

so that *he* be and appear before our Justices at *Carlisle,* at our County Court of Common Pleas, there to be held the *Eighteenth* Day of *October* next, to answer *James Gourley*

of a Plea of *Trespass on the Case &c.*

And have you then there this Writ. WITNESS *John Armstrong* Esquire at *Carlisle,* the *twenty third* Day of *July* in the *fourteenth* Year of our Reign.

John Agnew

Figure 13. 1774 order for service of summons from a court to a sheriff. See ***fined nisi***.

fits: See *conniption* in *What Did They Mean By That?*; sudden and lasting contractions of any larger muscles especially of the legs, arms, or feet, e.g., "Maggie knew that a conniption was an outburst of energy and movement, while severe and continuing cramps were a sure sign of fits."

fixt to take charge of powder: a cannon or other heavy gun that was in working order and ready to be loaded, e.g., "In 1652 one of the standing orders to the Virginia militia was that the men maintain all artillery 'fixt to take charge of powder.'"

flag bottom chairs: a chair with a seat of woven, dried flower-bearing reeds ("flags"), e.g., "The inventory revealed six walnut flag-bottom side chairs, those apparently for use anyplace in the home."

flat: as now; also that land lying between high and low tide of any inlet, bay or tidewater river, e.g., "The court early considered the *fleet* (q.v.) and the rights to the flat of the James River at Scotland in Surry." See *fleet*.

flatulent colic: See *appendicitis*.

fleet: as now; also a river, creek or marsh, the depth of which is affected by the tide. See *flat*.

flesh mark: See *stock mark, stock brand*, etc.

flies, white man's: See *honeybees*.

flitches of bacon: See *smokeloft*.

flook, fluke: latter, the wide part of an anchor; a fin of a whale; though not mentioned by *Johnson* or Walker, yet now commonly used, a gain or advantage won without direct intention to that conclusion; an advantage gained almost by accident, e.g., "The boy's discovery of the rare book while playing in the old barn surely was a flook."

flotsam: a partial amendment to the *What Did They Mean By That?* flotsam definition: any material that floats and is not a part of a ship and is cast overboard to lighten the load, e.g., "Many were the sailing vessels that threw flotsam overboard in a storm, hoping to retrieve that material after the danger passed." See *jetsam*, and see *ligan*.

flour, meal, corn meal: because without such the colonies could not have bread or cornbread, flour and meal were critical to life here; two grades of wheat flour were commonly made, the best being sold in 1800 for about eight cents per pound at the mill, and other for approximately seven cents, e.g., "In the 1870s Hellings Mill near Phoenix also sold a coarser product called 'semetilla' (from the Spanish), as well as offering bran for three cents"; "Numerous mills sold cracked corn and lesser qualities of flour called middlings, samp, sharps, shorts, and semetilla, those middlings especially favored by Native Americans for trading purposes." Also see *bolting, etc.*

fluke: See *flook.*

flummery: fruit, usually berries of any sort, but also plums, cherries, and peaches, sweetened and with a little water, thickened slightly and served with custard, e.g., "The children looked forward to springs and summers, since it was then that flummery was often prepared by their mothers."

flux: any excessive flow of fluids or waste from the body, such as diarrhea or hemorrhages, e.g., "Before death took him in 1597, it was said that Sir Francis Drake suffered greatly from the *bloody flux*." Also See *dysentery* in *What Did They Mean By That?*

fodder: the stalks, leaves and residue left after removing the ear corn from a shock, e.g., "Dalton told Carolyn that he had pulled the ear corn and had fodder left for the cattle." Also see *bind of fodder.*

folio: a leaf in a book, as opposed to a page; one hundred words of a legal writing; a large book, e.g., "In early days the leaves of a book were numbered, and the pages were not"; "Early law reports sometimes were designated by the number of words contained per page, one hundred words being a folio."

for cause: those reasons or justification that the law and public perception consider sufficient for the doing of some act, e.g., "Hux was ordered to show cause why he did not attend church in September of 1694"; "Parker revealed that there was good cause why he should not destroy the dam he built that resulted in the flooding of Drake's pasture."

forced respite: See *respite, etc.*

forestallers: those who evaded the collection of taxes and particularly of duties levied on merchandise or commodities arriving or leaving colonial ports, e.g., "The collection of taxes on Meharrin River and many other such government duty posts was undergoing 'great abuse' and by the mid-seventeenth century the Virginia Legislature had provided stiff penalties for those agents who did not collect those duties and for those who had not paid such."

forged nails: See *cut nails, square etc.*

fornication: not commonly understood now, means sexual intercourse only between two unmarried people, e.g., "Many early courts have held that when one of the two people having intercourse is married and the other not so, the crime is adultery for the married person and fornication for the single person; two separate and distinct crimes."

forswear, forswore: to give oath or swear to the truth of some factual matter, knowing that the statement is false, e.g., "While perjury means swearing to the truth of some matter that is material to a legal cause and involves an oath in a court or before an officer of the court, forswear is a broader concept"; "While he knew that he was lying, in swearing the truth of a matter in an affidavit to buy a car, Mike was not guilty of perjury, but was guilty of having foresworn in the matter."

fortnight: two weeks; fourteen days, e.g., "Myriad historical writings speak of a fortnight as a measurement of time."

forty, a: a very common abbreviation referring to forty acres, which is one-quarter of a one-quarter of a Section of land in surveys done on the basis of Sections, Townships, and Ranges, e.g., "Barbara found that in 1835 Joseph Drake had patented a forty in Section 20 in Wood County, Ohio."

four corners: a common legal expression meaning that in interpreting a document such as a will, contract, or deed, one must consider the entirety of that writing, as well as the environment and context in which it was formed and executed, e.g., "When Walker quoted only two paragraphs of a contract in making his case, the judge admonished him that the document was to be considered 'from its four corners.'"

fourth, marital: See *marital fourth.*

frank, franking: in old law, free; now, the privilege of some to use the facilities of the postal system at no cost, e.g., "Our senators and representatives and many other members of government have franking rights and use that privilege with abandon."

freehold interest, freehold estate: an interest in land that has no duration limit, and will last till the death of the freeholder, unless he or she terminates that tenure by sale or other voluntary conveyance away, e.g., "Though there was a mortgage on the property in favor of the bank, Mr. Delozier would remain a holder of that freehold till his death, unless he sold, transferred or otherwise lost it from some action of law before then." See *fee simple* in *What Did They Mean By That?*

freeman, freeman's roll: that list or venue of citizens who were entitled to whatever privileges were offered for and by the government and were enrolled as Burgesses, thereby having several privileges, including the duty to select judges and their own deputies and other officers of the town, e.g., "The duties of the Burgesses set forth in the freemens' roll of New England were first adequately set forth by John Cotton and approved by the Crown in 1641."

French fall: See *dowlas shirt, lockram etc.*

French pox: See *syphilis* in *What Did They Mean By That?*

wing sections, townships, etc., and several "forties." See *forty, a.*

Frenchman: See *outlandish, etc.*

fuero: in Spanish law, meaning a law or ordinance, e.g., "Considering his age, Teresa's son, Christopher was well versed in the fuero de El Salvador."

full age: Twenty-one is the number of years after which one is of full age, is the age of adulthood, and is the age of majority in the eyes of the law in this country, however in the Civil Law that age is twenty-five years, e.g., "Adulthood (or full age) in the eyes of the law is very different from being old enough to drive, serve in the military, or be married."

furniture, ships': See *ships' furniture.*

fustian: a heavy stuff—fabric, cloth—woven with linen and cotton, or cotton and wool, and mentioned by Shakespeare, e.g., "Constance related that fustian was not difficult to handle and cut." And see *stuff*, in *What Did They Mean By That?*

G

galingale: a spice from the East Indies, and used as a flavoring and to give cheap wine an oily and more desirable flavor, e.g., "The highly regarded galingale is said to lend a very pleasant aroma to wine and other drinks, and has an intense ginger-pepper taste." Also see *hippocras, yprocras.*

galvanic battery, voltaic battery: an apparatus first patented in the U.S. in 1887 by Carl Gassner, consisting of copper and zinc plates each facing the other, to which when acid and water were added, generated an electrical current, e.g., "Many, if not most, of the physicians of the last half of the nineteenth century thought that the current that could be generated by a galvanic battery had important medicinal value."

garbanzo soup: a spicy soup from Southwest, e.g., "Teresa told that garbanzo beans are loaded with potassium, and that the ingredients in her early garbanzo soup were garbanzo beans cooked with saffron, water, much garlic, pork, sausage, potatoes, tomatoes, onions, and carrots." Also see *chickpeas.*

garnishment, garnishee, garnished: a warning through court order directing that the garnishee not pay or give over money or credits he owes to a debtor; an aid in execution, e.g., "For a garnishee to pay wages to one who is garnished is to risk *contempt of court* (q.v.)." Also see *alius,* and see *lawsuits, common, procedural steps.*

gee-gaw, geegaw: curios, trinkets, "pretties," souvenirs of events; small decorative items purchased for their value as novel decoration, rather than for any utility value, e.g., "Lincoln occasionally laughingly spoke of Mary's habit of buying gee-gaws."

gelatin dry plates: the successor to *collodian* (q.v.) wet plates, dry plates came upon the scene in the early 1880s, e.g., "The gelatin dry plates provided Bill Midlam with a means by which his glass plates could be prepared and stored for days or even weeks before deterioration rendered those unusable."

gelt, geld: verb, to geld a horse, e.g., "Until the eighteenth century the word gelt was frequently used in describing the neutering of a stallion."

genealogical evidence: See *evidence, genealogical.*

General Court: that name given to the legislatures of the New Hampshire and the Massachusetts colonies during the early colonial period, e.g., "Though the title implies actions in the law, the General Courts, instead, were the colonial general assemblies of the early times in those colonies."

General Sessions Courts: See *state court web sites.*

gentle family: See *gentle born* in *What Did They Mean By That?*

gentling: opposite of "breaking" a horse. See *horse whisperer.*

George Washington cake, fruitcake: as now, though nearly always laced with brandies, e.g., "Though such cakes are laden with preserved cherries, dates, raisins, both light and dark, and apricots in a dark sweetened dough, and colored by molasses, the presence of such on the American continent is credited to George Washington."

George Washington, rations orders of: See *rations for soldiers, etc.*

German measles: See *rubeola.*

get his living: a description of a physical condition or health sufficient to be able to earn a livelihood, e.g., "In May of 1695 the court found that by reason of age and weakness of body, both Richard Last and John Newsum were unable to get their living and so should be exempt from the tithes."

gibbet: a gallows, and also, per Johnson (1755 and 1802), that structure with cross members from which the carcasses of criminals were left hanging for display after execution, e.g., "As in many countries, throughout the American colonies criminals were left hanging from the gibbets in order that all know of the wages of criminal conduct."

gift causa mortis: Latin; a very common legal term meaning a gift of personal property given to another by one who is near death and knows of that imminency, e.g., "The law has long ago determined that gifts causa mortis may be revoked if the dying person survives."

gifts during life: See *gifts inter vivos.*

gifts inter vivos: a gift made during life that takes effect when both are yet alive and is without conditions that extend beyond death, e.g., "When Jane gave Beth a chair and also endorsed over to her a ninety-day certificate of deposit, those were gifts inter vivos."

gimp: twisted silk or lace, used as decoration of the apparel of women and occasionally men, e.g., "Elizabeth's dress was trimmed at the collar and hem with gimp."

gist: somewhat unlike now, the gravaman or fundamental proposition central to a lawsuit or criminal investigation, e.g., "Though he had introduced theories and a wide array of evidence tending to establish innocence, the simple gist of the matter was that he was found with a recently fired revolver in his hand standing alone over the body of the dead man."

glacis: a bank of earth sloped from the outer wall down, often early to a moat and on this continent often from a fort wall down to a trench or pit, e.g., "The existence of the glacis rendered it much more difficult for attackers to scale a wall, their ladders and devices slipping down the slope, especially when made wet by defenders."

gland, glands: as now; early, Johnson wrote, "a kind of internal strainer to separate some particular fluids from the blood," e.g., "In 1886, Dr. Pierce described eleven different glands, the names assigned to some of which are now unknown."

glandular fever: mononucleosis, e.g., "As now, glandular fever was well known to our ancestors."

glasee of the old fort: unknown; may be from the French, *glacís* meaning a bank of dirt or earthwork, e.g., "General orders, Ticonderoga, Sept. 25, 1776 '...All persons bringing ... the above articles immediately for sale are to carry them to the foot of the glasee of the old fort where the markitt is constantly to be held....'" See *What Did They Mean By That?*, **sutler.**

glassolalia: See *speak in tongues.*

glebe, glebe house: the land that is part of the property of a church or parish and usually produces income or is otherwise beneficial to that church or group of churches; that land upon which a glebe house may exist, e.g., "The glebes of many early Virginia churches are yet the property of those churches, and many glebe houses are now museums or otherwise used by the church, a community, or a historical society."

goiter: See *thick neck.*

gold-wine: wine in which gold has been placed and allowed to stand, and for centuries reflective of the mediaeval idea that gold had medicinal value, e.g. "Several seventeenth-century mentions of gold-wine may be found, as follows, '...it is made by quenching plaits of gould in good wyne IV or V tymes, let it stande to cleere, and when it is...streined let it be kept, for it hath vertue to comfort the hart, and it drieth up the superfluities of al other dregges from the bloud....'"

good and lawful men (and ***women***, now)*:* very common early expression referring to those citizens who were eligible legally and in fact to serve on a jury, e.g., "The order of the court that the sheriff find twelve lawful and good men was common parlance and meant only that the sheriff should bring in such folks to serve on a jury."

Good Book: quite usually, a Bible, and occasionally a prayer book or other religious writing, e.g., "Ida often admonished the children to spend some time every week reading the Good Book."

grammar school: in the very early colonies, a school that prepared students for college; now, any school between grade/primary school and high school, e.g., "The Massachusetts statutes of 1647 required every town to provide a grammar school for those who intended further learning."

grass widow: probably pre-sixteenth century, and variously meaning a woman separated from her husband, a mistress abandoned, and a woman with an illegitimate child, e.g., "Myron suggests that the expression, 'She's a widow, whether by grass or by sod I have no idea' refers to an event of pregnancy after illicit sex in a hayloft or on the grass and away from the house."

Figure 15. "Union" schoolhouse for all grades. See *grammar school*.

Figure 16. 1869 headstone revealing "Feb. 31" as a woman's date of death. See *gravestone symbols and carvings*.

gravestone symbols and carvings: Mrs. Castillo and the *Genealogical Society of Southern Illinois* list the following symbols as having these meanings; **anchor**-hope; **angels**-God's messengers; **archways, pillars and gates**-entrance to the next life; **broken pillar or column**-loss of the head of the family; **broken ring**-family circle severed by death; **broken tree stump**-life cut short; **butterfly**-child and short life; **cherub**-a child or young woman or angelic; **chopping hand with hatchet**-life cut short, youth; **corn**-ripe old age; **cross**-devout, faithful; **cut tree stump**-member of Woodmen of the World; **fingers pointing skyward**-soul gone to Heaven; **flower bud** or **morning glory**-beginning of a new life; **folded hands**-prayer or Scripture; **full bloomed rose**-the prime of life; **open Bible or book**-the book of life; **hand reaching down**-God reaching for the soul; **handshake**-God's welcome to heaven; **harp**-praise to the Almighty; **heart**-earthly sorrow and grief; **hex signs**-to ward off evil; **ivy**-friendship and immortality; **lamb**-innocence, usually on stones of children; **laurel**-victory over death; **lilies** or **lilies-of-the-valley**-innocence and purity; **oak leaves and acorns**-maturity, ripe of age; **palm leaves** or **lilies**-the resurrection; **poppy flower**-asleep here; **rose bud**-morning of a new life; **sheaf of wheat**-prepared for death; **star**-reward of Heaven for the soul; **torch** (pointed down)-life gone; **tree stump with curled ivy**-immortality or head of the family; **urn draped with a wreath or crepe**-mourning; **urn with a blaze over it**-undying friendship; **urn**-death; **weeping willow tree**-emblem of deep sorrow; **willow tree**-death of the flesh.

gray: a badger, e.g., "Several early Pennsylvania references reveal that the American badger was also known as a 'gray.'"

grease wool: a common early fabric woven from wool in its near natural state, washed, but yet containing the natural oils of the animal, rendering it almost waterproof and very warm, e.g., "Evan's favorite cold weather garment was a collared sweater of double woven, heavy, grease wool."

Great Awakening: that groundswell of religious fervor that overtook many of the American colonials in the decade of the 1730s, resulting in a decline of Quakerism, Anglican influence, and of Congregationalists beliefs, e.g., "The Great Awakening brought an increase in Presbyterianism, as it did the number of Baptist congregations." Also see *New Lights, Old Lights.*

great hunter: presumed to be a hunter of large animals for hire, probably buffalo and bear, e.g., "The 1856 state census of Iowa reveals a man whose occupation was given as 'great hunter.'"

Great Law, the: the first acts of the legislature governing Pennsylvania and promulgated in 1682, e.g., "Included in the Great Law was a right of liberty of conscience; that, a move toward freedom of religion and a forerunner of the activities that made us a free people one hundred years later."

great men, greate men: the very early American Indians who were the Chiefs or otherwise in high office or command, e.g., "The Surry reports of 1655 reveal that the judges of that time also referred to chiefs of the Native Americans as 'the Greate Men.'"

great pox, French pox; See *What Did They Mean By That?*, **syphilis**, also see *What Did They Mean By That?*, *chancre* and see *clap*.

greatest creditor: a common expression in estate administration, and meaning that the person or business so named was of the highest priority among creditors, e.g., "The court spoke of Stephen Sherwood as the 'greatest creditor' since he was 'secured' and was owed more than any other creditor." Also see *secured*.

green fever: anemia, *Bright's Disease* (q.v., *What Did They Mean By That?*), e.g., "Of the many 'fevers' viewed as ailments and not symptoms, green fever was viewed as a distinct illness."

green sickness: see *chlorosis.*

greenhorn: a neophyte, one who is new to a required duty, task or obligation, e.g., "A newly grown horn or antler is labeled 'green' meaning not yet ripe or hardened, that fact being a metaphor for one who is assigned a task or has a duty for which he is not yet prepared or capable."

grinder, coffee: See **coffee mill, etc**.

grindin' of bread corn, could not raise a: a superlative meaning totally or very unproductive, e.g., "Carolyn remembered that an acquaintance had said his land was so poor that he couldn't 'raise a grindin' of bread corn', meaning he could not grow even enough corn to make meal sufficient for corn bread."

griot: As now in modern communities, a griot was an African village storyteller. His role is to preserve the history, genealogies, and traditions of his people and to pass that information on in order that future generations may know of their heritage, e.g., "Charee, Quan and Teresa pointed out that, though overlapping in purpose, the art form of the 'Alex Haley' type griots with their anecdotes and character descriptions of individuals should be differentiated from those griots who dedicate their stations, efforts, and memories to the more general history of the community, its leaders, and its communal activities."

grist: See **gristmill, etc.** in *What Did They Mean By That?* and see here **bolting, etc.** and see *flour, meal.*

grizzle: See *gristle, etc.*

grocers' itch: said to have been an arm and hand skin irritation common to grocers of the period, e.g., "Grocers' itch is thought to have been caused by mites or other parasites from the bags sent from the mills and suppliers."

grogram: fabric (*stuff*, see *What Did They Mean By That?*) woven with long woof and heavy pile, e.g., "Grogram appears occasionally in very early New England inventories."

grub stake, grub-stake: a common term for the many agreements, often written and sometimes quite formal, by which one person supplied the transportation, tools, and other goods needed by another person to go to the gold fields, after which the miner was obligated to divide the proceeds or benefits he gained in prospecting and mining in accordance with the agreement, e.g., "In 1850 Jane grub staked Wesley to the extent of $500.00, however try as he would, he found no gold."

gruel: oats or oatmeal boiled in water with a tad of salt, e.g., "What was known for centuries as gruel (Johnson, 1755) is now called simply oatmeal by Americans."

guarantor: quite similar to a *surety* (q.v.), however a guarantor typically has been paid for his agreement and willingness to make whole the creditor, e.g., "In 1872 the bank of Bledsoe County told Walker that it would only loan the money for the repairs on the old house if he supplied a guarantor or co-signer of reputation." Also see *co-signer.*

guardians' bonds: See *probate bonds.*

guinea: early gold coin often found in American records and valued variously, but usually at 21S (£1,1S), e.g., "Many records of Virginia merchants reveal payments in guineas."

gullah dialect, gullah people: See *sweet grass, etc.*

gumbo punch: See *punch.*

gutta rosaccea: See *eczema.*

guy, guy lines, to guy: as now, slang for a grown boy or man; a rope (usually hemp early) line used in hoisting or securing heavy items, e.g., "The captain ordered that the ship's guy lines be secured to the wharf stanchions."

H

hack stand: same as the cab stands of today, served by operators of horse-drawn short-distance carriages of people; points central to traffic of those who would need transportation to and from the areas of a city, e.g., "At the turn of the twentieth century there was a hack stand on West

Center St. near the depots that served incoming and outgoing passengers of the C&O, the Erie, the Pennsylvania, and the Big Four railroads."

hackney: a horse for hire, e.g., "Anthony's *livery stable* (q.v., *What Did They Mean By That?*) in Marion offered hackneys to those needing a riding animal or a draft animal."

haint: a ghost or apparition, e.g., "Dr. Charles remembered the use of the term being used in his Southern upbringing."

hair sifter (cilice): a sifter made of cloth for such as starch or other food or material that requires a very fine sieve, and in the American colonies usually made of the hair of horses' tails or manes, e.g., "Before inexpensive wire could be made and then woven, horse or other animal hair woven into a fabric provided a quite usable material with which to make sieves"; "A 1787 order to a Kentucky merchant included thirty yards of fine sheeting, one tin funnel, six yards of linen, and one hair sifter."

haircloth: See *hair sifter.*

hake: as now, a fish; otherwise perhaps forgotten, it seems; a utensil for cooking or at the fireplace, e.g., "The inventory records of Essex County, Virginia reveal 'Two hakes and a gridiron' and several other mentions of hakes, including one valued at 3S,6d, none of which refer to the fish of that name."

hand money: cash given from a buyer to a seller to bind the parties to a bargain or sale, e.g., "In 1774, Lazarus paid Mr. Amos 12 shillings as hand money, the balance being £14."

harpsichord: a fifteenth- to nineteenth-century (recently again popular) musical instrument with keys attached to picks which struck or plucked the strings; the earliest of the pianos, e.g., "Allison, from a wealthy Southern family, enjoyed learning and playing the harpsichord." Also see *spinet* and see *pianoforte.*

harquebus, arquebus, hakbut: a very early firearm, probably as early as the fourteenth century, quite usually of less than 90 caliber, fired from the shoulder, of long barrel, and having a *wheel-lock* or a *matchlock* (q.v., *What Did They Mean By That?*), e.g., "The 'guns' in the 1698 estate of Judith Parker of Surry likely were harquebuses." Also see *flintlock* and see *matchlock* in *What Did They Mean By That?*

hasty pudding: a popular and very early dish, e.g., "Mikaila made hasty pudding by boiling Indian corn in water till it was thick, then adding molasses, honey or maple syrup as a sweetener."

hatchel, hetchel, flatchel: a small, rather thin oblong or square block of wood with sharp metal points or nails protruding from one side, used to separate straw and foreign matter from flax, before spinning it into linen thread, e.g., "Hatchelling the flax was difficult for Maggie as she grew older."

hauking bag, hawking bag: a bag or pouch, usually of leather with a flap cover, and having space for hawk food and reward treats (and doubtless for man also), hoods, and other items, not including the bird, that might be needed by a man engaged in hawking, e.g., "Though rare, there are instances of early colonial inventories revealing the presence of hawking bags."

hay-weigher: an appointed officer of a New England town; a man of modest salary whose task it was to prevent cheating of the citizenry by those selling hay in the community, e.g., "The fact that the very large percentage of early town dwellers had a horse and often a cow required someone employed to prevent dishonest and unscrupulous dealers from cheating people over the weight and sometimes the quality of hay being sold."

headboroughs: a most ancient Saxon term, yet surprisingly found in 1699 in Virginia, and meaning the leader or head of a town or borough; an office later usually incorporated into the office of constable, e.g., "In 1699 headboroughs were included by the Virginia Council as among those who were issued a commission to administer oaths." Also see ***escheators,*** see ***dedimus potestatum, etc.***; and in *What Did They Mean By That?* see ***constable.***

headmoldshot, headmold shot: when the sutures of the skull, generally the coronal, overlap when closing, that is, have their edges overshot, which condition is frequent in infants and often caused convulsions and death, e.g., "While not common, of the 25,000 deaths recorded in London in 1720, sixty-six were attributed to headmoldshot." Also see ***death, causes, etc.***

headright certificate: from 1 October 1837 till 1 January 1840, the Republic of Texas awarded 640 acres (a Section) to every head of household who with his or her family moved to the lands of the Republic and remained there, e.g., "Many Tennesseans moved to Texas with their families and gained headright certificates for having done so."

headrights, laws of: (seventeenth and eighteenth centuries) as found in *Henings Statutes at Large*, vol. 3, p. 304, "...all and every person male or female imported and coming into this colony dominion free, has a right to fifty acres of land; and every Christian servant, male or female imported after he or she becomes free, or time of servitude is expired, has a right to fifty acres of land for his or her importation; and every person coming into this colony, and importing a wife or children under age, hath a right to fifty acres of land for himself, his wife and every such child so imported..."

Bolton, _____ 178_

at a ___ of Hay weigh'd this day, belonging

_____ of the Town of _____

C.	qrs.	lb.

ed   3_ — 0 — 0

     1_ — 0 — 0

ay 19 — 0 — 0   Fees for weighing; 1/_

    _____ _____   Hay-weigher.

ate by a *hay-weigher* as to the nineteen-ton load of a teamster.

headstones, carvings on: See *gravestone symbols, etc.*

healer: one who claims to affect cures by other than drugs or other material substances, usually by thought and non-touching exchanges, e.g., "In the early days of the discipline of Christian Science, the New York courts permitted the use by that group of the word 'healer' in describing themselves to the public."

heart asthma: feeling of being unable to breathe, especially at night or when reclining; probably heart disease or attacks of angina, e.g., "Though many early people wrote of heart asthma, Dr. Patterson wrote that the frequency of death from that complaint probably reveals that it was a manifestation of heart disease."

heat eruption: See *eczema.*

hedge wizard: See *wizard, etc.*

heir: early and usually now, one who inherits anything by virtue of intestate death, e.g., "Though for centuries the word heir described only those who inherited by intestate succession, in recent years it is used to describe one who inherits, whether by intestacy or by testate death."

heir apparent: See *apparent heir.*

heir-at-law: in the popular sense, a term to describe one who inherits property by will or by intestate death, yet more properly meaning only those who gain such assets through statutes of descent and distribution applicable to intestate death, e.g., "Though John referred to himself as an heir under his father's will, he more properly should relate that he was a devisee of his father." Also see *heir,* and see *heirs and assigns* in *What Did They Mean By That?*

heirs at law: See *legal heirs.*

Henings Statutes at Large: that thirteen-volume compilation by William W. Hening of colonial law in Virginia and published 1819-1823, and covering the period 1619-1794; indispensable to understanding life and the law in the seventeenth and eighteenth centuries, e.g., "Henings Statutes, though difficult to understand for those not working within the legal system, was made easier to use in the *Swem Index* (q.v.)."

Heralds' College: that royal corporation of Edward III in 1483 that had the authority make grants of arms, record the pedigrees of those men of arms, and permit changes of name by such citizens of the realm, e.g., "While now the Heralds' College may yet grant and register arms and pedigrees, the same is a quasi-private corporation and needs no authority from the sovereign to design and grant arms."

hereditaments: anything capable of being inherited, both real and personal property, e.g., "Though hereditaments are usually thought of as structures attached to or a part of the operation of land, in fact the term includes everything of any nature on or associated with land that one might pass to his or her heirs."

Hetty Green, meaner than, the witch of Wall Street: a truly remarkable woman with uncanny investment senses and techniques, and as absolutely frugal as she was rich, e.g., "Mrs. H. found the expression 'meaner than Hetty Green' (1835-1916, the richest woman in the U.S. during her lifetime) worthy of comment and reflective of the excesses and extraordinary characters sometimes found in American history."

hide: an ancient and now obsolete term meaning 125 acres of land, e.g., "Because of the enormous quantities of inexpensive land available on the American Continent for the most part bordered by streams, roads, or natural barriers, and because surveyors were not easily found on the western edges of settlement, acreage was estimated between such natural boundaries, and so the term 'hide" was almost never used." Also see ***virgate.***

hippocras, yprocras: an ancient and favored strong drink still mentioned in the nineteenth century and thought to have medicinal value; a spiced wine, e.g., "It was noted that one recipe of many for hippocras was red wine mixed with cinnamon, ginger, nutmeg and sugar, and then strained through a woolen cloth, and another was red wine with ***galingale*** (q.v.), ***grains of paradise*** (q.v.), ***cubebs*** (q.v.) and long pepper, this too strained and served." Also see ***hippocras, yprocras.***

hobby: unlike now, a small horse or a general name for an unspecified falcon, e.g., "When he said that his hobby weighed about 290 pounds, it was apparent he was speaking of a small horse and not about a bird or falcon." See ***stone*** in *What Did They Mean By That?*

hoes and stocks: farm tools, meaning hoes and the removable or replaceable handles for such; also perhaps wood planes, e.g., "Clay and Marilyn all explained that the 'stocks' listed in the 1863 Alabama inventory of John A. J. Whitehurst that included '1 chest tools, 1 broad axe, 1 set plows, hoes & stocks, (and) 1 set irons,'"; "Cabinetmaker Harold noted that plows and hoes are names of cuts made by planes in wood, stocks being basic components of planes, and irons are the cutting parts (blades)."

hoes, sweeps, bats: metal arrowhead shaped (thus appearing as do bats in flight) very strong pieces of metal (iron in early days, and steel now) from eight to ten inches in length that attach to a cross bar, e.g., "Cotton plantation owner Joe mentioned that sweeps are sometimes known as hoes, especially when the reference 'is to those one, two, or three inches across.'"

hogshead: a large barrel varying in capacity and weight, said by Johnson (1755) to be sixty-three gallons, and by modern dictionaries defined as 100 to 140 gallons, e.g., "There being no established or recognized weight or capacity of a hogshead, all merchants yet using the same are careful to specify the weight or liquid content of those barrels in which they are trading."

hold adverse to: See *adverse possession: hold adverse to, etc.*

holland pillow beares, pillow beares: Holland was a fine linen; beare was a very early word, seemingly abandoned by the nineteenth century, that meant simply a pillow case, e.g., "Interestingly, neither Johnson (1755, 1802) nor Walker (Boston, 1823) mentioned the term, yet one finds many references in inventories across the colonies to 'pillow beares.'"

holographic will, olographic testament, olograph: the first spelling is expected in early American law, latter spelling is preferred under the Civil Code; a will written and signed entirely in the hand of the one so intending, e.g., "Though the will was written entirely by hand, the handwriting of the signature did not match that of the body of the will, so the court labeled it onomastic and refused to admit the writing as a holographic will." See *onomastic.*

home guards: see *meets, meets of, etc.*; see *militia* in *What Did They Mean By That?*

homunculi: the imaginary microscopic men that were imagined to be in the head of individual spermatozoon, e.g., "Early sources, before the invention of the primitive microscope, reveal the beliefs in the likelihood that a tiny man with his feet toward the tail existed in every sperm cell."

honey tamarind: a plant of India, and imported to Britain and the colonies very early, e.g., "The leaves, flowers, and seedlings of the tamarind were made into a pleasant and invigorating soup by a few affluent colonials, and the pulp of the fruit was sweet, was used as a delicate spice, and was mentioned in a few early American recipes."

honeybees: as now, but unknown to the American Indian, called "white man's flies," and brought from the old countries by the earliest immigrants, e.g., "Very soon after the first settlements in New England, colonies of bees were brought in order that there be sweeteners other than maple syrup and maple sugar." Also see *molasses.*

hooky, hookie, play hooky: very early and difficult to trace, to be absent from a duty, usually of attending school, and perhaps arising from the fact that early boys were usually those who missed school, and did so in favor of going fishing, e.g., "Very few were the boys of the nineteenth century who did not occasionally play hooky."

hops: A plant thought to have medicinal value. See *nervines*.

hornets: See *house hornets*.

horse power, horsepower: a measure of usable power from any source, and being of the capacity to lift 33,000 pounds the distance of one foot in one minute, e.g., "Though it once was said to do so, whether or not the term *horsepower* in any way now relates to the capacity for work of a draft animal is now largely unknown."

horse whisperer: a term apparently of nineteenth century America, meaning to break a horse to the bridle by gentle, quiet, and soothing talk—whispers, e.g., "An 1882 Lawrence, Kansas newspaper referred to D. C. Bater as a 'famous horse whisperer.'"

horseman's coate (coat); a long overcoat worn by a man astride a horse, with a divided back and no buttons below the waist in the front, e.g., "A horseman's coat, such as found in early inventories and lists of dry goods, kept the rider's legs warm and also dry, depending on the fabric from which it was made."

horseman's sword, cavalry sword: a heavy bladed sword designed for slashing, as with a cavalry sword, e.g., "The inventory of the 1800 estate of Thomas Mason revealed the presence of several weapons, including a 'horseman's sword.'"

horseshoe head: a disease of the very young, wherein the plates of the skull are too far apart at birth and do not join, causing the crown of the head to appear like a horseshoe or a "U" shape, e.g., "Many early children who suffered horseshoe head were doomed to die young from injury to the top of the head."

hose tops, boot: See *boot hose tops*.

hotch pot, hodge pot, hutspot: a stew of Early New England, consisting of corned beef, carrots, turnips, salt pork, sometimes wild game, and often with a bit of cornmeal or rye meal, e.g., "The winter staple for all of the family was hotch pot kept gently simmering in the big pot in the fireplace."

hotchpot: the mixing together in theory of property, real or personal, of two or more people, the whole of it to be divided as agreed or intended, e.g., "In their efforts to equally divide their father's property at his death into equal parts for the four children, the hotchpot included forty acres advanced early to Connie, twenty-five acres advanced to Beth, and 215 acres remaining in the estate, for a total of 280 acres, or the equivalent in value of seventy acres to each child."

house hornets: those nests of hornets brought into the very early houses soon after being built by hornets, those hung above head height in the houses with windows opened, and intended to rid the residence of flies and other insects, e.g., "Drue often told of house hornets, and how as a result there were virtually no flies inside throughout the summers." (Editor's note: it works, and my grandchildren were never bitten when I tried the idea.)

house of ill fame: See *bawdyhouse, etc.*

house of ill repute: See *bawdyhouse, etc.*

household measures: See *measures, household.*

housekeeper: the head of a single household occupying a residence, e.g., "Early Virginia law prescribed that 'all housekeepers, whether freeholders, leaseholders, or otherwise tenants shall be only capable to elect burgesses by Major part,' and only one housekeeper was permitted per family." Also see *Burgesses, electors of.*

Housing Courts: See *state court web sites.*

huckleberries: from the same family as blueberries, e.g., "As now, blueberries, though much smaller than those of today, for centuries have been a very favorite fruit for preserves, wine, pies, and sauces, e.g., "It is interesting that even as the very late nineteenth century, Mark Twain yet named a favorite character, 'Huckleberry Finn' for the tasty fruit we know as blueberries."

humid tetter: See *eczema.*

humpback: See *Pott's Disease.*

hundredweight: 100 pounds avoirdupois and 112 pounds in the English system, e.g., "Most seventeenth- and eighteenth-century mentions of a hundredweight were of the English system and were equal to 112 pounds."

hunkers: Conservative Democrats of the period 1840-1850, usually from New York, New Jersey, and eastern Pennsylvania, e.g., "In 1846 John Karner wrote of his attendance and small donations during meetings of the Hunkers."

hunting or shooting, prohibitions of: by 1645, and thereafter to now, hunting and shooting on the land of another without his permission has been prohibited, e.g., "As early as 1642, in Virginia, the fine against those who hunted or shot guns without permission of the landowner was a hefty four hundred pounds of tobacco, half to the landowner and half to the county."

hurtleberries: See *whortleberries.*

hydrathras: See *white swelling, etc.*

I

ibid, ib.: Latin *ibidem*, meaning on the same page in the same book being considered, read, or written, e.g., "While the abbreviation *ibid.* means previously cited on the same page, *op. cit.* means the same source was previously cited elsewhere in the same book or writing."

idem, id.: Latin, the same reference as was the one immediately preceding, next above, e.g., "It was a relief to Paul that when citing Philip Bruce's *Economic History of Virginia in the Seventeenth Century*, once he had written the complete title and reference, he could use *id., ibid.,* or *op. cit.,* with only an abbreviation of the title and the different page numbers, such as 'Bruce, *Econ.*' when making further references to that same source." Also see **ibid, ib.**

ignoramus: now, ignorant; early and now obsolete, the endorsement of a grand jury placed upon a presentment to them and indicating to the world that they found that charge to be untrue and not warranting a prosecution, e.g., "The 1772 notation that the charge was labeled 'ignoramus' had nothing to do with the education of anybody."

ill fame, house of: See **bawdyhouse, etc.**

ill repute, house of: See **bawdyhouse, etc.**

imparlance: early, a grant of additional time for legal response; recently more commonly known as "a continuance," e.g., "Many are the mentions by early courts of granting imparlances to parties to a lawsuit."

impertinence: early, unlike now, the offer or evidence of legal pleading that had no relevance to the issues before the court in a lawsuit, e.g., "The eighteenth-century entry stating that the motion of the plaintiff was impertinent had nothing to do with the attitude or demeanor of that person."

impetigo: See **eczema.**

implead, sue and: almost redundant, both meaning to bring action in enforcement of the law, criminal or civil, and in pursuit of matters of personal rights or of equitable relief, e.g., "Early colonial records, especially of the South, reveal numerous instances of the term, 'sue and implead' meaning to file a law suit or seek prosecution and to further file such pleadings as required."

implements, farm: See **plows**, and see **hoes and stocks**.

impostume: any collection of purulent matter in a bag or cyst anywhere on the body, e.g., "It is interesting that of 25,450 odd deaths in 1720, forty-seven of those were listed as having been caused by impostume." Also see **death, causes, etc.**

imprimis: first in order, the first consideration, in the first place, e.g., "The term imprimis is often found throughout the law reports of the English and American legal system, meaning the object or action following first next is to be considered."

Improved Order of Red Men: See *Redmen, etc.*

in course, in due course, payable in due course: as now; events are to or have taken place within ordinary, required or expected time periods and deadlines; duties to pay are not to vary beyond the terms of the bargain, e.g., "The court ordered that the fine of 'five hundred pounds of tobacco and cask will be paid in due time at the risk by Daniel Pierce of being in contempt.'"

in esse: Latin, presently in being, alive, in existence, e.g., "While 'in posse' would describe the condition of an unborn child of a pregnant woman, 'in esse' describes the same child soon after birth."

in hoc: Latin, with regard to this, in respect of, within or in this, "'In hoc' was and yet remains a common term of legal reports and has the same meaning as our presently common expression, 'as to this matter.'"

in kind: of the same class, category or nature, e.g., "When the council declared that the constable was to take his fees in kind, it meant that he would be paid from what money he collected in his work in that capacity."

in the breast of the court: See *breast of the court, etc.*

in the place of: a very common early expression seen throughout the colonies, having nothing to do with a residence or physical location of anybody, and meaning instead or in the "stead of" and having the same duties as some prior person so occupied, e.g., "In April of 1775, as to his duties as road inspector, Jonathan Coleman of Edgecombe County was said to be in the place of Joseph Pitman." Also see *in the room of* in *What Did They Mean By That?*

in travail: See *travail, in.*

in ventre sa mere: common early expression, Latin, a fetus; an unborn child, e.g., "many were the early wills and courts' decisions that gave consideration to or provided for a child that was in ventre sa mere."

inanition: described by Johnson (1802) and Walker (1823) as "emptiness of body" and "of the veins"; exhaustion due to malnutrition, such weakness as to be unable to eat or for an infant to suckle, e.g., "Cheryl described the inanition of her uncle, who weighed but two pounds at birth."

inchoate: underway, not accomplished yet, imperfect, unfinished, e.g., "With the 1785 marriage of John and Elizabeth, her property became his, however she would have an inchoate dower in those lands until he died, at which date her rights would vest and be complete and for her use to the exclusion of anyone else."

incorporeal property: See *corporeal property.*

incorporeal right: those rights which have no material existence; may not be found by the physical senses, e.g., "Todd's rights, if any, to cash the certificates of deposit that belonged to his wife were incorporeal."

increpid or infirm: a term of the colonies describing a person of such physical debility that he/she was exempt from taxes, e.g., "In excusing Kinchen from the poll tax, the Delaware court described him as an 'increpid and infirm fellow.'"

indentures, ordered that ___ be drawn: See *be drawn, etc.*

Indian chiefs: See *great men, greate men.*

indictment See *information.*

information: the same as an indictment, however an information is sworn to by a competent public officer and not a Grand Jury, e.g., "Knowing that he might be found out for his part in a separate fraud, the prosecutor filed an information against the man, rather than present the matter to the Grand Jury for indictment."

ingress, egress, regress: as now, in common parlance; in law, right to movement into property, out of the same, and to return to that land at will, e.g., "From the earliest days, courts and those who enter upon a lease as lessee or lessor have used the words ingress, egress, and regress to describe the rights of tenants to come and go as they choose."

inherit: As commonly used, but early meant one who gains assets or property as a result of the death of another intestate, e.g., "Constance suggested to Charlene that it is poor genealogical usage to say that Jane inherited the land by the will of her father."

in-laws: as now; as late as the nineteenth century stepparents were occasionally referred to as in-laws and sons-in-law as stepchildren, e.g., "In his seventeenth-century will in Surry Co., Virginia, John Parker referred to his stepson as his son-in-law."

inn, common: See *common inn.*

inquest, coroner's: See *coroner* in *What Did They Mean By That?*

inquest: a group of citizens called or summoned together to determine facts that are or may involve matters before a court or other administrative or legislative panel, e.g., "Likely the best known of the inquests are those of coroners, however other factual matters might be subject to such inquiries, such as inquests of lunacy, inquests of sheriffs or other officers of government, and inquests of arrests."

insanity, partial: See *partial insanity,* and see *lunacy.*

insanity: See *lunacy.*

inspector of meat: a county appointee of North Carolina and most other colonies whose duty it was to inspect meats, especially pork, that was to be sold at the public markets or otherwise in commerce, e.g., "In January of 1775, James Hill was appointed inspector of meat in Edgecombe County, and was required to post a performance bond equal to £500, a very high sum."

instanter: at once, immediately, without any delay, forthwith, e.g., "Though in colonial times it was a very common legal term in court orders directing actions by others, the word 'instanter' is now nearly obsolete."

instigation of the Devil: early New England particularly, and the colonies in general, firmly believed that Satan personally brought about crimes and breaches of the faith, e.g., "In Salem, in 1665 it was said by the court that a woman servant of Philomen Limbry '...acted at the instigation of the Devil while not having the fear of God before her eyes...'"

intangible assets, intangible property: assets that have no material existence, yet have value, e.g., "Perhaps the most common intangible assets we have are insurance policies, since those have value, yet that worth is not in the paper evidence of the policy but in the benefits that may come to one who has paid for the agreed future benefits."

inter vivos: Latin, during life; matters between living individuals, e.g., "Probably the most common early use of the term 'inter vivos' was in reference to gifts during their lifetime made by parents to their children or to other persons."

interlocutory: often found both in early courts records and now, refers to orders, actions, or activities during the pendency of a lawsuit or other proceeding, also costs that arise during the pendency of such cases, e.g., "The court made several interlocutory orders as a result of motions by both parties to the case."

internal taxes, See *external taxes, etc.*

intrusion, writ or action in: an action at law against one who by his presence intrudes on or otherwise disturbs the land of another, e.g., "Since time immemorial, intruders under color of title or otherwise have been the subject of intrusion actions to ouster such violators of the rights of landowners."

ipso facto: apparent by the fact itself; the facts require no explanation, e.g., "Ipso facto, a shotgun and a steel trap are dangerous."

iron rust (ferrous oxide): a very common compound early thought to have medicinal value, and administered by early physicians, mid-wives, and *granny women* (q.v., *What Did They Mean By That?*), as iron carbonate, iron citrate, iron pyrophosphate, "iron by hydrogen," and iron chloride, e.g., "In 1879 Dr. Pierce wrote that 'salts' of iron were beneficial for anemia, would 'tone up' the nerves and organs, and would increase the vitality."

irons: cutting parts of wood planes, e.g., "Harold pointed out that plows and hoes were irons, and *stocks* (q.v.) were the upper structure of the planes by which the irons were held in place and adjusted."

issues and profits: the term contemplates all benefits, income, resources and products that might arise from a tract of land, e.g., "Simply stated an agreement, lease or deed that transfers all the issues and profits grants to the recipient every opportunity or asset that can be derived from operation of the property, and that would include value derived from mining and drilling beneath the surface."

itinerant records: See *paripatetic, etc.* and see *miscellaneous records.*

J

jail fever: see *typhus.*

jailed for debt: See *lawsuits, common, procedural steps.*

jangle, jangler, makebate, makebater: to quarrel, e.g., "Fred was accused of being jangly and a makebater, tending to cause quarrels—jangles."

january fever: See *winter fever.*

Japan, japanned: varnished and with portions of the glass or metal molded or pounded into a raised style, as in our Nippon ware, e.g., "In 1820 Mrs. Geier bought thirty-one Japan *waiters* (q.v.) from the Kennedy estate for fifty cents each."

jaundice: See *biliousness.*

jean: fabric, a strong, cotton fabric—*stuff* (q.v., *What Did They Mean By That?*)—used for daily work apparel for all, yet usually for men and boys, that fabric from which came the term jeans meaning pats for men or women, e.g., "The Thomas Mason estate of 1800 Virginia revealed, among many yards of other stuff, '4 yards jean.'"

jersey: a *stuff* (q.v., *What Did They Mean By That?*); early, a fine wool yarn; now a fabric made of cotton or synthetic material, e.g., "The jersey gloves and stockings of the early days were much warmer than those made today of cotton and plastic."

jesses: a term of falconry found occasionally in the inventories of estates and of merchants to the American rich, e.g., "Jesses were hoods and leg straps for falcons and hawks, those removed when the bird sighted the prey."

jetsam: a partial amendment to jetsam in *What Did They Mean By That?*: cargo or personal property aboard a ship that will not float and that was thrown overboard to lighten the ship in an emergency, e.g., "When the violent storm came upon them, the passengers on the *Mary Ann* in 1714 were ordered to throw overboard as flotsam and jetsam all personal belongings other than the clothes they were wearing." See *flotsam,* and see *ligan.*

Jim Crow laws: See *Black Code, etc.*

jincy punch: See *punch.*

jitney: a powered vehicle to move people and light freight such as their luggage and wares, advertised and available for hire and other than a bus, streetcar, elevated railroad, or trolley car, e.g., "The little three-wheeled open vehicles common to many nations in the twentieth century were known as jitneys."

joint ownership: See *undivided interest.*

jointure: a freehold interest in real estate, either established in a wife or to ripen into a possessory interest for her at the death of her husband, e.g., "A jointure was created in 1687 by Hunt when he transferred their home to his wife and by that deed provided that she was to be the owner at his death."

joynt stool: joint stool; a very well made early stool in which all the joints are mortised, e.g., "The 1669 Virginia Bushel estate listed 'joynt stools' in association with other furniture."

Judge Advocate, Judge Advocate General, JAG: in a court martial proceeding, that person or persons who administer oaths, advise the court, act as prosecutor, and also advise those charged in order that they not answer improper questions or respond in a way that incriminates themselves, e.g., "As a member of the Judge Advocate General corps, Charles often was called upon to advise prisoners concerning the complex rules of military justice."

judgment dockets: those lists, books or files of orders or judgments made by courts, kept and maintained by the clerks, and open to all citizenry, e.g., "Where such have been preserved, judgment dockets are vital in a search for ancestors."

judgment of peers: trial by jury, e.g., "The expression 'judgment by his peers' dates to Magna Charta and originally meant a determination of innocence or guilt by twelve men of the same status and station in life as the person charged, and now meaning a decision in any matter by a jury of whatever number of persons the law of that jurisdiction requires or permits."

judgment, confession of: See *confession of judgment.*

judicial divorce: a now obsolete term formerly used to distinguish a divorce granted by a court from one determined by the legislature, e.g., "Maggie Cody obtained a judicial divorce from Worth, while her grandmother obtained hers from the Tennessee legislature."

judicial separation: a divorce *a mensa et thoro* (see *divorce* in *What Did They Mean By That?*), e.g., "When early courts could not find the authority or adequate proof of grounds for a permanent divorce, yet realized that the parties could not continue to live together, a judicial separation often was granted."

jumbles: See *schnecke.*

jump the broom: an early expression, especially of Blacks, indented servants, and the poor of the Old South meaning to become married by voluntary act and without formality, e.g., "Loreda asked permission of her owner to jump the broom with David."

jurat: probably the most common of legal writings; a certification by one appointed to administer oaths that a document or writing has been acknowledged and signed by the person who appeared before that notary or other officer, e.g., "Tyler signed the certificate, the notary public had him swear that his signing was his voluntary act and deed, and then the notary placed his jurat below Tyler's signature, that jurat revealing when, where, and before whom Tyler affixed his signature and swore to the act."

Justice of the Peace Courts: See *state court web sites.*

justices' courts: now largely abolished; courts held by justices of the peace and having jurisdiction over only minor claims and misdemeanors, e.g., "When Drake and Evan both claimed the heifer that had wandered on a neighbor's land, the matter was settled at the justice court of the county."

juvenile courts: See *state court web sites.*

K

Kaintucks: flatboatmen traveling back north on the Natchez Trace, e.g., "The many men from Kentucky, as well as Ohio, Indiana, Illinois, and neighboring states who steered loaded rafts down the rivers to the lower Mississippi ports and to New Orleans, and made their way back home for another round trip were widely known as Kaintucks."

kickshaw: known to Milton, though unknown now; obsolete noun, meaning remarkable, mysterious, fantastical, and sometimes, ridiculous, e.g., "An early New Hampshire newspaper referred to a two-headed turtle as a kickshaw."

kindred, kin: relationship by blood; kin by consanguinity, e.g., "Elizabeth's mother's sister is kindred of Elizabeth, that is, she is related by blood through that mother, thus also is kin to Elizabeth."

King's Counsel: See *Bench, King's Bench, Queen's Bench, etc.*

King's Evil, scrofula: draining and widespread eruptions on the body and, as were many diseases, thought subject to being cured by a touch from the king (or queen); also meaning a disease or affliction apparently affecting glands in the neck, e.g., "Seventeenth-century New England physician, Dr. Josselyn, wrote that Indians were susceptible to scrofula and to King's Evil."

kit and kaboodle (caboodle): has had several meanings; kit usually in the American colonies meaning pouch or small leather or cloth container or a small box that were carried with the person, and kaboodle probably most used to mean "the entirety of the lot or activity" or "a bundle", e.g., "The pouch and bundle of a *tramp* (q.v.), often being the entirety of his belongings and property often were referred to as his 'whole kit and caboodle.'"

kith, kith and kin: those with whom you share considerable affection; a good and sincere friend, e.g., "In 1878 Jane commented that she was very happy that all her kith and kin had joined her in welcoming Beth, her new daughter-in-law." Also see *kin, etc.* in *What Did They Mean By That?*

knee tuberculosis: See *white swelling, etc.*

knot tray, knot dish, knot holder: a open small container, sometimes with a lid, used to hold/store fancy head or dress decorations, often called knots, e.g., "Colleen had a flow blue knot tray on her dresser."

know all men by these presents: See *presents, etc.*

L

labor, benefit of his/her: See *benefit of his/her labor, etc.*

Lady Day: observed occasionally in English colonial America, and often a day designated for the payment of debts in deeds and contracts; the twenty-fifth of March (Feast of the Annunciation), e.g., "Prior to the change to the *Gregorian calendar* (q.v., *What Did They Mean By That?*), in addition to often being the approximate date of the vernal equinox, Lady Day was the first day of the New Year and the first day of spring."

lady's slipper: A plant thought to have medicinal value. See *nervines*.

lance corporal: a rank of the U.S. Marine Corps between private first class and corporal, usually reflective of excellence at duty in the former rank, e.g., "All expected that Ryan would achieve the rank of lance corporal very early in his term of service."

lancer, lancers: a series or "set" of quadrilles, usually four in number and danced one after another, e.g., "Christine adored to dance and a lancer followed by a waltz truly pleased her." Also see *quadrille* and see *Virginia Reel* in *What Did They Mean By That?*

land certificate: that document representing an obligation by a government, state or Federal, to transfer a quantity of land to the holder of the certificate if and when that holder meets certain requirements of law, e.g., "Early clerks, especially in Virginia, very often issued certificates for land that had been abandoned by the former grant or patent holder, those certificates standing in the same legal place as had the prior patent or grant." Also see *bounty* and *What Did They Mean By That?* generally.

land courts: See *state court web sites*.

land grants: See *bounty,* and see *What Did They Mean By That?*

land, patent: See *patent land, etc.*

landlord and tenant: early, referred to the relationship between a lessor and a lessee in a lease of land; recently, the relationship of any tenant to a landlord or owner, e.g., "One should always further check in the land records for a recorded lease when an early writing refers to a landlord or a landlord and tenant.

laneret: very early, a small hawk or falcon, e.g., "An early North Carolina notebook referred to a young boy who had a handsome laneret."

lantern: as now; also seldom seen and meaning a dome skylight in a church or other tall structure, e.g., "An early Massachusetts church record referred to the 'sun light flowing in from the dome lantern.'"

lascivious carriage: from early Connecticut, acts between a man and woman which do not violate laws relating to public decency, adultery or sexual intercourse; acts short of intercourse that are against the will of the other partner, e.g., "Fondling of a woman in early Connecticut, with or without her consent, sometimes was considered a crime if she was not of age and if that woman or her parent chose to charge the man."

last will and testament: See *testament*.

laus Deo: Latin, praise be to God, e.g., Many early wills, deeds and other legal instruments carried the expression at the beginning or at the conclusion of the writing."

laver: a large pan or bowl used for washing oneself, e.g., "Maggie called the extra bowl kept at the commode a laver." See *commode* in *What Did They Mean By That?*

law of similars: See *similars, law of.*

law, to read: See *read medicine, etc.*

lawful heirs: See *legal heirs.*

Laws, the Duke of York's: See *Duke of York's Laws.*

lawsuit, suit, bring suit, to sue: to file an action seeking relief or other remedy in any court, e.g., "The word 'suit' in the expression 'bring suit' is mysterious in origin, however all recognize that it means to timely and properly lodge a formal complaint in a court having jurisdiction"; "Though her manner of expression left much to be desired, when Diane said she had brought suit against her partner for $50,000, all knew what she had done."

lawsuits, common, procedural steps: depending upon the rules of the colony or state in which the **case** was filed, the procedural steps in the advancement of an early simple civil lawsuit might well proceed as follows*:* a **petition** or **complaint** was filed by a **plaintiff** against (vs.) a **defendant**; then such as **motions** might have been filed by the defendant in order that he learn more of the allegations. After the court **rules** on such motions, the defendant next must file an **answer** (a **counter claim**); the defendant then may file **motions** (again, often **heard in open court**) or could file a **pleading** called a **demurrer**. A **demurrer** argued that even if all the **allegations** of the plaintiff were true, that defendant should win. Then, the defendant filed an **answer** (**counter-claim**) and, should he choose, also may file a **cross-complaint** (**cross-petition**) against the plaintiff alleging that the plaintiff also had wronged him, the defendant. Thereupon the plaintiff similarly filed an **answer** or **cross complaint** against the charges alleged by the defendant; next, **motions** again might have been filed and heard, including a motion by the defendant alleging that the plaintiff should be **non-suited** (should lose). Then too, a **motion for summary judgment** (which differed slightly from a demurrer) might be filed. The party filing such a motion was asserting that based upon the totality of allegations and responses in all the pleadings up to that point and without further proceedings, the party filing that motion was entitled to a judgment in his/her favor. As before, all motions brought decisions out of hand or **hearings on the motions** were held and the court would then **decide** those matters. If the court decided that all of such motions that might end the case should be denied, then the case again moves forward. **Depositions** may be taken by any o the parties up to the time of trial. Then, the judge and the parties agree that the issues had been **joined**—an order directing that a deposition be taken in Tennessee shortly after the Civil War—and a **trial** would **be set**. A **trial** required that a **jury** be selected from a **venire** or the parties could elect to **try the case before a judge** instead. A **trial** will ensue, all the while the parties and the judges would be encouraging settlement. **Witnesses, affidavits, and demonstrative evidence** would be presented in that trial, and the jury or the judge would make a decision, in a **civil case** called a **judgment**, which usually was for **money damages** to be paid by the loser to the winner as compensation for the loss the winner had suffered at the hands of the loser (said **"to make him/her whole"**). The losing party, however, usually could **appeal** that decision to a higher court, however in criminal cases, quite usually the **prosecutor**—**state's** or **district attorneys**—could **not** appeal. When no appeal was advanced within the prescribed time, if the loser did not pay the winner or otherwise do as he have been ordered to do to make the winner whole, the judgment would be enforced by what is and was called an **execution** (does not mean put to death). Often next, the **sheriff** was ordered by the judge to **levy execution**, which meant to use any of several **proceedings in aid of execution**, including **garnishment** and **attachment** (secure or impound any monies or assets) then owed by others to the loser, or to go gather up and take **(seize)** enough of the loser's property to pay the judgment against him, plus the **court costs**, but not the winner's **attorney's fees**. Frequently, those assets seized up by the sheriff were (and still are) sold at **public auction**, often then called **public outcry**. Then too, before the nineteenth century, when men yet were jailed for debt, the sheriff often **arrested** the loser and physically brought him before the court for further enforcement of the judgment or to be ordered to jail. If an **appeal** was filed, usually the court required that the loser file an **appeal bond** in an amount equal to **twice the amount of the judgment**, that bond continuing in effect till the appeals were completed and the matters were at an end. Also see *limitations, statutes of.*

lawyers, early, conduct of: See *attorneys at law, early, etc.*

lay a child, to: particularly common in New England, the acts and words of a mother of an illegitimate child that serve to identify the natural father, e.g., "In 1666 the Salem court ordered Ann Simpson to 'lay the child to the right father.'"

leaf: See *folio.*

leasehold, leasehold interest: an interest or estate in real property for a term of years, e.g., "Though the recorded document revealed that Mark might occupy the land for eighty years, in the law the interest remained a lease."

You are hereby notified that o[n]
[th]e 15th day of March 1867, [p]roceed at
[th]e to open and State an account,
J & L. Cunnigham vs J. P. & H. C. Rogers
[in] Chancery Court at Pikeville
[you] are required to attend and produce
[what] you may have touching the matters, &c.,
[said] account will be taken from the

Respectfully,
H. A. [Henninger] Com[r]
By F. E. [White] Sol[r].

ourt that a deposition be taken. See *lawsuits, common*.

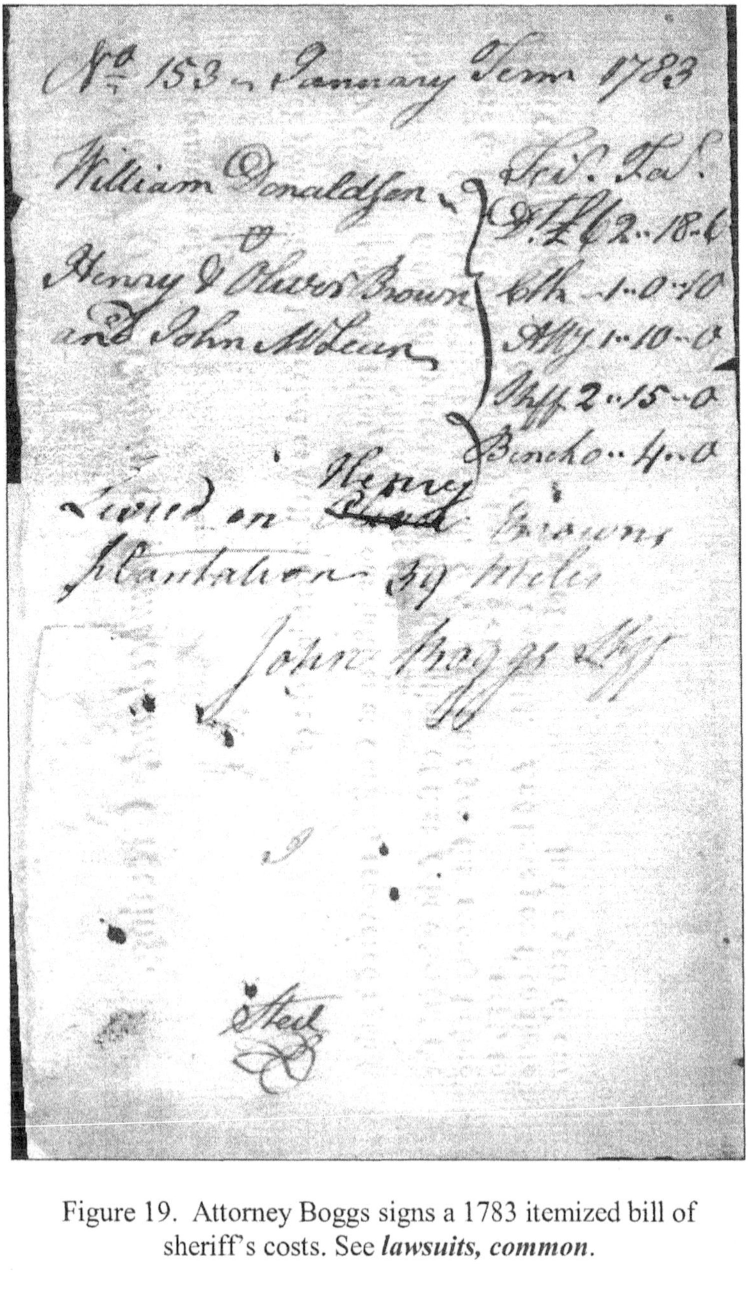
No 153 – January Term 1783

William Donaldson v Henry & Oliver Brown and John McLean

Sci. Fa.

Plff £ 2..18..6
Clk 1..0..10
Atty 1..10..0
Shff 2..15..0
Bench 0..4..0

Levied on Henry Browns plantation 30 Miles

John Boggs Shff

Figure 19. Attorney Boggs signs a 1783 itemized bill of sheriff's costs. See ***lawsuits, common***.

leather britches: green beans in the pods drying for later use, e.g., "Each year, Teresa's Georgia grandmother would hang green beans in a dry place, so-called because when the pods turned brown those appeared as tiny pants for men, or leather britches."

leeching: the ancient practice of using live leeches to cure disease and to remove bruising resulting from bleeding beneath the skin, e.g., "Leeches were applied to the head of George III as a treatment for his mental aberrations and recurring mania."

legacy, legatee: a transfer of personal property by will; one who receives a legacy, e.g., "Though early the words legacy and devise were not synonymous, the two terms often are now so used, e.g., "In early records the researcher must be aware that the word devise often reveals a transfer of real estate by will, and a bequest was of personal property only." Also see here ***first devisee***; in *What Did They Mean By That?* see ***devise*** and see ***bequeath.***

legal age: that age at which one is or was legally permitted to act in some way; an age at which one was fully or partially permitted to act in a specified fashion; an indefinite term, requiring knowledge of what activity is in question, e.g., "Legal ages for various activities have varied greatly over the centuries, and whether one was to marry, vote, serve in the military, own a firearm, hunt and fish, drive an automobile, hold office, etc., the law applying to that activity must be examined." Also see ***of age*** in *What Did They Mean By That?*

legal heirs: of elusive definition, but courts have held that the term means those persons who would gain a portion or all of a decedent's property if he or she died intestate; very often "next of kin" when used in many early estate records, e.g., "Heirs at law, legal heirs, and lawful heirs have been used synonymously, and refer to those who would receive property by the laws of descent and distribution."

legal residence: not synonymous with ***domicile***; where one lives and receives mail, has a telephone, sleeps, prepares meals, stores clothes, used frequently and at which place others might reasonably expect to find the person when not working, e.g., "While 319 South State Street was her domicile, Baker Hall was her legal residence." See *dwelling house, etc.,* and see ***domicile*** in *What Did They Mean By That?*

legatee: See ***legacy, etc.***

leprosarium, leprosy: a hospital or facility for the treatment of the dreaded leprosy, e.g., "Dr. Bater suggested that since mottled or light skin appearing here and there on the body at birth is not always a forewarning of leprosy, early records of diagnoses of that terrible scourge, after which the patient survived, reveal that the condition may have been of some other cause."

let out: to lease land to another, e.g., "In 1666, in New England, Francis Gray did let out forty-five acres to a man named Hiltard." Also see ***demise*** and see ***lett and farme sett.***

let, to: See ***demise.***

lett and farme sett: Johnson, 1775, defines both "lett" and "sett" as "to lease," and "farm lett" meant that the land was leased as a farm, such leases often carrying provisions having to do with crops, the produce, and timber from the land, e.g., "The diligent researcher will find lease documents of record in the early colonies, many stating the purpose of the parties being that the lessee 'sett and farm lett' the property."

leucorrea, whites: a vaginal or uterine disorder, the symptoms of which are a distracting discharge, e.g., "Dr. Pierce wrote that virtually all women suffered from leucorrea at once time or another, and he prescribed his own concoctions and a tea made of slippery elm bark or a cleansing solution of glycerin and water, or all of the above."

levy court: no longer in existence in the District of Columbia, where it was a body of appointees who managed the financial affairs and administered aspects of *local* government there; in Delaware, a board of equalization in matters of taxes and levies, e.g., "Records of the levy court of the District of Columbia are kept in the National Archives, and those for recent years of the body of the same name in Delaware are kept in the administrative offices in Dover."

levy of distress: See ***distress, levy of.***

libel: See ***slander and libel.***

licence: one who, charged with a crime, has permission—license—as a result of a bond or release on his recognizance or that of another to be free pending trial or further order, e.g., "The term licence, meaning usually a bond, though common in the colonial period, is virtually unknown today in the U.S." See ***bond*** in *What Did They Mean By That?*

liege: an ancient term meaning that one was bound to the Crown, both in honor and in fact, e.g., "In the Surry records of 1664, William Strong posted a bond of 10,000 pounds tobacco, assuring that he would '...well behave himself towards all his majesties leige people more especially toward the right Worshipfull Court of Surry County.'"

lien; mechanics, tax, etc: several in number and name; debts, formal or as a chose in action, and chargeable against property; a statement of debt formally lodged, filed and constituting an encumbrance against the title to property, personal or real, e.g., "A mechanics lien or a tax lien are well known, both being charges against real property of the person who benefited from the work or a person who has not paid taxes as assessed." See *chose in action.*

life tenant: one who has privileges in uses of land for the period of his or her life, or for the length of life of another person, e.g., "The deed granted to Marty a tenancy for the life of her younger brother."

ligan: cargo or personal property aboard a ship that was attached to a flotation device or buoy in order that it might be thrown overboard and then later recovered, e.g., "When a violent storm came upon them, all aboard the *Mary Ann* in 1714 were ordered to throw overboard as flotsam and jetsam all personal belongings other than the clothes they were wearing, and to attach to those anything that might float in order that such be later recovered." See *flotsam* and see *jetsam.*

Lights, New and Old: See *New Lights, Old Lights.*

limitations, statutes of: acts of legislatures that prescribe periods of time during which claims and legal actions may be filed, and after which time periods specific rights and remedies may not be sought and gained, e.g., "In most states the statutes of limitations concerning negligent damages to the person are two years, that is, after exactly two years a suit may not be filed seeking redress and if such are filed, a motion for *nonsuit* (q.v.) was appropriate." Also see *lawsuits, common, procedural steps.*

liquidated claim: a claim or lawsuit, usually for money, the amount or the remedy for which has been agreed by all parties prior to judgment, which sum or action will be paid or performed when and if the claimant or plaintiff proves the debt or claim, e.g., "Paul and Kyle agreed that if the court determined that Kyle was entitled to be paid for the carpentry work, the liquidated damages would be $240."

liquor, distilled, bottled spirits: terms referring to all beverages containing alcohol except beer, ale, and other drinks containing malt, e.g., "Since early families might make all the beer they needed, yet liquor was subject to regulations of the quantity distilled, many early cases distinguished beer and ale from liquor, no matter the alcohol content of the former."

lis pendens: Latin meaning pending lawsuit; a lawsuit in process, the status of which often prevents any change being made in the material facts, subject or details of that suit, e.g., "Because of lis pendens he could not use, hire, or drive the backhoe, the payment for which he was being sued"; "Ray's attempts to manipulate to his benefit the profits from the oil venture were improper because of the doctrine of lis pendens."

living, get his, get a: See *get his living.*

lockram: See *dowlas shirt, lockram etc.*

locomotive: the name given the steam or electric driven power sources for moving trains of cars, e.g., "When he was eight years old Paul was allowed to ride on the locomotive of a Erie Railroad passenger train." Also see *yard locomotive* and see *trimmer.*

locus: a place, e.g., "There are many early reports and orders that mention the 'locus' of the act or of a crime, those meaning where such took place."

loden: occasionally found in early American inventories, a soft, thick wool fabric, usually of a green-brown color when natural, and used in capes, outer coats and jackets, especially in the northern colonies and states, e.g., "Mikaila's loden coat was her favorite on cold days, very warm, and almost windproof."

loggets: a game, perhaps a thousand years old, and not unlike horseshoes, in which each competitor throws a logget (a wooden sphere with a handle) at a stake driven into the ground, and the one whose logget lands nearest the stake wins; Shakespeare and Ben Jonson (*Every Man in his Humour*, 1599) also used the term for a game or sport, e.g., "The word logget appears early, occasionally in association with the game of *quoits* (q.v.), both being casting or throwing games."

londen: lime for treatment of the soil and to destroy the waste in a latrine, outhouse, or garbage dump, e.g., "In those colonies that had limestone near or outcropping the surface, that mineral soon and very early was being ground for use in and about the facilities of the settlers."

London Company: See *Virginia Company, __ etc.*

long ton, short ton: in Britain, twenty *hundredweights* (q.v.) or 2240 pounds; a ton as we know it in the U.S., 2000 pounds, e.g., "The difference between a long ton and a short ton was of great importance in early times when contracting, especially for large quantities, bulky, or heavy materials and merchandise."

lost property, mislaid property, misplaced property: the differences have been important to the law over the centuries, especially in matters involving insurance; "lost" is personal property that the owner has parted with intentionally and is unable to relocate; mislaid and misplaced are said to be synonymous and are property intentionally placed in a certain place, the location of which the owner cannot recall, e.g., "When Paul left his keys in the yard and could not again find those, he lost the keys, but when he placed those on his work bench and forgot that he had done so, he mislaid or misplaced those."

Figure 20. Union Pacific *locomotive* #23 and crew, c.1870.

ocomotive of the First World War. Photo courtesy of Mrs. Diane Peterson.

lot: as now; an early and now common term used in listing several, yet an indeterminate number of items to be sold or appraised together as one unit, e.g., "The 1848 estate of Ohioan Lewis Fridley listed a lot of 'sacks,' one of 'old tools,' one of 'harnessing' and one of 'old iron.'"

love apples, Devil's fruit: tomatoes; see *tomatoes* in *What Did They Mean By That?*

lunacy: a medical condition involving actions or conduct by one who previously was in possession of the faculties of the mind, yet is later thought to have lost that condition in the judgment by the community and physicians at one's place of abode, and distinct from insanity, which is a legal determination, based on medical conditions, of one's capacity to conduct his or her own affairs as society expects, e.g., "The physician's affidavit of 1872 filed in the matter of Susan Cole revealed she had been insane for some number of years, whereupon the court ruled her to be insane and she was committed."

lycanthropy: madness, lunacy, e.g., "Early New England writings by physicians occasionally speak of lycanthrophy."

lying in of a child begotten of her body, expenses of: those sums ordered paid to the mother by a father of an illegitimate child for the period during which she was preparing for or after birth of that child, e.g., "In February of 1780, Mr. N. Bell was ordered by a New Hampshire court to pay Pamela's expenses for her lying in and her convalescence after the birth of a child '...he had begotten of her body.'"

M

maceration: softening in water, usually of some foodstuff, e.g., "Many recipes of the American colonies speak of macerating vegetables, fruits, or spices in either cold or warm water for some period of time, parboiling meaning in boiling water."

machine: as now; also, an expression of the first half of the twentieth century meaning automobile, e.g., "John Endicott invariably referred to his automobile as 'my machine.'"

made from whole cloth: See *whole cloth, etc.*

madhouse: where those are kept who were beieved "mad," a lunatic asylum, e.g., "Many people were placed in the madhouses who today would be given sedatives or anti-depressive drugs."

magistrate: a term without precise meaning; an officer of government having authority in minor judicial, legislative or executive matters, contests, and activities, e.g., "Justices of the peace ("JPs") and *police magistrates* (q.v.) are but two of the lesser officials that have been labeled as magistrates across the years."

maiden: a young unmarried woman, and not necessarily a virgin, e.g., "The naming as maidens of Barbara and Elizabeth in the 1706 indictment of Weller did not reveal their virginity or lack of the same."

mail routes and carriers: at the coming of the Civil War the population west of the Mississippi and "in the valleys of the Missouri" was sufficient to have brought about regular mail to and from California and places in between, e.g., "On March 24, 1860 the *New York Herald* set forth the mail routes then supported by the U.S. government as follows; 1) **Pacific Steamship Mail**, twice monthly from New York to New Orleans and to San Francisco; 2) **Butterfield Overland Mail**, twice weekly from St. Louis and Memphis to San Francisco; 3) **San Antonio to El Paso**, weekly connecting there with Butterfield; 4) **St. Joseph to Leavenworth to Salt Lake City**, twice weekly; 5) **Salt Lake City to Camp Floyd and Carson Valley to Placerville**, twice weekly; 6) A spur from 3) at the **forks of the Platte to Denver and the Rocky Mountain Gold Mines**; 7) **Independence to Kansas to Santa Fe**.

mail, government: mail or notices were required to be transmitted from plantation to plantation or community to community by the landowners or sheriffs until such reached the destination or objective, e.g., "No mail services being present till the eighteenth century, by 1642 it had become the law of most colonies that all people were responsible to further messages and notices having to do with government business."

mainprize: an ancient term abandoned here by 1750; a bond-like security given to assure appearance or performance of the duty secured, however, unlike bail, the person secured could not be given over before the due date of the performance or debt, e.g., "Virginia records before the mid-seventeenth century reveal that mainprizes were yet accepted to secure the duties or debts of another person." Also see *bail* in *What Did They Mean By That?*

majority: twenty-one or more years old, e.g., "'Of age' and 'majority' are not synonymous in the law, and the researcher should draw inferences only with great care, so a young woman may be eighteen and 'of age' for marriage, yet still not be of majority or qualified to vote." Also see *legal age*.

make a note: See *note, promissory, to make* and see *non fecit*.

make distress and sale of the goods to: See *distress, levy of distress, etc.*

make whole: See *lawsuits, common, procedural steps*.

makebate: See *jangle*.

malaria: as now, and common, especially in the South, e.g., "Early physicians, including Dr. Pierce as well as many other caregivers, believed that malaria was caused by 'noxious gas emanating from decomposition of vegetable matter.'"

malediction: a curse, e.g., "A number of early writings speak of persons overtake by a malediction."

malignant fever: See *typhus.*

malignant pustule: See *anthrax.*

malitia: militia. See *meets, meets of the militia, etc.*

mandamus council, establishment: See **Coercive Acts, etc.**

mangling board: See *mangle* in *What Did They Mean By That?*

marasmus: any progressive deterioration of the body or health, e.g., "Old Dr. Rhu believed that marasmus was an identifiable disease, and not merely symptomatic of any number of other ailments."

marital fourth: has nothing to do with a one-quarter interest or a twenty-five percent portion; an award by a court to a widow who is in poverty or destitute, e.g. "Though rare, courts occasionally granted marital fourths to very poor widows who had no other means of support, those sums coming usually being in lump sum and from the general funds of the county."

marriage bonds: See *bonds, surety, etc.*

marsh rubies: New England cranberries, e.g., "Since the earliest days of the Northeastern colonies, cranberries, known early as marsh rubies, have been popular with meat and salted meals, though very tart without a heavy addition of sweetener."

Maryland, Colony of: See *fiefdom.*

Massachusetts Bay Regulating Acts: See *Coercive Acts, etc.*

master, master in chancery: an appointed assistant, now male or female, to the chancellor (equity judge) who was/is an administrator, e.g., "Though it was thought inappropriate by some, Judy was appointed Master to Chancellor Martin in Pickett County." In *What Did They Mean By That?* see **chancellor** and see **chancery court.**

matron: a mature, married woman usually; an unmarried elder woman, e.g., "At age forty-five, Mrs. Sherrill was a young matron of the community and was highly regarded for her many civic activities."

mayor's court, municipal court: minor courts established by many cities and some states, and quite usually having jurisdiction in traffic matters and small criminal matters and quite usually with authority to hear minor civil claims for money, e.g., "Dexter Hazen was the mayor's court judge for many years and was a favorite of all for his fairness and understanding of difficulties"; "Judge Vogt ably conducted the municipal court at Kettering."

mea culpa: See *culpa.*

meadow: see *field.*

meaner than Hetty Green: See *Hetty Green, etc.*

measles: See *rubeola.*

measures, household: measures of food have been a convenience to homemakers since writing was widespread and brought the trading of recipes among women, e.g., "In 1879 Marion Cabell Tyree listed the following common measurements in her book, *Housekeeping in Old Virginia*: "butter (soft) one pound = 1 pint; drops, 60 = 1 teaspoonful; eggs, 10 = 1 pound; flour, 8 quarts = 1 peck, (4 pecks = 1 bushel); gills, 2 = one-half pint; Indian meal (corn meal), 1 pound 2 oz = a quart.; sugar (best, brown), 1 pound 2 oz. = 1 quart; sugar (loaf, broken), 1 pound = 1 quart; sugar (powdered), 1 pound 1 oz = 1 quart; tablespoon, full = one-half oz.; tablespoons, 16 large = one-half pint; tablespoons, 8 large = 1 gill; teaspoons, 4 = 1 tablespoonful; wheat flour, one pound = 1 quart; tumbler = one-half pint.

meat: food, now obsolete; e.g., "It is supposed that the use of the term 'meat' by Shakespeare in referring to any food was ancient even then."

mechanics lien: See *lien; mechanics, tax, etc.*

medicine, to read: See *read medicine.*

meets, meets of the militia, militia meets, militia drills, malitia drill: those early and frequent gatherings of the local, district or county militia for drill and training, e.g., "The meets were enjoyed by all, especially those who came for the refreshments and social exchange, as well as the children." Also see *militia* in *What Did They Mean By That?*

melancholia: an early term for severe depression, early without known cure and not understood, e.g., "Tragically, listed within the Toledo Asylum records are numerous inmates whose cause for commitment was shown as 'melancholia.'"

memorandum of agreement: a properly executed and usually acknowledged document setting forth the terms of an agreement, e.g., "In the law a contract is intangible and exists only in the minds of those involved with it, and the written evidence, though commonly called 'a contract' is really but a memorandum setting out the terms of that agreement."

memorial: as now; also early and now, a petition or written request by several or many and presented to a legislature or early courts, the same seeking redress or action by the body to which it was presented, e.g., "In 1722 some citizens of the area of South Quay, Virginia presented a memorial to the Colonial Council, the same seeking a movement of the tax collectors on Meharrin River."

mess, to: early, to eat; early and now, to waste or not efficiently utilize time by doing unnecessary tasks or by being in the company of another to no particular advantage, e.g., "Paul disdainfully said he would not mess with anyone in the Nickles family"; "The 55th Ohio was at its mess along the Orange Pike east of Chancellorsville when Jackson's Corps attacked."

middlings: See *flour, meal.*

might have benefit of his/her labor: See *benefit of his/her labor, etc.*

migration West, supplies suggested for: thanks to Ms. Peggy Batchelor Hamlett, the following is from *Wayne County Kentucky Marriages and Vital Records*, Vol. 2., pp. 499-500, and is the list suggested there for the supplies needed for a wagon trip "west" from Kentucky: **FOOD PER PERSON,** 150 pounds of flour, 25 pounds of bacon, 10 pounds of rice, 15 pounds of coffee, 2 pounds of tea, 25 pounds of sugar, 1/2 bushel died peas, 1/2 bushel dried fruit, 2pounds soleratus (baking soda), 10 pounds salt, 1/2 bushel corn meal, 1/2 small keg vinegar, pepper; **CLOTHING PER PERSON, Men**, 2 wool shirts, 2 wool undershirts, **Women,** 2 wool dresses, **For Both,** 2 pair drawers, 4 pair wool socks, 2 pair cotton socks, 4 colored handkerchiefs, 1 pair boots and shoes, poncho, broad rimmed hat, **MISCELLANEOUS PER FAMILY,** rifle, ball, powder, 8-10 gallon keg for water, 1 axe, 1 hatchet, 1 spade, 2 or 3 augers, 1 hand saw, 1 whip or cross-cut saw, 1 plow mold, at least 2 ropes, mallet for driving picket pins, matches carried in corked bottles, **Sewing supplies,** (carried in a buckskin or stout cloth bag) stout linen thread, large needles, thimble, bit of bee's wax, a few buttons, buckskin for patching, paper of pins, **Personal items,** 1 comb and brush, 2 toothbrushes, 1 lb. castile soap, 1 belt knife, 1 flint stone, **Cooking wares,** baking pan (used for baking and roasting coffee), mess-pan wrought iron or tin mess pan, 2 churns, one for sweet, one for sour milk, 1 coffee pot, 1 tin cup with handle, 1 tin plate, knives, (forks, spoons, per person), 1 camp kettle, fry pan, 1 coffee mill, wooden bucket for water, **Bedding per person,** 1 canvas, 2 blankets, 1 pillow, one tent per family, **Medical supplies,** Iron rust, rum and cognac (both for dysentery), calomel, quinine for ague, Epsom salts for fever, castor oil capsules.

milk pans: See *set pans, etc.*

mills, fees, share of grain ground: in early England mills often retained one-sixteenth of the grain ground for others; here, with the notable exception that because of their religious disciplines, Quakers were not permitted to charge more for flour (or anything else) than their actual cost, less than that fraction was very common, and the usual percentage retained by millers in our colonies was ten to twenty percent, and often twelve percent for corn and sixteen percent for wheat, e.g., "Grist mills were on virtually every stream that carried water sufficient to maintain a mill pond, and were said to have been the most important businesses in the colonies; many were highly profitable."

miniver: white, white/gray or white/black fur of ermine or mink, e.g., "Early inventories occasionally reveal the presence of apparel trimmed with or made from otter, lynx, beaver, or minivers; fox, muskrat, bear, and wolf being less desirable."

minstrel, roving: an itinerant who wanders about the countryside playing one or more musical instruments, usually for small sums or money, e.g., "As were gypsies and peddlers, roving minstrels were common throughout the colonies, especially during hard times."

minutes, courts' minutes, court orders: minutes are those notes made by a judge or at his direction during hearings or appearances before his court; orders are transcriptions of rulings made by judges before, during or after a hearing or other court functions wherein decisions are being made, including orders made in chambers, e.g., "An examination of courts' minutes and orders in those counties where an ancestor lived are an absolute necessity for thorough genealogical research."

Miscellaneous Records: the proper title for the volumes of records that result from actions of any of the three elements of government for which there is not a specific depository otherwise, e.g., "The registrar regularly filed copies of materials in the Miscellaneous Records when he knew of no other place for such records to be preserved and recorded." Also see *paripatetic, etc.*

misdemeanor: a crime of less import than a *felony* (q.v.), quite usually punishable by a fine or a jail term, that term usually being limited by state legislatures to less than one year, e.g., "In Ohio and several other states the maximum jail term that may be imposed on one found guilty of a misdemeanor is eleven months and twenty-nine days."

mislaid property, misplaced property: See *lost property, etc.*

misprision of treason, misprision of felony: next to treason itself, perhaps the most serious of crimes during wartime; both crimes involve having knowledge of a crime, yet not assisting in the planning, the crime itself, or in actions of the criminal after the event, e.g., "In August of 1850 Shawnee Indians, William Rodgers and Paschal Fish were charged with   misprision   of   treason   and   jailed   without   bond."

…harge against a man named Hankins. See *misprision of treason*.

Mistress, Miss: now, a common title—Miss—for an unmarried young woman; early, a young unmarried lady who was a daughter or a ward of a gentleman or a gentlewoman, e.g., "In eighteenth-century America, to address a woman as 'Miss' revealed an elevated measure of affluence in her family and also a high degree of respect for her by the speaker."

mobby: Johnson (1802) defines it as potato whiskey; Teresa describes that distilled by her ancestor, John Stewart, as having also been made from peaches or apples, e.g., "The inventory of Allison's sixth-great-grandfather listed 'mobby stills and tubs.'"

modest amount, modest sum: a term of comparative price; requiring but small sums to purchase compared to other items of the same sort requiring relatively more, e.g., "While the word cheap meant inexpensive and did not mean poorly made, the adjective 'modest' meant requiring a small sum to buy and did not reflect quality."

moiety: one-half of anything, e.g., "If you and another person are joint tenants of a tract of land, it is said that you have a moiety of the rights in that property."

molasses: as now, a valuable sweetener, first brought to Virginia from the Caribbean islands as a by-product of processing cane sugar, and at once introduced to the other colonies, e.g., "With the seventeenth-century importation of sugar cane molasses from which rum was made in New England, the colonists had a sweetener other than maple syrup and honey."

mollycoddle: from "molly" meaning to appease, to calm, to pacify, or to gently deal with another, and probably from caudle, meaning to boil and soften, e.g., "Thelma's gentleness with her children led her family to say she mollycoddled her kids to an extreme."

money damages: See *lawsuits, common, procedural steps.*

Monmouth cap: very much like a stocking cap; described as heavy wool, very warm, easy to wear and without a bill, these have been popular in Britain since the fifteenth century, e.g., "The seventeenth-century lists of what a settler would need in the American colonies usually included a Monmouth cap"; "Shakespeare mentioned that men in Wales wore Monmouth caps with leeks attached as an 'honorable badge of the service.'" (Henry V, Act 4, Scene 7)

mononucleosis: See *glandular fever.*

monument: anything that serves as a reminder of the existence of a contract, relationship, person, event, or past life or presence, e.g., "Just as a headstone is a monument to the memory of a person, so too is a painting or a framed or preserved memento to that individual."

moon-stroke, moon-stricken: partial lunacy, loss of reasoning or of control over one's body and senses as a result, it was thought, of exposure to certain phases and activities of the moon, e.g., "It was commonly believed that one could become moon-stricken by being exposed to certain phases and appearances of the moon."

Moravians: a fundamentalist group, more prominent in the nineteenth century, and believing in strict construction of the Scriptures and adhering to those as the only guidelines of life, e.g., "The Moravians of early Pennsylvania were well known for their austere lifestyle and fine horses."

morphew: blisters, perhaps resulting from ***scurvy*** (q.v., *What Did They Mean By That?*), e.g., "Though scurvy was well known in the colonies, morphew was often misdiagnosed as 'severe fever blisters.'"

mortification: gangrene (q.v., *What Did They Mean By That?*), e.g., "Drue Drake's mangled arm was declared mortified beyond help and was amputated in 1883."

mortiis est: Latin meaning, "is dead," e.g., "Kristina noted that following a date of birth, the term 'mortis (sic) est' appeared, so she knew that child was born dead or died immediately after death."

motions: See ***lawsuits, common, procedural steps.***

mourning bell: See ***passing bell, mourning etc.***

muck cart: See ***muck, etc.***

muck, muck cart, muck wagon: animal waste and manure, usually in such a quantity that boots are worn to clean it up for use on the fields or otherwise, e.g., "Armies of all wars before World War II had men assigned to drive muck carts in order that manure could be removed from the areas where the horses were kept."

municipal court: See ***mayor's court, etc.***

muniments: documentary and explanatory material pertaining to the title to land, e.g., "The muniments presented to the court to prove title to the land upon which stood the factory ran to many pages and exhibits."

Murder Act: See ***Coercive Acts, etc.***

muslinet, muslinette, muslin: a very common, woven cotton fabric used for "everyday" apparel, warm weather shirts, undergarments, and linings in many items of wear, e.g., "The 1796 estate inventory of the estate of Thomas Phenix of Charles County, Maryland listed '21 yards of muslinet,' among many other fabrics (***stuffs***, q.v., *What Did They Mean By That?*)."

mutual wills: separate wills made by two people, each providing the same terms for the other, e.g., "Mutual wills were and are common since women have come to have the rights of inheritance equal to those of men with the exception of *dower* (q.v.) rights in some states, e.g., "The wills of Diane and Todd each first provide for the care of their minor children, and then make the same bequeaths and devises each to the other, depending on who dies first."

N

nail rod: long thin strands of iron or steel from which *cut nails* (q.v.) were made, e.g., "The Thomas Mason estate revealed the presence of '2 faggots of nail rods.'"

nail: a measurement equal to two and one-quarter inches, e.g., "In the early American colonies a nail was a common measurement and well known to every blacksmith, carpenter, housewright, cabinetmaker and craftsman."

*nailmaking machine:*as it sounds, a machine, early water- or animal-drawn, that shaped "cut nails," e.g., "Thomas Jefferson had a very early nail-making machine on his Virginia plantation." Also see *cut nails, square nails, nail rod.*

nails; forged, cut and wire: See *cut nails, square nails.*

Nantucket sleigh ride: an expression of the days of New England whaling, and meaning that a whaleboat had been pulled by a harpooned whale in its attempts to escape, e.g., "It was common to hear of Nantucket sleigh rides in the days of sailing ships and harpoons hurled by hand from the small boats launched from a mother ship."

narrow bleares, fine bleares: See *bleares, narrow bleares, etc.*

nascituris, natis, nati et nascituris: Latin for born thereafter or born previously, now obsolete, *natis (nati)* meaning already born, e.g., "Some early wills referred to 'children (or issue) nati and nascituris,' meaning already born to the testator and those who might be born of the marriage after death of the *testator* (q.v., *What Did They Mean By That?*)."

natis, nati et nacituris: See *nascituris, etc.*

natural child: offspring related by blood, and not by adoption, formal or informal assumption of parental duties of the child, e.g., "She had two natural children and one who she 'took in' out of pity." Also see *adoption, system, etc.*

natural father: the sire of a child, and not necessarily one who is married to the mother of that child, e.g., "All knew and acknowledged that Drue was the natural father of the little girl of Elizabeth, though both were unmarried at the conception of the child in 1782."

natural life: as it sounds, and often applied in wills as the means by which the term of a bequest or devise was apparent, e.g., "Many early wills, especially in the South limited the rights of the spouse throughout her natural life, 'her widowhood or until she remarries.'"

natural son/daughter/child: contrary to common belief, the terms also may mean that the child so described is related by blood to the parent, e.g., "Though Owen Griffith referred to Andrew as 'a natural son,' the boy was a son of Owen's brother."

ne exeat, writ ne exeat: Latin; an order of court preventing a person from leaving the jurisdiction, be that the county, state or country, e.g., "By reason of the likelihood that Wilson would steal off to the frontier, in 1834 the judge issued a writ ne exeat directing that he not leave Buncombe county."

necessary house: an outdoor toilet; a pit latrine within a shelter; any structure within which one might relieve himself or herself, e.g., "The old Hotel 1880 boasted that the 'necessary house is heated.'"

neck clothes, neck cloths: Johnson, 1755, defines clothes as "anything woven for dress or cover," e.g., "Neck cloths presumably are what we now know as "neck scarves" or simply "scarves," and often appearing in early inventories."

neck verse: benefit of clergy (q.v., *What Did They Mean By That?*) was a privilege of those sentenced to death, and to claim that benefit a convict who was eligible could request that the priest present open the Bible to any Scripture that priest chose, and if the convict could read that selection, he literally saved his neck, e.g., "Words from the 51st Psalm (in Latin) were a popular early neck verse, a few of those words being, 'Misere mei Deus.'"

nee: born; usually a maiden name; a prior surname of a woman, e.g., "The expression 'Jane Roberts nee Jones' reveals to all that Jane was either born Jane Jones or previously had been married to a man of that surname."

nephew and *niece:* as now, however in early records, the term may mean grandsons or granddaughters or cousins, e.g., "The 1868 will of Walter Williams made bequests to 'my granddaughters, Mikaila and Allison,' however those women were in fact his nieces."

nephew: derived from the Latin term "nepos" meaning grandson, e.g., "When the word 'nephew' appears in very early wills, one should be cautious in concluding that such was the relationship we now presume it to mean."

nephritis, nephritic, acute uremia: very common, but not understood early; any serious affliction of the kidneys; any remedy thought appropriate for "the stone," e.g., "Dan Carner was diagnosed with acute nephritis, for which Dr. Pierce recommended as nephritics, warm bathes, alcoholic vapor bathes, flannel worn next to the skin and 'jalap' (a purge) given four or five times a day.'" Also see ***Brights' Disease*** in *What Did They Mean By That?*

nepos ex filio: nieces and nephews, e.g., "Early records, especially in the Southwest occasionally refer to nieces and nephews with the Latin words shown."

nervines: herbs and plants thought to have value in "calming the nerves" were many and included ***black cohosh*** (q.v.), hops, skull-cap, lady's slipper and pulsatilla, e.g., "Several of the monthly difficulties of women being thought associated with 'nerves,' herb nervines were commonly prescribed for such and also for 'excitability,' restlessness due to excessive energy, and 'quick temper.'"

nervous prostration: a term for most nervous conditions, ***mania*** (q.v., *What Did They Mean By That?*) or exhaustion from no obvious cause, e.g., "Elma was certain she suffered from nervous prostration and regularly took 'nerve medicine' having alcohol as an ingredient."

nester: apparently unknown outside America before the eighteenth century; a "squatter"; a person or group of people who take up residence upon or assume the use of the land of another without permission, express or implied, e.g., "The vastness of the forest here and the lack of accuracy in frontier property lines during the early centuries caused frequent legal complaints about nesters."

New Lights, Old lights: as to the "New," non-conservative religious party associated with the Quakers; others have written, two groups of discipline who debated the issue of God during the Great Awakening, the Old Lights who rejected the Great Awakening and the New Lights who accepted it, e.g., "The New Lights often suffered heavy persecution since their views disrupted the 'old institutions.'" Also see ***Great Awakening***.

new mother, new father: a stepmother or stepfather, e.g., "Before the terms 'stepmother' or 'stepfather' were in common use, early records occasionally refer to those relationships as 'new mother' or 'new father.'"

next devisee: the person to whom a remainder interest in real estate is given by will, that interest to vest at the extinguishment or end of the term of the life estate holder, e.g., "The will devised a 'remainder' to Bethany, thus when the life estate of her mother ended by that mother's death or otherwise, Bethany would be the owner of the entirety of the rights in that land." Also see ***devise***.

next of kin: a term most common to genealogy and to proceedings in intestate administrations; the nearest kin, whether one or more, of a decedent, e.g., "When Miss Wells died, her next of kin were her four first cousins."

niggardly: a very early term meaning miserly, avaricious, e.g., "While the word niggardly is now quite politically unacceptable, the original meaning had nothing whatever to do with African-Americans."

nigger consumption: distasteful as is the term now, a commonly appearing early reference to tuberculosis in African Americans; at times, perhaps asthma, e.g., "Ms. Gorin in 'Old Definitions (continued, #132, N through P)' defines it as 'Black person's TB.'"

night riders: men of the post-Civil War years who rode about the countryside bringing fear to the free Blacks, e.g., "What had been nightriders continued that horrific practice to the twentieth century as members of the *Ku Klux Klan* (q.v., *What Did They Mean By That?*).

ningimmer: a low and disrespectful term and slang for a physician who held himself out as being able to cure venereal diseases, e.g., "Ningimmers, though very discreet, were held in low repute and often said to carry the diseases they were claimed to cure."

nisi, nici: See **fined nisi**.

NMI, NMN: no middle initial; no middle name; many official, legal, and quasi-legal writings and documents reveal the fact of but one forename by the use of the initials NMI or NMN, e.g., "Paul's application to join the U.S. Navy during the Korean War recited his name as 'Paul NMI Drake.'"

NMN: See *NMI, NMN.*

no asset administration: an order by a court that he/she had determined that the assets of a decedent were insufficient to justify probate proceedings, e.g., "In 1671, the Surry Court noted that the estate of William Judson amounted to not more than 330 pounds of tobacco 'which not being worth the administration it is ordered that the widow pay her fees and the remainder of such sums be paid to any Just creditor.'"

nolle prosequi: Latin; a formal entry in a case revealing that the plaintiff or the prosecutor will not further press the matter against the defendant, e.g., "Though the nolle prosequi had been entered, to protect the defendant Glover, in 1839 the court required that the prosecutor amend that entry to show that the matter would not be pursued later."

nolo contendere: Latin for "no contest"; I will not contend the matter; the equivalent of pleading guilty to a criminal charge, e.g., "Though he pleaded nolo contendere to the indictment for robbery, he knew that his plea could not be used against him in any future legal matter."

non assumpsit: obsolete; the person did not assume a debt by law or in fact, e.g., "The formal early legal defense of non-assumpsit has now almost disappeared in favor of a simple denial by one that he owes someone else."

non-com, non-commissioned officer: an enlisted person in the military force, who has not been commissioned as an officer, e.g., "Paul was a petty officer 2nd class, a 'non-com.'"

non compos mentis: See *What Did They Mean By That?*

non est inventus, n.e.i.: Latin for "he is not found"; a very common notation on any warrant when a sheriff did not find a person charged or ordered served, e.g., "In 1763 when the sheriff was ordered to summons the Hines brothers in Sussex County for a debt they owed, the summons was returned marked 'non est inventus, went to the Carolinas.'"

non fecit: Latin, now obsolete; he/she did not *utter* (q.v., *What Did They Mean By That?*), sign, agree to, or *make the note* (q.v.) revealing a debt; a legal answer to a charge that one owes or has assumed a contractual debt or obligation, e.g., "When sued on the promissory note, Dr. Don asserted non fecit, meaning that he had not signed it." Also see **promissory note**.

non obstante: Latin for notwithstanding, e.g., "A legal term often used even to now is 'non obstante veredicto,' meaning the judge has found a person not liable even though the jury's verdict was that he was so."

nonpareil: excellence; very highly regarded as being of high quality manufacture; many newspapers bore as part of the title, the word "Nonpareil," e.g., "Though her article was published in the *St. Albans Nonpareil*, Eva Watkins was outraged and voiced that resentment with unequalled terms."

nonsuit: a very common term early and even now, often meaning that for whatever reasons the court has ruled the case closed because the person who filed a claim against another has not pursued his demands in a timely fashion or even at all, e.g., "Many early cases were nonsuited because the plaintiffs simply did not or could not return from a distance to press the matter." Also see *lawsuits, common, procedural steps* and see *nolle prosequi*.

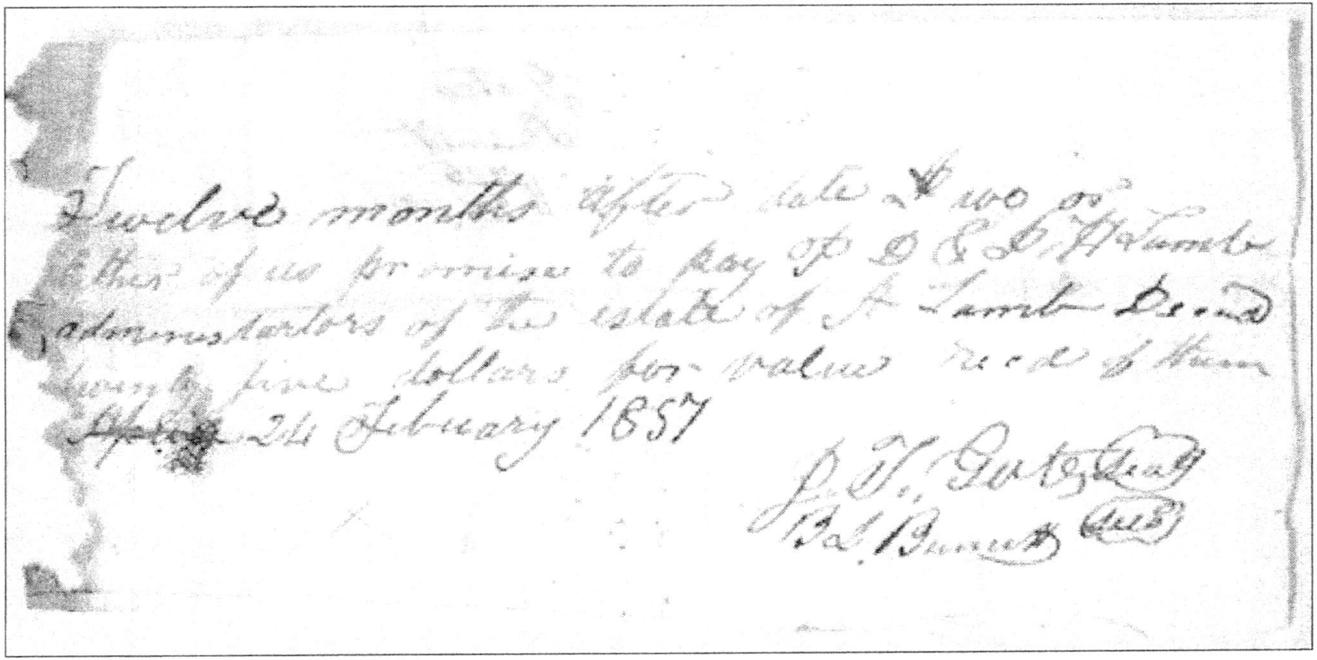
Twelve months after date we or
either of us promise to pay [illegible] Lamb
administrators of the estate of [illegible] Lamb Dec'd
twenty five dollars for value rec'd of them
24 February 1857

Figure 23. Tennessee promissory note of 1857. See ***non fecit***.

Figure 24. An 1870s newspaper ad showing *nostrums* and patent medicines for sale.

North Carolina headrights: The standard headright of fifty acres per person established in Virginia was adopted in the Carolinas about 1697. Before that time a sliding scale was used that granted one hundred acres to heads of families but only six acres to female servants when their terms expired. The governor also was allowed to sell tracts of 640 acres or less to those without headrights, or who had used their headrights for free land. To keep people in North Carolina, the Assembly forbade the sale of headrights until the claimant had been in the colony for two years. Copies of the proprietary land patents are available at the North Carolina State Archives and on microfilm at the Family History Library. Seven of the original proprietary shares were sold to King George II in 1729, and North Carolina became a royal colony. Only John Carteret, second Earl Granville, chose not to sell the share he had inherited. The Crown continued the headright system instituted by the Lords Proprietors, but modified the system in 1741 to allow one hundred acres for a head-of-household. The Crown land office first opened in 1735, six years after the Crown purchased the province.

nostrum: a quack medicine or patent medicine; a mixture supposed to cure one or another illness, yet having no proven medical efficacy, e.g., "Dr. Drake's '1861 Plantation Bitters' was little more than a nostrum with high alcohol content."

not satisfied: a common endorsement by a sheriff on a writ ordering him to seize assets or money of a defendant and revealing that the defendant or other person against whom the order was issued did not have assets sufficient to meet the debt, or that the sheriff could not find sufficient assets for that purpose, e.g., "In a 1755 judgment against Lazarus, the sheriff endorsed the writ 'levied on one cat' revealing with humor that the judgment would not be satisfied."

note of hand: an early term now seldom seen and referring to a promissory note or other written memorandum of debt or obligation; an "IOU," e.g., "From colonial times to the present, the records often reveal the presence of a written memorandum revealing a debt by the expression 'in possession of his note of hand.'"

note, promissory, to make: See *promissory note* and see *non fecit.*

novation: the substitution of a new contract or agreement between two or more persons or between other parties with the agreement of those original parties, e.g., "When Dee was injured and could not pay Cody as agreed, he and Cody agreed that there would be a novation and from then on Robert would make the payments and be responsible."

now wife: often found in early wills, a former wife is to be inferred, e.g., "The words 'my now wife' in John's will reveal a former wife whose identity has not been established."

nuisance: actions or conditions that render uncomfortable to a person of ordinary sensibilities such a person's peaceful possession of his property, e.g., "The hog lot adjoining the new apartments were alleged to be a nuisance." Also see *attractive nuisance.*

O

oakum: unraveled rope, very often used to *caulk* (q.v.) ships, boats and other structures that would otherwise be damaged by water or wind passing through seams, e.g., "Every shipbuilder in the days of wooden sail-driven ships well knew the use of oakum."

oath, corporal: See *corporal oath.*

obligee: See *debtor, etc.*

obligor: See *debtor, etc.*

obsolete twentieth-century U.S. terms, some: Many earlier terms and words have only recently been abandoned or nearly so in one or more parts of the country. As Colleen has suggested, here are but a few: *adding machine*-mechanical device to add numbers; *more money than Ben Gump*-cartoon rich man from 1930-1950; *brassiere*-bra; *bomb, the*-meaning the atomic bombs dropped at Hiroshima and Nagasaki; *carbon paper*-to make copies; *caboose*-final car of a freight train, nearly obsolete; *career girls*-not needed now; *Charles Atlas*-now forgotten advertised body builder and idol of the first half of the century; *cistern*-no longer used; *coast to coast*-now world-wide; *continental kit*-not now used; *curb feelers*-for autos; *dinner*-lunch; *emergency brake*-parking brake; *express train*-obsolete; *fender skirts*-wheel covers; *flue covers*-decorative metal covers for over chimney flues inn the summer; *foot feed*-accelerator; *in a family way*-pregnant; *ink well*-a container for ink; *interurban*-one or two-car passenger trains between towns; *loaf bread*-bread not sliced; *lumbago*-almost unheard now; *machine*-automobile; *outhouse* and *privy*-for toilet outdoors; *percolator*-coffeemaker; *rumble seat*-a seat on the outside back of an auto no longer made; *running boards*-not used now; *sliced bread*-nearly all is now; *steam shovel*-heavy excavating shovel powered by steam; *steering knob*-not needed after power steering; *store bought*-as opposed to home-made; *summer kitchen*-cook stove no longer moved out of doors; *street car*-a multiple passenger horse, later electric powered, car on tracks in and about a city; *supper*-dinner; *threshing machine*-a horse or tractor drawn, mobile separator of wheat from chaff; *typewriters*-no longer manufactured; *unmentionables*-meaning underclothes for women; *uptown* or *downtown*-central shopping areas of communities before malls and shopping centers; *window curtains*-no longer found except on the most expensive autos.

Occupations, some synonyms for, and origins of some surnames:
Bailie-bailiff; *Baxter*-baker; *Binman*-a very old term, still used, a trash
collector; *Bluestocking*-female author/writer; *Brakeman*-one who
originally tended mechanical brakes on trains and other wheeled
transportation; *Brewster*-beer maker/seller; *Brightsmith*-decorative metal
worker; *Caulker*-one who caulks ships, etc., with tar or resin and hemp
or similar fiber; *Chaisemaker*-maker of better carriages; *Chiffonier* and
Peruker-wig maker; *Colporteur*-book peddler; *Conductor*-one who has
charge of a railroad train, trolley, subway, or elevated railroad;
Costermonger-fruit and vegetable seller; *Crocker*-a maker of pottery;
Docker-dock laborer; *Drayman*-heavy or large wagon driver; *Dresser*-A
surgeon's assistant, usually in a hospital; *Duffer*-Peddler (unknown to
Johnson); *Faulkner*-falconer; *Fellmonger*-a dealer in hides and skins;
Fletcher-one who makes bows and arrows; *Glazier*-installer of paned
glass; *Hatcheler*-one who combed and carded flax; *Haymonger*-dealer in
hay and straw; *Hayward*-a tender of fences; *Higgler*-an itinerant peddler
of provisions; *Hillier*-a roof tiler; *Hind*-a peasant or farm laborer, a
female red deer; *Hostler, Hossler*-one who tends horses, sometimes at an
inn or hotel; *Huckster*-sells insignificant wares; *Jagger, Fishmonger*-
one who sells fish; *Journeyman*-one who has mastered his craft, usually
after an apprenticeship; *Keeler*-sometimes one who tends barges;
Lardner-one tending the food staples of mansions; *Lavendar*-laundry
woman; *Lederer*-said to be a leather maker; *Longshoreman*-a stevedore,
both unknown to *Johnson*; *Lorimer, Loriner*-one who makes leather
horse tack; *Lormer*-harness maker; *Maltster*-one who tends to malt for
beer, a brewer; *Manciple,* steward-a manager of community affairs;
Mason-brick, tile and stone artisan; *Mintmaster*-manager or
superintendent of a mint; *Monger*-one who sells any goods, foods or
products to the general public (See **fishmonger, fellmonger**, etc.);
Muleskinner-a person skilled in driving teams of draft animals;
Neatherder-one who tends *neat cattle* (q.v. *What Did They Mean By
That?*); *Ordinary Keeper* or *Ordinary Keep*-a keeper of an inn with
regulated prices;one who owns or manages an *ordinary* (q.v., *What Did
They Mean By That?*); *Peregrinator*-a traveler, a wanderer; *Porter*-early,
a door keeper, now one who tends to passengers; *Quarrier*-one who
owns or works in a quarry; *Rigger*-one who works with ropes and cables;
Roper-a maker of nets, rope, string and tackle; *Schumacher*-a
shoemaker; *Scribler* (Scribbler)-little known writer/author, and see *What
Did They Mean By That?*, **Scrivener**; *Scrutiner*-one who judges
elections; *Slater*-a roofer (and see roofer *What Did They Mean By
That?*); *Slopseller*-rare, one who sells ready-made clothes in a slopshop,
slop meaning trousers and open pants (very early, Shakespeare); *Snob*-a
shoemaker's or cobbler's apprentice; *Sorter*-from Pope, very early, a

tailor, to suit or fit; *Steward*-see **Manciple**; *Thatcher*-very early, one who applies roofing woven and made of straw; *Tide waiter*-an officer in a customs house; *Tidewaiter*-a customs agent or inspector; *Traver(s)*-said to be a collector of toll bridge fees; *Wagoner*-one employed as a wagon driver, a teamster; *Wainwright*-wagonmaker; *Waterman*-ferryman, boatman; *Webster*-a weaver or operator of loom (obsolete even for *Johnson*, 1802); *Wharfinger*-one who tends and may own a wharf; *Wharfman*-tender of a wharf; *Whitster*, *Whitester*-one who bleaches fabrics. Also see *surnames as occupations* in *What Did They Mean By That?*

octogenarian, nonagenarian, septuagenarian, etc.: ancient terms derived from the Latin for numbers and in age of a subject, signifying the decades, e.g., "The nonagenarian Henry T. Cline was born in 1797, became a nonagenarian (began his ninth decade of life) on his ninetieth birthday in 1887, and died in 1894." also see *September as 7BR.*

odd years, censuses within the states of the U.S.: Over the years, the several states have sometimes conducted censuses in odd years, any of which may be extremely valuable to the researcher. Those known to be **open and available** for researchers are **Florida** (1935, 1945), **Iowa** (1856, 1925), **Kansas** (1925), **New York** (1925), **North Dakota** (1925), **Rhode Island** (1925, 1935) and **South Dakota** (1925, 1935, and 1945). **Censuses yet closed to the public** are **Colorado** (1885), **Florida** (1885, 1895), **Iowa** (1885-1895), **Kansas** (1885, 1895), **Nebraska** (1885), **New Jersey** (1885, 1895), **New Mexico** (1885), **New York** (1892), **North Dakota** (1885), **Rhode Island** (1885), **South Dakota** (1885, 1895), and **Wisconsin** (1885, 1895).

of counsel: See *a conciliis.*

off binding: outside the terms of an agreement, exclusive of, or not included in a specific contract or bargain, e.g., "When asked why he did not also convey the five acres adjoining the 120 acres, Frank stated that it was off binding, meaning outside of and not contemplated in the agreement of sale that bound both him and the buyer."

oil cans: referred to any size lidded containers of tin or other metal used to store whale, "coal," lubricating, or other oils used about the house and farm, e.g., "Martha had a small, tin, lamp oil can that was kept filled and carried about the house each evening to fill oil lamps as needed."

old milk: skimmed milk, e.g., "Many early recipes and letters of women refer to what we call skimmed milk as 'old milk.'"

olographic will: See *holographic will, etc.*

Figure 25. Nonagenarian Henry T. Cline, 1797-1894.
See *octogenarian, nonagenarian, etc.*

omnibus, omnibus bill: a pleading or a proposed act of the legislature that contains unrelated subject matters, e.g., "Wills that contain details of prior relationships, as well as gifts, devises and bequests are known an 'omnibus testaments' or 'omnibus wills'"; "Legislation that has 'pork barrel' spending mixed with quite unrelated legislative provisions often is called an omnibus bill."

onomastic: a will, writing or document with handwriting that clearly differs from that found in the signature or elsewhere in the document, e.g., "It was apparent that more than two people had assisted in writing the document purporting to be a will of the old man, so the court refused to admit the document into the record as the last will and testament."

onset: now obsolete, a closable structure or outbuilding attached or closely related to a house, e.g., "An early Pennsylvania Freeburn family will spoke of 105 acres and 'the onsets' for the youngest son of the family."

op. cit: See *ibid, etc.* and see *idem, id.*

opiate, opium: a sedative or narcotic, early used very frequently to induce sleep or to calm those with such as epilepsy or *mania* (q.v., *What Did They Mean By That?*); a drug made from the juice of the poppy plant, e.g., "Dr. Weaver, Dr. Lewis and most of their counterparts are known to have frequently prescribed opiates, even for colicky children."

oral will, spoken will, death-bed will: See *nuncupative will* in *What Did They Mean By That?*

orange bitters: See *bitters.*

Order of Redmen: See *Redmen, etc.*

ordered that indentures be drawn: See *be drawn, etc.*

orders, courts': See *minutes, etc.*

ordinance: legislation; usually a statute, but also a law from a lesser political subdivision, e.g., "Virtually every city has passed and maintains access for the public to its ordinances."

ordinary license: a license issued by the county court and allowing the operation of an *ordinary* (q.v., *What Did They Mean By That?*) at prices usually prescribed by rule of court or the county commissioners, e.g., "A common ordinary bond amount to be posted usually ordered by eighteenth-century South Carolina courts was £30, a lot of money then."

Ordinary, Court of: the name given early courts having jurisdiction over matters of probate, wills, and administrations, e.g., "Early Georgia, New Jersey, South Carolina and Texas had Courts of Ordinary, meaning simply 'probate courts' having authority over decedents' estates."

organic act: those actions and legislation of Congress that transfer the powers of a state to a territory; legislative action by which a city becomes a municipal corporation, e.g., "Alaska was the last state to come into existence by virtue of an organic act of the Congress of the U.S."

original, original document: the first or earliest copy of any writing archetype, e.g., "Well known to genealogists is the fact that even writings that purport to be or are labeled 'original' may contain errors resulting from incomplete or inaccurate transcription by early clerks who worked without any copying devices."

orotrix: an early term, and meaning a female plaintiff, complainant or petitioner, especially in an action in *chancery court* (q.v.), e.g., "Though the reasons are difficult to understand, early *chancellors* (q.v.) often made note in minutes and orders if a petitioner was a women, lest they be found not legally permitted to so file." Also see *chancellor.*

orphan: a minor child who has lost one or both parents, and often a minor who had lost only its father, e.g., "The legal hurdles over which early women could not leap, their lack of education, and the fact that there were virtually no sources of income for them, led the law to presume that if a father was dead a child was as disadvantaged as if the mother too was deceased."

Orphan's Courts: those usually county courts of general jurisdiction that are also probate courts, e.g., "Probate courts permanently designated 'Orphans' Courts' in the U.S. are found in Delaware, Maryland, New Jersey and Pennsylvania." See *states of the U.S., etc.* and see *websites of states' courts*

ostery: See *family hotel.*

ostler: one who tended teams of or individual horses, mules, and oxen at an inn or hotel, e.g., "Myriad inns of the early days hired ostlers, usually boys with a measure of knowledge of horses and draft animals." Also see *common inn, railroad hotel,* and *family hotel.*

out of term, after term, between terms: those days, weeks and months when there are no regular sessions of court, and the court is said to have adjourned, e.g., "As were most American courts, the Massachusetts courts were out of term during the months of July and August of 1754 by reason of the suffocating heat in traveling to, from, and within the courthouses." Also see *recess.*

out-boundaries, outboundaries: those arbitrary boundary lines established by the Mexican government before the Mexican War, and within which smaller tracts were described and sold, smaller in size but not unlike such American land as the Western Reserve lands, e.g., "After parts of Mexico had become a part of Texas the even then old outboundaries were very helpful in determining locations of lands that were to be designated as Texas properties."

out-crier, outcry: an auctioneer, a sale by auction, e.g., "An ancient term describing an auctioneer, and revealing that before modern voice amplifiers, he was required to speak loudly—'cry out.'"

outlandish, Frenchman: interestingly, a very early term meaning that someone is acting in a remarkable, bizarre, or most unusual way, just as one might expect of a person from a different country—"a foreigner," e.g., "In early England and in these colonies and because they conducted themselves quite unlike English men or English women, those whose conduct was outlandish were called Frenchmen until sometime shortly after the American Revolution."

outlay: the total overhead, costs, and expenditures required in the manufacture or production of any product, e.g., "When the court ordered that Haskins receive the income, lest the outlay, he was awarding what we now know as gross profit."

outriders: usually bailiffs, and sometimes deputies paid by sheriffs to ride long distances to summon or otherwise serve process upon defendants, witnesses, etc., e.g., "Often county lines were twenty, thirty, or even more miles from courthouses, thus requiring outriders willing to travel days in service for the courts and sheriffs."

outsettler: an early expression meaning someone who had moved to the outer edge of a populated area, e.g., "When Dan Carner and his family moved to western Illinois in 1820, he was said to be an outsettler."

over sea, over-sea: See ***beyond sea, etc.*** in *What Did They Mean By That?*

overlaid: a child smothered by being laid upon inadvertently by some person with whom the child was sleeping, e.g., "The numbers of small children who regularly slept with their parents in the early eighteenth century is revealed by the fact that in 1720, it is written that of 25,000+ deaths, sixty-nine were said to be caused by being overlaid."

overseer of highways: q.v., *What Did They Mean By That?*, and herein see ***road orders.***

owelty: those sums paid by one co-owner of land to another co-owner, such payment resulting from the difference in value of one tract over the other, e.g., "The impossibility of dividing the land by survey and the necessity of rendering equal the inheritance of Mikaila and Drake in the tract resulted in her forty acres being worth $400 less than Drake's forty acres, so he paid her that sum as owelty."

Oyer and Terminer Courts: Latin for 'hear and end,' meaning to hear cases and end disputes. See *Oyer and Terminer* in *What Did They Mean By That?*

oyle glas: meaning perhaps lost in the deep past; may be a glass in which oil thought to have medicinal value was poured, e.g., "As early as Chaucer, the words spelled 'glas' and 'oyle' were common, and in the mid-seventeenth century an early Surry inventory reveals the presence of an oyle glas."

oyster hut: a cabin or small building near oyster beds designed to house those who sat and shucked oysters for transport to market, e.g., "Since the earliest days of commerce in oysters, oyster huts were a sight along Chesapeake Bay."

P

p:Cent: per Cent (%) or per:hundred, e.g., "Mrs. H. commented that North Carolina and Virginia records reveal numerous incidents of a "p:" or a "crossed p:" followed by either 'Cent' or the word 'hundred' indicate either percentage or weight totaling one hundred pounds (112, including tare, then)"; "In a Gale Inventory 'per:hundred' is written as 'p:H.'"

P:Hundred, p:hundred: See *p:Cent.*

pace: an early rough measure of distance and being the supposed length of one pace by a man walking at a rapid walk yet not running; approximately thirty inches or two and one-half feet, e.g., "Early approximate measurements, especially in battle, often were given in such terms as, 'the enemy had to advance across a field of about 500 paces.'"

pack of wool: a very early term of commerce and meaning a measure of wool equal weighing 240 pounds, e.g., "The manifest of the steamer *John and James* revealed that it had twenty packs of wool as part of its cargo moving from Paducah to Memphis."

painters' colic: See *appendicitis.*

Pale, English: See *Anglo-Irish.*

pan handler: a very old term describing a beggar or one who holds a pan or hat in a public place, hoping thereby that charitable passers-by will give him/her money, e.g., "After the Civil War, the streets of cities were often frequented by pan-handlers who were destitute veterans hoping for gifts of coins from citizens who walked by."

pantalets, pantaloons: undergarments for women; men's long narrow pants or trousers with a strap extending from the cuff under the instep and back to the opposite cuff, e.g., "Though there were a few ads for such apparel in the very first years of the twentieth century, such are almost exclusively of the nineteenth century."

papular rash: See *eczema.*

paradise: a favorite seasoning of the fourteenth through nineteenth centuries, having a flavor that is much like *cardamom* (q.v.), ginger and pepper, e.g., "Paradise spice, occasionally seen in early America, has been popular in common dishes of West Africa and the Indies since very early times, and it is said to have been chewed on cold days to warm the body."

paraph: In Louisiana, the signature of the notary or other person before whom an oath was sworn, e.g., "Gowland stated as a part of his defense against Mr. Harz that the paraph in the *jurat* (q.v.) of the contract was not that of the notary who was said to have signed it."

paraphernalia: unlike now, personal property of a wife that was hers alone, and of which she had the right to bequeath, convey, give or otherwise make disposition with or without permission of her husband, e.g., "Though all else became the property of her husband at their marriage, Diane had the privilege of doing as she pleased with her paraphernalia." Also see *extra-dotal property, etc.*

parboiling: See *maceration.*

parcel, P:cell, percell, or pursel of hogs: See *sounder, drift, parcel, etc.*

parcel: a very general term meaning a tract of land of unstated size, e.g., "The term 'parcel' was and is very often followed by a description in courses and distances, in metes and bounds or by a measure of acreage." See *metes and bounds* in *What Did They Mean By That?*

parceners, co-parceners: in early times, when there were no sons, only daughters, sisters, or females as heirs of a intestate decedent, those women inherited real property as co-parceners, not in their individual right as to strangers, but individually as between themselves, e.g., "When the descendants of a daughter who inherited land are females only, in early law the outside world viewed the estate created in that land as a joint tenancy, but not so as between themselves, since upon death of any of those the share of each descended to the heirs of each, rather than to the survivors." See *joint tenancy* in *What Did They Mean By That?*

parchment: See *vellum.*

paresis: See *softening of the brain.*

paripatetic, paripatetic records: files of miscellaneous and itinerant activities, not a part of regular or long term courthouse record keeping, e.g., "The paripatetic records of Maryland may be found at the county level or, instead at the state archives, and may include categories of materials such as licenses for occupations/professions, schools and boards of education, records of such as toll services, roads and ferries, boards of elections, on and on, and should be carefully searched by all family historians with roots in Maryland." Also see *miscellaneous records.*

parish church: difficult to generalize, but usually and in the law a church structure with buildings for public worship by the members or by the public generally and often having a cemetery, and to some fundamentalist disciplines the church was considered the congregation itself, e.g., "Many are the pastors who include in their sermons an assertion that those gathered there or might have done so are 'the church.'" Also see *parish.*

Parish Court: that Louisiana court of limited jurisdiction over minor civil and criminal matters, but having wide responsibilities and jurisdiction in probate matters, and often corresponding to such as the county or justice of the peace courts elsewhere, e.g., "While parishes in early Virginia had wide authority in matters of the religious conduct of the citizenry and were complementary of the circuit court in probate matters, the Parish Courts of Louisiana had wide authority in probate matters and very little in civil and criminal matters."

parish vestry: See *vestry, parish.*

parish: a very common term of various definitions; generally, a sub-division of land, a number of congregations, or several church structures of sizes manageable for administration by a church officer, e.g., "In most states where the term was commonly used, a parish was a established precinct administered by the a parish priest; in New England, a parish early was a subdivision of a town by territory and later by church congregations and structures used by any particular discipline; in Louisiana, it was and remains a territorial division usually corresponding to or often the origin of a county; and in many states the term is not used as it relates to other than the internal organization or ordering by a church such as Roman Catholic." Also see *parish church* and see *parish vestry.*

parochial: matters that have to do with the business and members of a parish, e.g., "Though now seeming remarkable, early Virginia and Carolina boundary disputes were often viewed as parochial in nature."

paroxysm: convulsions, e.g., "Not knowing the paroxysms were a symptom of some other illness, early doctors often prescribed cold baths and the application of snow or ice."

partial insanity, half-crazy: that mental imbalance early thought to exist at all times, yet revealed only occasionally, e.g., "Many individuals of the early days who displayed short temper were considered persons of partial insanity." Also see *lunacy.*

parturition: giving birth, e.g., "Many early reports of physicians reveal the deaths of mothers during parturition."

passage money: the sum paid for trans-oceanic travel, e.g., "The sums paid for the transportation of *indentured servants* (q.v., *What Did They Mean By That?*) were commonly known as 'passage money.'"

passes, passports: as now; a grant of privilege, either in writing or otherwise, permitting a person or group of people to move from one political subdivision to another, e.g., "But two of the many examples of passes being granted to early citizens might be those of the eighteenth and nineteenth centuries by North Carolina permitting passage westward through the Cherokee lands of western North Carolina, and those of the mid-seventeenth century permitting Virginian debtors to pass by boat or ship to another colony."

passing bell, mourning bell, death bell: those bells either of church or community that were rung to announce a death, e.g., "There being only word of mouth throughout our early history, bells announcing deaths and events of common interest were commonly and often heard throughout the colonies." Also see *bellman* in *What Did They Mean By That?*

patent entry books, local: very valuable research aids for genealogists; a book—journal—required usually by county governments where land patents were commonly issued and traded, and revealing of those patents, dates of the issue of the same, from what government, the patentee's name, a very general description, and in some cases the name and date of the warrant and survey, e.g., "Among others, many early counties of Virginia, North Carolina, South Carolina, Georgia, Kentucky, and Georgia kept patent entry books. Also see *patent land.*

patent land, patented land: the subject of an original title; that land that had been the subject of a perfected grant and thereby transferred from a government that first owned it, or from a government to which a former patent had been forfeited or seized through legal process, to a person or persons, e.g., "John Drake failed to perfect his grant from Virginia, and in 1692 that patent was reissued."

patents, land: See *bounty*, and see *What Did They Mean By That?*

path, common: See *common path.*

Patriot War of 1837: those debates, clashes of arms, and conflicts in the lower east provinces of Canada in which Canadians sought independence from Britain, just as the Americans had done in the American Revolution, e.g., "Though the conflict is more well known in

Canada, there were two events of consequence in upstate New York, the burning of the *Sir Robert Peel* in the Thousand Island region in 1838, and the expedition and 'Battle of the Windmill' which sent some Jefferson, Lewis, and St. Lawrence County men to their death, and others to exile in the penal colony of Great Britain, Van Dieman's Land, now called Tasmania."

patrolers: those men hired by communities to walk about at night, maintain order, and report disturbances and unacceptable behavior to the constables or sheriffs, e.g., "Daniel Sutherland and James Stockdale were employed as patrolers in Concord for the period August 1778 to July 1779."

pauper: in early Virginia and the Carolinas a pauper was defined as someone whose total personal assets were valued at £10 or less. Such a person might not live in utter poverty, as with a widow who, owning virtually nothing, could anticipate that her family would care for her, e.g., "A single man might well be, and often was termed a 'pauper' and yet live and work on the plantation (farm) of his parents."

pauper's corner: See *potter's field.*

payable in due course: See *in course, etc.*

peaces (pieces), lending of, to Indians: Early colonial law prohibited anyone from lending or otherwise supplying American Indians with firearms or any means of firing such, e.g., "The prohibition against providing Native Americans with weapons provided that it was a crime to lend 'peace, pouder and shott' (powder and shot)."

peake, woompompeak, and Roanoke: Indian shells, bone, metal, beads and metal coins used as currency during the seventeenth and early eighteenth century, e.g., "In 1655, at a 'Grand Assembly' in Jamestown, it was determined that peake, woompompeak and Roanoke might be accepted as currency, along with pieces of eight, at an exchange rate at first determined by the parties to the bargain, after 1652 by the council, and by 1700 the council ruled that if the piece of eight was 'good and of silver,' it would have an exchange value of 5S." See *milled dollar* in *What Did They Mean By That?*

peake: other than as Indian "money," unknown, e.g., "The following clearly written passage appeared in 1757, 'I Desired him that there might not be no peake on such an occafsion as this was, and he say'd how can I believe it when he did not write to me....' (See *Letterbooks of Governor* [SC] *William H. Lyttleton, 1756-1760*, to be found in many larger libraries.)

pease: beans, soup, navy, etc., e.g., "Beans of all sorts—including what we now know as peas—were commonly referred to as peas (pease) in colonial America."

peck: one-half a bushel, a dry measure for grain, corn, and many other dry foodstuffs for man or animal, e.g., "The peck measure was very commonly used in the retail sale and pricing of fruits and vegetables." Also see *bushel, etc.* in *What Did They Mean By That?*

peers, judgment of: See *judgment of peers.*

pellicane: unknown or forgotten; from a context, perhaps a tall circular container made of crockery and having handles, and used to store liquids, wines and other juices, e.g., "There was left but one or a very few references to pellicanes in our Colonial records, one of which was, 'when it is therfor prepared in this wyse, let it be put into a pellicane, that is a vessell with eares or handles on ether syde one.'"

pendens: pending, and see *lis pendens.*

Pennsylvania, The Great Law of 1682: See *Great Law.*

pennyroyal: A plant of the mint family found in many parts of Kentucky and the nearby states and thought to have many medical uses, e.g., "Diane spoke of the use at the turn of the twentieth century of pennyroyal by her grandmother."

per diem: as now; by the day, e.g., "In 1779 General Silliman directed that Sherwood be paid per diem for his service to the Massachusetts colony."

per poll, per person: an action directed toward each individual in a certain class or category of people, e.g., "The 1697 levy of two pounds of tobacco was 'per poll,' meaning that the sum was to be paid to the county for every individual residing in the parish."

perambulation: processioning (q.v., *What Did They Mean By That?*); the ceremony of walking the bounds of a tract of land within the parish, very early done during Rogation Week (the second week before Whitsunday (the seventh Sunday after Easter), and later upon request by landowners who differed as to the location of boundary lines, e.g., "In 1722 Richard and Thomas Drake had their common Isle of Wight boundary line perambulated." Also see *Rogation Week.*

percell: See *sounder, drift, parcel, etc.*

perch: as a measure of a solid, an indefinite term and often not defined by statute, e.g., "Often used as a term of measurement of brick, a perch is sixteen and a half cubic feet, however in other locations it is twenty-five cubic feet." Also see *perch* in *What Did They Mean By That?*

perishable estate: those assets subject to spoliation or decay in short periods of time and those that will deteriorate or lose substantial value in the time expected to pass before disposition or settlement, e.g., "A Michigan court ordered that Darlene be permitted to sell the many rolls of printing paper that remained of the property of her brother, since those were part of the perishable estate."

perjury: See *forswear, etc.*

pernicious fever: See *typhus.*

perquisites: any reward or benefit gained by purchase, trade, etc., or by investment or co-relations in a business, e.g., "One of the perquisites of his work on a local plantation was that he had *toting privileges* (q.v., *What Did They Mean By That?*)."

pesthouse: a facility used to house those having smallpox and other serious infectious diseases, e.g., "In the mid-nineteenth century the 'pesthouse' was located on the ground now occupied by the music hall, and within what is today known as Lincoln Park."

petition: See *lawsuits, common, etc.*

petty officers: lesser Naval officers and equivalents of the sergeants of the Army and Marine Corps, e.g., "When discharged from the Navy in 1914, John was a second class petty officer, that rank then being equal to the tech sergeants of the Marine Corps."

Peychaud bitters: See *bitters.*

phrenitis, cephalitis: A most serious, long and early known disease said to be an inflammation of the brain, that brings raging fevers, delirium, stupor, headache, neck pain and drowsiness, nausea and fever, e.g., "In 1888 Dr. Pierce suggested 'copious perspiration' should be induced, baths of 'hot lye salt, pepper and mustard,' and then rubbing the 'body with hot pepper.'" (Author's note: how anyone survived I have no idea!)

phthiriasis: infestation by head or body lice, e.g., "Many were the cures for infestations by lice, including powdered arsenic rubbed on the skin and in the hair, and borax applied in the same way, both usually associated with shaving hair off the affected areas."

Phthisic, asthma: as now, with the symptoms being, according to Dr. Pierce, sudden tightness or difficulty in drawing a breath, flatulency, and fullness of the stomach, e.g., "Physicians of the Civil War years prescribed emetics, inhalations of chloroform or ether, a teaspoon of chloroform on a handkerchief and held over the nose, hot, black coffee, and breathing fumes of potassium nitrate."

phthisis, black lung, white lung: tuberculosis or black lung from years breathing coal dust, and white lung from years in a textile or weaving business where lint and particles of cloth are ever in the air, e.g., "It was suggested that phthisis might be cured by healthy nutrition, open air, exercise, and a diet heavy in 'milk, rich cream, eggs, wheat flour bread, cracked wheat, oatmeal, good butter, beef, game and fowls.'"

physiognomy: Johnson (1802) says, 'the face, the cast of a look,' e.g., "A seventeenth-century Virginia coroner's inquest determined that the body of an unidentified dead man, washed up on the bank of James River and dressed in the clothes of a servant, had drowned, as was apparent by the condition of his body and his 'physiognomy.'"

pianoforte: a piano, the suffix "forte" meaning loud, as opposed to those harpsichords and spinets that were softer in volume, e.g., "The pianoforte mentioned in the 1855 inventory of the Weaver estate was what today we know simply as a piano." Also see *spinet* and see *harpsichord*.

piece: as now; early and to some branches of the service, a firearm. See *peaces (pieces), lending of, to Indians*.

pieces of eight: it was determined in seventeenth-century Virginia that pieces of eight, if of gold or silver, would have a trading value of 5S, e.g., "The extreme shortage in the Americas of English currency in the seventeenth and eighteenth centuries made it necessary to use any medium of settlement having a 'true value,' such as these Spanish coins." Also see *peake, etc.*

piercer: probably a tool for piercing leather or thick fabrics, e.g., "The Surry inventory of 'Widdow Creed' dated October 15 1668 listed a 'piercer' and a 'long piercer' in association with other farm utensils and hand tools."

pigeon pair: twins, a boy and a girl, e.g., "There are numerous American colonial references to someone having give birth to or of having been a parent of a 'pigeon pair.'"

pillow sheet, pillow slip, pillow cover: now, usually called "pillow cases," e.g., "Pillow sheets were used to contain any insects within stuffed pillows, also to keep the oil and dirt of the hair from the pillow fabric (usually oznaburg), and to keep the pillow soil in the pillow fabric from the hair and skin, e.g., "Pillow sheets covering the coarse fabric of early pillows and head rests were common in homes of the more affluent, though much less so among the poor families."

Pinkerton, Alan: See *private eye*.

Pipe Rolls: those earliest records of our British ancestors; the accounts of rents and profits of the king that commence in 1156 and continue through the colonial years until 1833, e.g., "Few are the serious genealogists who have not referred to the Pipe Rolls when researching early ancestors of the British Isles."

pityriasis, rubra, negra: See *eczema.*

place of, in the: See *in the place of.*

plaintiff, complainant: See *lawsuits, common, etc.*

planet-struck, planet struck: probably arising from the belief that suffering sunstroke, *moon-stroke* (q.v.), and planet-stroke were not remarkable happenings; any sudden madness, paralysis, epilepsy, or loss of control over one's muscles that had no other obvious cause, e.g., "We can not now infer the probable causes of what was described as being planet-struck."

plank road: a roadway or pathway with planks or lengths of lumber laid perpendicular to the path of travel and, because of the expense of constructing such, the planking was often was placed only on the right side of a road leading to a town; a travel surface of planks for use during periods when otherwise the road would be mud, e.g., "As well as on the right side of roads leading into towns, early armies and merchants with year-round businesses often were called upon to construct plank roads to move their materials, merchandise and supplies to and fro." Also see *turnpike* in *What Did They Mean By That?*

plank: unspecified, usually rough sawn lumber, e.g., "Surry resident William Newsum gained an order from the sheriff, dated March 5, 1671, for lumber needed to build the jail, that lumber described as 'sixteen hundred and fifty foote of inch plank,' meaning lumber one inch thick, twelve inches wide, and totaling 1650 feet long."

plantation, plantation house: Johnson says, a large planted tract of land, and a "place planted," and makes no reference to grandeur or wealth, e.g., "While by 1860 the word plantation brought images of affluence, wealth and large size, it was less so regarded in the seventeenth century, when the expressions meant the principal dwelling house on what now we would describe as a farm."

planted and seated: an expression of the law of land grants and patents, and meaning that a patentee had gained a warrant, filed his survey, been issued a land patent, and had planted a crop, and built a residence on a tract of land gained from government, e.g., "Planting and seating were required if one were to perfect his title and gain a patent." Also see *deserted land* and see *seating, etc.* in *What Did They Mean By That?*

planter: one who plants; by the eighteenth century meaning a person who engaged in planting and growing crops on a rather large scale, e.g.,

"In 1770 Jesse Drake was spoken of as a 'planter' having 170 acres." Also see **husbandman** in *What Did They Mean By That?*

pleadings: formal written documents pertaining to and setting forth the issues in a lawsuit, and usually having the purpose of revealing to all that some issue, contention, complaint, assertion, or allegation is lodged against another or that the other party is denying or contesting such assertions and intends that the matters be settled or tried by evidence, etc., e.g., "When Mr. Delozier's attorney alleged libelous statements by Jane in his complaint against that woman, Judy's lawyer filed a pleading denying all allegations set forth in the complaint, thereby contesting everything said." Also see *lawsuits, common, etc.*

plot: a small tract of land; the converse of *plantation* (q.v.), and usually what we now would describe as a "lot," e.g., "A small tract of land that in town might be described as a 'lot,' if outside the community boundaries often would be described as a 'plot'"; "Mrs. Kennedy maintained a garden plot at the back of her property."

ploughman: an ancient term not common in the American colonies, yet meaning a manual farm laborer, e.g., "Seventeenth-century records, especially of New England, only occasionally refer to farm laborers as ploughmen."

plow tree: the wooden handle or handles pushed, pulled or guided by a man and usually a draft animal, e.g., "Guiding a horse- or mule-drawn plow by the plow tree was as back-breaking as it was common."

plows, implements: early, were of two large categories, a "bull-tongue" plow which was long and narrow, and the "shovel plow" which was broad and short, the former used to break up the ground, preparatory to planting, and the latter employed to cultivate, e.g., "Glynda remembered that the plow-stocks were made from wood and trees grown on the farm, and the plows were forged from iron in the crude blacksmith shop, also on the farm.

plum pudding: a favorite over now many centuries, and brought here from old England, it was made of raisins, currants, almonds, dried orange peels, suet or beef fat, flour, sugar and salt, and served with a sweet sauce, e.g., "Olga's plum pudding was very much enjoyed by all who knew her, though little kids snickered since, as with all such puddings, it contained NO plums."

Plymouth Company: See *Virginia Company, etc.*

podagra: See *gout* in *What Did They Mean By That?*

Podunk: a Hartford County, Connecticut village, now within the city of Hartford and dating from at least 1680; named for an American Indian tribe, e.g., "While Podunk was the name of what is now a portion of

Hartford, Connecticut, for reasons difficult to understand the word has come to be slang for a community in which nothing of excitement happens and there is no recognizable government, industry, or organization."

Poke Day: said to be an ancient British term meaning that day after harvest when an allowance of grain was given to each farm laborer who had earned that wage, e.g., "Though there was said to be a Poke Day here as in Britain, we have found but one such reference in the American colonies."

pole, rod: a measure of length, equal to sixteen and a half feet, e.g., "The pole (rod) was a standard of measuring distance, especially in deed descriptions and the surveys for those."

poleman: a surveyor's assistant; that man who moved ahead of the transit to a convenient spot, held a graduated pole straight up and down, and was signaled by the man at the surveyor's tool when the difference in elevation between those two spots had been ascertained, e.g., "As the poleman moved ahead at the direction of the surveyor, the chain carrier measured the distances between the poles, all of which data was recorded and became part of the survey." Also see ***pole, rod.***

police magistrate: a lesser judge whose jurisdiction is very often under control by the government of the city in which the office exists; a judge of a lesser sort having jurisdiction in minor criminal matters in police courts and who also has committing authority for more serious crimes, as distinguished from a magistrate who maintains jurisdiction in some civil matters, e.g., "Scott was required to appear before the police magistrate for having disturbed the peace." Also see ***magistrate.***

poll: unlike now, one person, often, but not always, over twenty-one years old; the term for a list of jurors or those persons subject to a tax, tithe, or charge, e.g., "Polls might be lists of those eligible for jury duty or those on a tax list."

polypus: somewhat unlike now, a growth within the body cavity, e.g., "While now we readily distinguish benign growths or tumors from those that are malignant, such determinations were not possible in the early stages throughout all the centuries down to the 1950s."

pone: See ***pone, etc.*** in *What Did They Mean By That?*

poor accounts: records of an English parish or government and believed rarely used on this continent, revealing those sums paid and who of the poor were so awarded, e.g., "Accounts of who of the poor were given sustenance seem seldom to have been so labeled here."

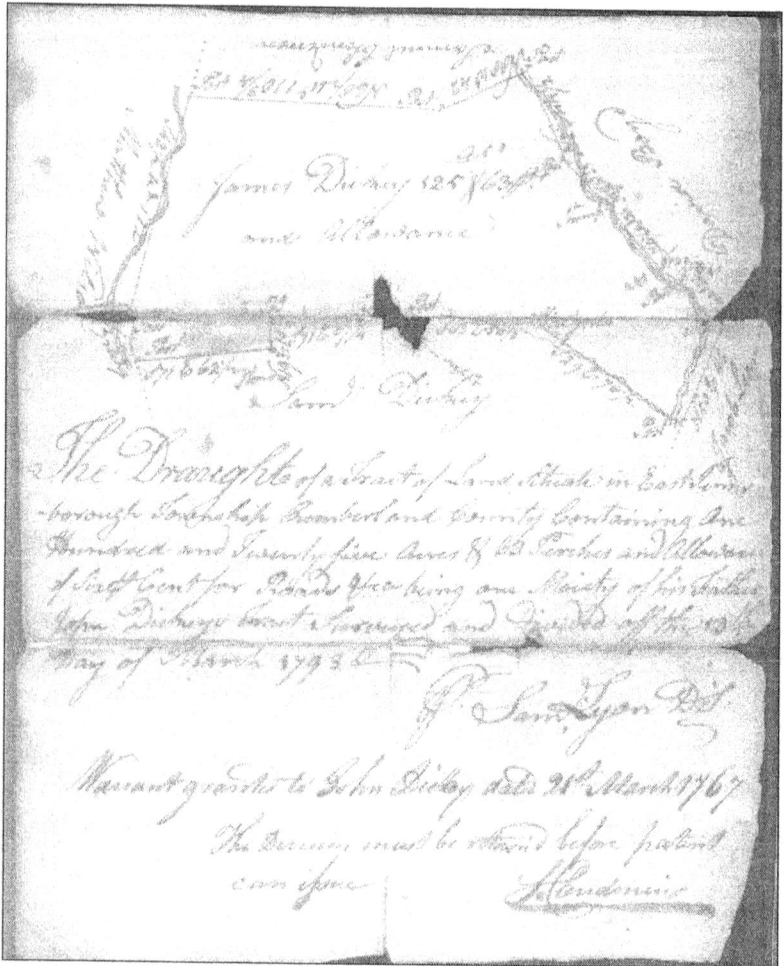

Figure 26. 1793 Pennsylvania survey for a patent for 125 acres.
See *poleman*.

poor laws: those laws and regulations, local and otherwise, that have to do with the maintenance, housing, and care of the very poor, e.g., "There were very few poor laws in the Southern colonies until the coming of the American Revolution, which for all practical purposes ended the authority of the parishes."

pork barrel: See ***omnibus, etc.***

post rider: one who carried mail by horse or mule and did so with no particular route or established stops, e.g., "Isaac was paid by the Continental Congress for errands of message delivery and was thereby labeled a post rider."

post road: a pre-selected route for mail delivery with or without a set schedule for service, e.g., "One of the post roads in early Cumberland County, Tennessee remains so labeled and carried as an address for the residents living along it."

post town: a term used widely in Britain, and only rarely here, and meaning a community in which a post office has been established, e.g., "While in Britain post towns are so called, here we often spoke of the town or community by the name of the post office, such as the communities known of 'Grimsley Post Office' and as 'Little Crab Post Office' in Tennessee."

post turtle: as a turtle found on the top of a post, a person occupying an office or position for which he obviously is not suited and did not achieve by his own efforts, e.g., "Reverend Jim called the Tennessee senator a post turtle"

postage currency, stamp money: in a few periods, mostly of the nineteenth century, our government provided postage stamps that also served as currency in specific sums, e.g., "Interestingly, until even the last decades of the twentieth century, stamps were frequently an alternative to paying with currency."

posthumous child: any child born after the death of the father, e.g., "Posthumous children sometimes posed problems in the administration of estates when the deceased father had not provided for that child in a will, and also when a child was posthumous, yet had a living grandfather." Also see ***pretermitted heirs.***

pot shot: a random shot with a firearm directed at any animal appropriate for the stew pot, and fired when the shooter seeks food, and is not engaged in serious hunting for trophy or rare animals, e.g., "When Jim shot the quail while deer hunting, and was asked why, he told his companions that it was merely a pot shot."

potter's field: a cemetery for paupers, suicides, those executed, and those not thought entitled to a Christian burial; may be a portion of another cemetery dedicated to those purposes, e.g., "Many years ago the Marion Cemetery reserved a corner distant from the entrance to be called 'paupers' corner.'"

Pott's disease: perhaps scoliosis; excessive curvature of the spine, usually in children from age three to post puberty, e.g., "Bethany suffered from Pott's disease and, as has been the treatment for many years, had to wear a brace that held her spine in the normal position."

præcipe, precipe: a writing filed with a clerk of court by a party to a lawsuit or by a prosecutor and requesting that a warrant or other process issue, e.g., "Though most have long ago been discarded, some early præcipes still remain and contain the actual handwriting of the attorneys."

prairie breaker: a large plow, suitable for the wet and hard soil of the prairies, such as from Indiana and Illinois westward; one who breaks prairie land to the plow for hire, e.g., "While early farmers found it easy to break the soil near a woods line, the hard prairies required bigger and more sturdy plows, those known as prairie breakers"; "The 1856 state census of Iowa reveals one man whose occupation was 'prairie breaker.'"

preaching, gone to the: very common expression where itinerant or circuit riding preachers appeared now and then, and indicating that someone has traveled to an event in which such is holding forth with sermons or revival, e.g., "Many were those who went to the preaching in Pickaway County, Ohio in 1804 when Bishop Asbury held services at the home of Shadrack Cole; that, the first Methodist preaching west of Zanesville."

prebendary: an employee or person appointed to the staff of a large church, e.g., "Though few churches in colonial America were large enough to justify prebendaries, records remain where those were so appointed."

precatory terms: words or expressions in a formal document or other writing that are construed as requests, hopes, wishes, or suggested courses of conduct, e.g., "When through oversight or otherwise it was seen to be impossible, the words in Terry's will stating that he was to be buried next to his deceased wife were ruled as precatory."

precinct: an indefinite term meaning a usually small geographical and political subdivision of some nature, and without specific meaning, e.g., "In 1725 it was ordered that from thence forward Nottoway Parish would consist of three precincts for purposes of listing the tithables."

pre-emption, pre-exemption, pre-emptioner, etc.: nearly synonymous terms; one who by filing for, settlement upon, or by cultivating some portion of Federal public lands or on lands so set aside by the states, and by those acts has gained the right to settle on public land in preference over all others, e.g., "In Wyoming one could pre-empt up to 160 acres, by paying a fee of $3.00 within thirty days after his settlement, and then within one year assume actual residency and cultivation of the tract."

prelate: an officer of the church of higher order, e.g., "The bishops and archbishops were the prelates for the early Catholics and members of the Anglican Church."

present, presents: verb (occasionally a noun), to hold or to represent to a court that charges have been determined and offered up to the court having jurisdiction of an indictment, e.g., "An 1834 Grand Jury of Morgan County presented that they had found evidence sufficient to believe that T. Ray should be tried for grand larceny"; "Many deeds, contracts, and legal writings commence with 'Know all men by these presents...,' meaning simply that the document represents certain facts." Also see *presentment.*

presentment: noun, a written notice to the court and prosecutor of a crime by named individuals that came to the attention of that jury through their own knowledge or evidence laid before them that did not arise from an indictment, e.g., "Many the presentments sent forth from grand juries against public officials, since those positions invite undue influence, bribery or chicanery." Also see *present.*

press, press to service: from the term *impress,* meaning to enlist or call to use or service, men and draft animals particularly, but the term might be used concerning any living person or animal, e.g., "On 27 May, 1666 the Court of Rappahannock Co., VA, ordered John Alexander to press six men and horses in order to learn more of Indian activities."

presumption, presumption of fact: in the law, an inference, short of positive proof, that natural consequences flow from ordinary events or actions; though we do not so label our thoughts, genealogists entertain presumptions at every turn, e.g., "While we should all confirm birth years from other sources, when a census reveals members of a family to be of certain ages, our presumption is that those named were born within a year or two of the years calculated by subtracting the ages given from the date of that census."

pretermitted heirs, pretermitted child: those children of a deceased person who, through oversight, error, loss of memory, or having been born after the death of that parent, were not included in his/her will, e.g., "While many do not, some states have statutes directing that pretermitted heirs should share in an estate equal to the share that child would have received if the death had been intestate."

prima facie: the fact reveals the truth without other evidence to establish it; a fact that will be assumed true unless acceptable proof otherwise is offered, e.g., "The fact that after the tornado of 1676 the Isle of Wight College (Coolidge) buildings and trees had been flattened surely was prima facie evidence that the great winds were the cause."

primary evidence: the best and most reliable evidence available at that time as to some fact though no evidence is primary for all purposes; primary evidence may become secondary or valueless if further and more reliable evidence is later uncovered, e.g., "A headstone of a woman who died at age forty is primary as to fact that the person named is dead, that in fact she was buried in that precise place, and that the age given is correct, yet it is surely purely circumstantial as to her cause of death, that she had children, that the date of death is accurate, that she is the mother of a namesake who died forty years later, or even that anyone attended her funeral, much less sobbed."

primogeniture, abolishment of: the ancient legal practice known as property passing by ***primogeniture*** (q.v., *What Did They Mean By That?*) ended in Georgia in 1777, in North Carolina in 1784, in Virginia in 1785, in Maryland and New York in 1786, in South Carolina in 1791, in Rhode Island in 1798, and the other New England states and Pennsylvania abolished the double portions allowed the eldest son in 1791.

private adoption: See ***adoption, system, etc.***

private eye; P.I.; Pinkerton, Alan: a term of the early twentieth century meaning private investigator, e.g., "Though he erred often, especially by overestimating Confederate strength, Alan Pinkerton is said to be the first American private eye that made a successful business of it."

Private Land Claims, Courts of: established by Congress in 1891 and having jurisdiction over claims of those who had Mexican or Spanish grants of land that fell within the public lands of the U.S., e.g., "While some of the abstracts of the records of the Courts of Private Land Claims appear in the records and archives of Texas, New Mexico, California and Arizona, including claims dating to 1879, the bulk of those reports for the years 1879-1904 are preserved in the National Archives."

privie to: having an interest in, affected by, having some relationship with; an ancient term used frequently in the law and otherwise, and revealing that a person so labeled will be affected by the result or actions mentioned, e.g., "When Paul did the genealogy for the estate problem of Attorney Looney, he became privy to the outcome, even though he was not a party in that matter"; "When Donna entered upon a contract exchanging the use of her road by Allison for Allison's maintenance of that road, when Allison moved out her tenant was privie to and bound by that agreement."

pro tempore: a very common legal term meaning for the present period of time, often for the present term of court, e.g., "The court order dismissed the jury 'pro tempore, subject to recall.'"

probate bonds: those bonds posted in amounts determined by the measure of responsibility and at the order of the probate court and including executor's bonds, administrator's bonds, guardian's bonds, etc., e.g., "Very often the amount of the bond required in probate matters is twice the value of the estate, however that amount falls within the discretion of the judge." Also see *bonds, surety, etc.*

probate proceedings: any matter falling under the jurisdiction of a chancellor or probate court, the limits of which vary somewhat from state to state, including but not limited to testate or intestate estates, e.g., "The word probate is not a verb, rather it is a noun or an adjective and should be used in those fashions only; to say the will was probated is poor usage of the terms. Also see headings here under probate, etc., see *states of the U.S., names and titles of probate courts in,* and see *probate, etc.* in *What Did They Mean By That?*

proceeding(s) in aid of execution: See *executed, execution* and see *lawsuits, common, procedural steps.*

proceedings in probate: See *probate proceeding,* and see *states of the U.S., names and titles of probate courts in.*

processioner: said to sometimes refer to a surveyor who established property lines, however for the broader meaning, see *processioning, etc.* in *What Did They Mean By That?*

promissory note: a written promise to pay that recites the sum, the names of the debtor and the creditor, the due date, and the nature of the payment required, e.g., "Virtually all bank loans are guaranteed by a promissory note of the maker (debtor)." Also see *non fecit.*

properly administer: a very common early expression meanings that the person so directed perform the duties of the task, and in no way a warning or meaning that the named was likely not to so act, e.g., "Honour Meade, with John Pulistone and William Jackson as her sureties, swore that she would properly administer an estate in 1696." Also see *bonds, surety, etc.*

prosecute the suit: to cause or bring about the required procedures that move a lawsuit toward conclusion, e.g., "The word 'prosecute' in matters relating to civil lawsuits means only that it is to move forward without undue delay, and has nothing to do with a criminal prosecution."

prothonotary: the chief administrator of the records of the court so named in several states, and as such has responsibility for all scheduling, paperwork and filings of a civil nature; where there yet are such officers, there also is a clerk to the court whose duties include the administration of all criminal cases, usually the calling, swearing and protection of jurors of all categories, and the adoptions and marriage records, e.g., "It is wise for all genealogists to remember that the clerks of courts in most states will have nearly all the courts' records, while in Kentucky, Massachusetts, Pennsylvania and Virginia, those duties are shared with prothonotaries, both of which places should be researched."

proximate, proximate cause: nearest, closest; in law the cause that is next before the event and when occurring in its natural and usual course brings about injury or damage, e.g., "Though it was the stumbling of the running horse that produced the horrendous injuries Gene suffered, the proximate cause of his pain and recuperation was the speed and terrain over which he rode the animal."

psoriasis: See *eczema.*

public adoption: See *adoption, system, etc.*

public days: See **court days** in *What Did They Mean By That?*

public domain: land or rights owned by, under the dispositive control of, or considered the property of a government or the citizens of any nation, state, colony, or government, e.g., "In addition to the land owned or controlled by the Federal government that was awarded as bonuses to Revolutionary War veterans, many states also had such land to use as awards or to sell very reasonably."

pudding mould: a small mould of wood, tin or pewter so designed as to shape puddings or other food placed in it to "set up" in a decorative or attractive design, e.g., "Jacque had several pudding moulds, all wooden except one very fine mould of pewter."

puffles, jumbles, wonders, and snickerdoodles: the names given any of the many Pennsylvania Dutch cookies and sweet pastries eaten with the fingers, e.g., "Though there was no sugar, molasses, or honey for pastries of preserves for the very first years of the Colonies, maple syrup and maple sugar had been known to the Indians for centuries, if not millennia."

puking fever: See *milk fever* in *What Did They Mean By That?*

pulsatilla: A plant thought to have medicinal value. See *nervines.*

a Pennsylvania *prothonotary* in the name of George III.

punch: Johnson (1802) says, "a liquor made by mixing water, sugar, spirits (alcohol) and juice of lemons," however the juice of many fruits has been used in place of lemons, e.g., "Teresa tells that in 1704 Madam Knight said that 'bare-legged punch' was 'awfull'; that Berkeley wrote that the strong drink of Virginia in 1710 was 'mobby punch' made either of rum from the Caribbean Islands or brandy distilled from apples and peaches; another Virginian traveler wrote in 1744 that 'Our liquor was sorry rum mixed with water and sugar, which bore the heathenish name of gumbo punch'; that pupello punch was made from cider brandy; sangry punch " was probably made from 'sangria'; that rack punch was made from arrack, and that the contents of jincy punch is now unknown."

pupello punch: See ***punch***.

pursell: See ***sounder, drift, parcel, etc.***

push boats: those flat bottomed, usually small, freight carrying boats early used on canals and rivers, the same being moved ahead by men on both sides of the waterway pushing with long poles, e.g., "Patty spoke of her nineteenth-century ancestor who, with his family, had made his way down the Ohio and Mississippi rivers by rafts, mule-drawn boats, and push boats."

putative father, putative marriage: a man believed or suspected of being the father of an illegitimate child or a child about to be so born; uncommonly a marriage wherein there were legal impediments unknown to either partner, e.g., "Though she and her family for many years had assumed that her young husband had been killed in the war, her subsequent marriage became putative in the eyes of the law when that first husband appeared."

putrid fever: See ***diptheria*** in *What Did They Mean By That?*

Q

q.v.: abbreviation for the Latin *quod vide*, meaning "which see" or "as to which, see"; move to or see the passage or word stated immediately before the symbol, e.g., "Throughout this dictionary one will find expressions such as ***mayhem,*** q.v., *What Did They Mean By That?*'"

quadrille: very early and occasionally yet, a card game; early and now, a dance much favored in the antebellum South, e.g., "Those at the party enjoyed several quadrilles and an equal number of waltzes and of

Virginia reels." See *lancers*, and see *Virginia reel* in *What Did They Mean By That?*

quahog: a very common hard-shelled clam of New England, eaten regularly by American Indians and the early colonials, e.g., "It has been written that but for quahogs, oysters, crabs and Indian corn, the first settlers of New England would have starved."

quarter: as now; early, a geographical area over which one had charge of listing the tithables; an area usually selected by the person doing the listing and was based upon the terrain, distances, and number of residences to be visited in the course of making such a tax list, e.g., "Since Robert was appointed to enumerate and determine the tithables in his Virginia quarter, his descendants may be confident that he was a man known for honesty and integrity and had a somewhat elevated standing among his peers."

Quartering Act: 2 June 1774; a leading cause of the American Revolution, e.g., "To the infuriation of the citizenry, the 'Quartering Act' required that at their own expense our colonists would furnish British soldiers with candles, salt, vinegar, fire, cooking utensils, five pints of small beer or cider or half a pint of rum mixed per man, quarters and bedding in empty houses, inns, barns, and even in private dwellings."

quarterly courts: the Kentucky near equivalents to *circuit courts, courts of common pleas,* and *courts of pleas and quarter sessions* elsewhere, e.g., "Since 1787 most civil causes in Kentucky have fallen within the jurisdiction of the *quarterly courts*, originally so named because those convened four times a year."

quarters: as now, a temporary residence, e.g., "Peter Jones and Richard Russell, an overseer, appear in 1764 Lunenburg Co as having 'quarters' on a tract owned by Jones."

Queen's Bench: See *Bench, King's Bench, Queen's Bench, etc.*

Queen's Counsel: See *Bench, King's Bench, Queen's Bench, etc.*

quid pro quo: what is traded for what; the something given over to another in exchange for something in return, e.g., "The quid pro quo for Sherwood's ride across the front of the British army in 1778 was the thanks of the people of Massachusetts, and a few dollars."

quit and discharge: quit being used as it is in the term *quit-claim* (q.v., *What Did They Mean By That?*), and meaning to absolve or forgive another of a debt, e.g., "As a rule, an act of quitting and discharging a debt was a private matter, however if a suit had been filed, then such acts of forgiveness were often recorded as courts' order."

quoits: a ancient game; Shakespeare uses the term to mean *to throw*; very similar to hurling the discus, e.g., "Though maximum distance is one of the objectives of quoits, accuracy in landing the quoit near a target spot is also part of the game."

R

rack punch: See *punch.*

railroad hotel: those small and modest hotels and inns that usually served food and were located near a railroad junction where the passengers and others might find a room for the nights between their arrival and the next train that would take them to their next destination, e.g., "The Crab Orchard, Tennessee railroad hotel, later known as 'Hotel 1880,' had no fireplace, but had pot-bellied stoves for each room, had a small dining room, a sitting room, a kitchen, two large sleeping rooms for guests, four smaller sleeping rooms, a cook stove, a water well, a cistern, and four entrances."

ranger: See *straymaster, etc.*

rapier: often viewed as a gentleman's weapon, long, thin, and with a double-edged blade designed for slashing and thrusting; Johnson (1802) says, "a small sword used only for thrusting," e.g., "It is the rapier that we saw so often used in duels and fights in early movies."

rapine: in no way associated with sex, a term meaning to take the personal property of another by violence or by breaking into his house or home, e.g., "The Sherman's men of the Union Army were guilty of repeated acts of rapine."

read medicine, read law: unlike now and early, the most common avenue to achieve training in either law or medicine, that education accomplished by working daily under the supervision of and usually for a practitioner in either calling, and so continuing until that practitioner is willing to recommend the student and declare that person to be adequately trained to enter the practice, e.g., "In addition to those who read medicine or law, in most of the colonies and states it was not illegal to simply hang out a shingle and enter into those callings, and that is true even down to the end of the twentieth century."

read the Riot Act: See *Riot Act, etc.*

read, sew and spin: a common expression in courts' orders or private agreements concerning the apprenticeship of a girl or young woman, e.g., "In September of 1697 the court in Surry ordered that James Ellis was to care for and have Anne Nash as a servant, and he was to teach her to '*read, sew and spin perfectly and...*(she also was to be taught)...*the rudiments of Xtian religion.*'"

Figure 28. Union Depot *railroad hotel*.

real evidence: evidence that arises by virtue of the existence of some memento, monument, road, grave, document, writing, or other object that has physical properties and is not an abstract, extract, summary, or interpretation by any other person, e.g., "Though a book is not real evidence, the ancient documents and headstones that guided the author in that writing were."

reale act and deed: real, true, actual execution of a deed; early phrase from deeds, affidavits or other acknowledged legal documents, e.g., "While now we are accustomed to the expression, '…true and voluntary act and deed….,' in early times the phrase 'reale act and Deed' had the same meaning."

recess of court: See ***out of term, etc.***

recess: in the law, permitting the jury members or other participants to leave the courthouse or remain nearby till court is back in session, e.g., "While courts adjourn between ***terms of court*** (q.v.), day to day proceedings often recess at the discretion of the judge and for the benefit of all."

red flannel hash: viewed as a healthy and filling meal, diced salt pork and leftover bacon or corned beef were fried with cooked beets, boiled potatoes, chopped onion, some parsley, with milk and butter added during the cooking, e.g., "The colonial wives wasted nothing, and red flannel hash made with leftovers was no exception."

Redmen: Order of, Improved Order of: formerly "Order of Redmen," a fraternal, charitable and patriotic organization, said to have been originated by the "Sons of Liberty" who, dressed as Indians, boarded British merchant vessels in Boston Harbor in 1774 and threw the chests of tea into the bay, e.g., "Their hatred for the tea duties exacted by George III led the Sons of Liberty, later known as the Order of Red Men, to bring about what forever will be known as the ***Boston Tea Party*** (q.v.)."

redneck: generally now, one of ***common*** (q.v.), unrefined, low or coarse actions or station in life or in the community, e.g., "Debra has revealed that the term redneck perhaps originated from the West Virginia coal miners who fought at the Battle of Blair Mountain during the coal mine wars of the 1920s and wore red bandanas around their necks as a badge of pride and in order that their neighbors know that they had defied the mine owners by meeting together, that being forbidden."

registrar: those in Britain who have custody over and administer the flow of paper and documents that pertain to all manner of legal affairs, as determined by the shires in England and by state law here; an officer of the county, known as a *register* in many states of U.S. and having duties as set forth in the statutes pertaining to that office, e.g., "While in Ohio there are *registers*, in many states that term is replaced by 'registrars' and will be recognized when the researcher asks the whereabouts of that office in a courthouse."

replevy, replevin: to recover personal property being wrongfully withheld by another person, e.g., "In 1671 a Surry resident ended his complaint filed with the court with the words, 'I Humbly prayeth the replevie of the said mare.'"

report of common fame: See *common fame, etc.*

residuary clause: that clause appearing in almost all wills stating the manner and method by which the executor is to distribute any money or assets remaining after all costs, expenses, devises and bequeaths have been paid, e.g., "The clause in Terry's will provided that the residuary sums, if any, should be divided evenly and distributed to his grandchildren." Also see *residuary estate.*

residuary estate: those sums or property of any sort that remain after all costs, expenses, devises, and bequests have been paid from an estate, e.g., "In a large majority of probate proceedings there remains a residuary sum or estate in property, that to be divided in accordance with a *residuary clause* (q.v.) in the will if there is one, or by the rules of intestate inheritance."

respite, respite a crime, respite of debt, respite of appeal: to delay or reset to a later date some action or proceeding at law, e.g., "Charlene's creditors, having failed to agree to a 'voluntary respite' giving her time to pay her debts, were ordered by the court to be subject to a 'forced respite.'"

respondent: a defendant in an equity case, e.g., "For centuries chancery courts have referred to the defendants as respondents and those bringing claims as *complainants* (q.v.)."

Revolutionary War, rations of soldiers: the diet of a Revolutionary soldier was hardly adequate by today's standards, however the rations of men at war seldom are, e.g., "Though many changes were to be made during the war years, in 1775 Washington ordered that rations were to be made available, viz., 'corned beef and pork, four days in a week; salt fish, one day; fresh beef, two days; as milk cannot be procured during the winter season, the men are to have one pound and a half of beef, or eighteen ounces of pork per day, half pint of rice or a pint of Indian meal per week; one quart of spruce beer per day or nine gallons of molasses to one hundred men per week. Six pounds of candles to one hundred men per week; for guards, six ounces of butter or nine ounces of hogs-lard per week. Three pints of pease or beans per man per week or vegetables equivalent, allowing six shillings (about $36.00 in 2000 money) per bushel for beans or pease – two and eight pence pr bushel for onions (about $14.00 in 2000 money), one and four pence pr bushel for potatoes and turnips (about $7.00 in 2000 money), one pound of flour pr man each day, and hard bread to be dealt out one day in a week, in lieu of flour.'"

revolutions: unlike now, descriptive of military marching and parading, e.g., "Christopher's sixth great-grandfather, Revolutionary War veteran, Frost Snow, and his fellow militiamen were '…proud to perform revolutions' for the audiences on court days."

rheumatism: as now, e.g., "In 1882, to treat rheumatism Dr. Walker prescribed 'spirit vapor baths' and '…acetate of potash, extract of black cohosh, extract of poison hemlock…' mixed with 'simple syrup.'"

right of action: the right by reason of the entirety of the circumstances to bring a lawsuit against another person, e.g., "When Parker built the mill dam and the water flooded the meadow of Hunt, the latter had a right of action, and when he exercised that right by filing a lawsuit it became a cause of action."

Riot Act, read the: years before the American Revolution, George I saw to the passage of the Riot Act in Britain, that measure providing that when twelve or more people were gathered together and were disturbing the peace or thought to be gathered for the purpose of being critical of government, or the king, any sheriff, deputy, constable, mayor or justice of the peace could read to them the *Riot Act* and thereby order them to disperse, e.g., "The expression 'she will read the Riot Act to you kids' employed that law as a metaphor for ordering children to cease with mischievous conduct."

rising of the lights: origin unknown, but "lights" was an ancient term meaning lung; probably croup, though early writers felt it sometimes was an "inflammation of the liver," e.g., "The term 'rising of the lights' reflects the fact that croup often results in a cough so severe as to bring up one's lungs, and that disease was said to be the cause of twenty-two deaths out of 15,455 in 1720." Also see ***death, causes of in 1720.***

rive, rive cut timber: trees cut down and split with a wedge or other blunt cutting and splitting tool; not smoothly cut, e.g., "It was not uncommon for leases to contain a provision that the lessee (tenant) might cut, saw and rive timber either in some specific places within the tract or generally."

roaches of the liver: cirrhosis of the liver, e.g., "Dr. Don smiled knowingly as he told of humble, poor, uneducated elderly patients of the Appalachians asking him if their ailment might be 'roaches of the liver.'"

road orders: in early counties the court directed work and repairs on the roads by conscripting able-bodied men who lived near that road, and the collective orders and courts' minutes pertaining thereto are/were so known, e.g., "Francis Drake was an *overseer of roads* (q.v.) in early North Carolina, and his reports are in the clerk's records known as 'road orders.'"

Roanoke: as now, the capital city of North Carolina and a river; currency of the seventeenth century. See *peake, woompompeak, and Roanoke.*

Rocky Mountain Spotted Fever: See *tick fever.*

rods, nail: See *cut nails, etc.*

Rogation Week: the week preceding Whitsunday, e.g., "In the seventeenth and very early eighteenth centuries during Rogation Week and a bit before or after, most Virginia parishes organized and undertook the processioning needed within the parish, however by the period 1720-1730 that activity often was being performed at other times of the year and as needed." Also see *perambulation.*

rollers: as now, a word of numerous uses, including an early word meaning tree trunks stripped of bark and placed under a building horizontally to the direction of movement, by which even a large building might be moved so long as trunks on a continuing basis were placed ahead of the movement, e.g., "In 1770 the Concord, Massachusetts jail was moved from one location to another using rollers and twenty-six pairs of oxen."

rood: one-fourth of an acre, e.g., "Early New England reports reveal many references to the rood as a measurement."

rose fever, rose cold, hay fever: allergies, so-called since such were expected in the spring and early summer, e.g., "Sarah knew that come every spring, little Diane would suffer greatly from rose fever."

roseola, rose rash, false measles: probably usually *rose fever* (q.v.); a rash or small eruptions on the skin that are rose color and appear as measles (rubeola, rubella), yet are not contagious, e.g., "The many early frequent diagnoses of roseola likely revealed the presence of allergies."

rosy drop: See **eczema.**

roving minstrel: See **minstrel, roving.**

rubeola, measles, German measles: well known to all, measles have been a scourge of man for millennia, e.g., "In 1762, Dr. Mottet of Charleston prescribed for measles an extract of smart-weed, sweating teas, and daily baths."

rubeola, rubella: See **roseola, etc.**, and see *measles* in *What Did They Mean By That?*

Rule of Three: To "cast accounts" originally meant to calculate and keep track of debits, credits and interest, however later the expression came to mean learning basic arithmetic: addition, subtraction, multiplication, division, fractions, and decimals, e.g., "After the Revolution 'rule of three' came to mean the study of ratios, that knowledge being summarized as the *Rule of Three* because the subject could be given three numbers and calculate the fourth, as in what we call basic algebra."

running scall: See *eczema*.

rye n' injun: bread made of both rye and cornmeal, e.g., "The use of the term 'rye and injun' for a bread made by those of the early Northeastern colonies seems to have disappeared before the American Revolution."

S

Sabbath, breach of: See ***breach of the Sabbath***

Sabbath-breaking, blue laws: any violation of those statutes or ordinances that restricted activities in order that Sunday be observed in a "Christian way"; the bank of laws and ordinances restricting activities on Sundays were known as "blue laws," e.g., "Though rarely now enforced, blue laws and charges of Sabbath-breaking are as old as the American colonies."

sack boy: a favored and common "job" of boys and quite young men of the centuries before 1900, e.g., "Because of the hundreds of thousands of grist mills before 1950, many needing a sack boy to bag up flour and meal for transportation or sale and for general labor around those mills, as many boys became sack boys just as later youth were 'paper boys.'"

Sally Lunn; the name said to have arisen from the ancient great resort at Bath, England; an early Virginia bread of meal of any sort with a lot of butter, eggs and a tad of salt, e.g., "Widow Jane Clemmons often made the very rich Sally Lunn by baking the dough in a pan and serving with yet more butter."

salt(ed) paper prints: the predecessor to the ***albumen print*** (q.v.) and the first of the paper prints; in wide use from about 1839 until the last years of the 1860s, e.g., "Without knowing the date of the print— photo—it is very difficult to distinguish a well made salt paper print from one of albumen."

salt-rheum: See **eczema**.

salvo: quite unlike now, an invitation, e.g., "Johnson (1802) quotes Addison in defining a salvo as an invitation."

samp: porridge made by boiling finely ground Indian corn with a tad of salt, and served with either butter or pepper or both or with a sweetener, e.g., "Just as Paul enjoyed his grits with milk and sugar, his New England grandson enjoyed samp with butter, salt and pepper."

sandwich board, sandwich board man: a means of advertising by which a man or boy for a fee would wear a board on the front and back of his body, advertising a product or merchant, e.g., "In the 1930s *Ralph's Snappy Service* in Marion, Ohio, hired a sandwich board boy to advertise his fast food, and paid the boy ten cents for all day Saturday." Also see *drummer.*

sangry punch: See *punch.*

scabies: See *eczema.*

scaler: one who is skilled at estimating the percentage of lumber of various grades that will result from the processing of logs, e.g., "It was said that Tyler was the best scaler in the timber country of Michigan's Upper Peninsula." Also see *timber cruiser.*

scarlatina: the dreaded, most feared and often fatal scarlet fever, thought to develop most often in three- and four-year-old children and advancing in three stages, *scarlatina simplex, scarlatina anginosis*, and *scarlatina maligna*, e.g., "Maggie correctly feared the worst when in 1904 little four-year-old Helen displayed all the symptoms of advanced scarlatina, for which there then were no cures."

scarlet fever: q.v. *What Did They Mean By That?* and see *scarlatina.*

schnecke, sticky buns, and cinnamon rolls: a favorite of all colonists, especially those from Pennsylvania Dutch country, e.g., "Hannah often made schnecke, a favorite of her children, since those were made of 'short dough,' brown sugar, cinnamon, and butter, then baked and served hot."

schnitz, schnitz un knepp: a favorite winter treat for all colonial families of the North, e.g., "Cheryl Bater made 'schnitz un knepp,' called usually simply schnitz by boiling the dried fruits of the previous summer, especially pears and apples, and adding dumplings."

sciatica: See *bone shave,* and see *lumbago* in *What Did They Mean By That?*

scienter: knowingly; having knowledge of consequences that would be criminal, e.g., "One of the defenses stated by the 1792 Virginia defendant was that his acts were not scienter as had been stated in the indictment."

scooner: obsolete; perhaps now unknown, and not mentioned by Johnson or Walker; may be a medium to large dish shaped like a gravy boat within which dressings and gravies were served, e.g., "A Delaware estate inventory of 1816 mentioned pewter, then '2 sass dishes and 2 scooners.'" Also see *What Did They Mean By That?*, *schooner.*

screws: See *rheumatism.*

scrofula: See *King's Evil, etc.*

scullery: that place in the homes of wealthy where large pans and pots were cleaned, e.g., "Only the Thomas Roberts family of Marion had sufficient space in their kitchen area for a scullery."

sealing wax: that wax which when melted, dripped on a document or letter and impressed with a seal, public or private, was used to designate as concluded or seal the cover of such writings, e.g., "Commonly the wax of preference for documents and letters was red, however green and blue also were used, and black wax designated death or mourning." Also see *seal* in *What Did They Mean By That?*

searchers, for a county, a paid officer of customs whose task it was to search all vessels that could or might carry goods or commodities that were subject to taxation or duties due the colony or the Crown; those men appointed by a community or county who were paid on a per diem basis for searching for miscreants, criminals, missing persons, and such as wild animals and dogs that were about to or had brought harm or injury to the citizenry, e.g., "In May of 1679 Bucks County appointed more searchers."

secondary evidence: is without precise definition, meaning generally that the evidence being offered as proof is not the most reliable that might be uncovered, or that the sources from which such evidence arises are no longer in existence, e.g., "An abstract or summary of any record is secondary, just as would be the words of a person who stated from memory the terms of a contract."

seconds, tobacco: See *clear from ground leaves or seconds.*

secured creditor: one who is owed money or a thing of value and who is assured of payment through a lien, a pledge of assets, one for whose benefit others have signed as sureties, or who, through judgment or other legal proceeding has a priority position among creditors, e.g., "The bank or finance company that holds a mortgage on your house, car, furniture, boat, etc., is a secured creditor, however a friend who loaned you money is not."

seeth, seether: to boil, and a pot in which to so boil liquids, e.g., "Colleen spoke of her two-quart iron pot as a seether."

selectmen: persons elected in much of the northeast with duties of managing the finances and business of a town and having some of the powers of a mayor, e.g., "The word selectman is variously used in New

England and elsewhere and the careful researcher will seek the duties of such persons in those local records."

Semayne's Case: frequently cited in the early records of the American colonies as a milestone in our law, a 1604 case that determined that a "man's house is his castle" and that no officer of the law could enter one's house without permission, unless that officer had gained a warrant to do so or had good reason to believe that a crime was being committed or that there was property within that legally should not be there, e.g., "The word 'house' in Semayne's Case was early construed as meaning 'home' or 'dwelling.'"

semetilla: See *flour, meal.*

September as 7ber, 7BR, & October as 8ber, etc: very common early, especially before the adoption of the "Gregorian calendar" here in 1752, abbreviations for September, the Latin root of which is "septa," i.e., the seventh month of the year, and so forth, e.g., "To the end that time was not wasted by writing the names of calendar months over and over, for centuries clerks, etc., have abbreviated for *September, 7ber* or *7BR;* for *October (octo), 8BR* or *8ber;* for *November (novem, 9BR* or *9ber;* and for *December (decem), 10BR* or *10ber.*" Also see *octogenarian, nonagenarian, etc.,* and in *What Did They Mean By That?* see *Julian Calendar*

septicemia, blood poisoning: a widespread infection resulting from any number of causes involving especially cuts or punctures of the flesh, e.g., "Elma knew that there was almost no chance of recovery when Bud was diagnosed with septicemia as a result of a cut on his hand that happened at his workplace."

servants without indentures, service of: the terms of those servants brought to Virginia without indentures was four years for those over sixteen years of age, and until age twenty-one for those under sixteen, e.g., "The differences between young servants and masters had so grown by 1650 that the council established those terms of service that had previously been bargained."

set pans, butter pans, milk pans: pans in which fresh milk was placed in order that it separate and the butter fat rise to the surface for skimming, e.g., "Loreda always covered the milk pans at once after the fresh warm was poured into those."

settled with prejudice: See *with prejudice, settled.*

shallop: a small boat, usually with oars, e.g., "Curiously, Henry Blair of Virginia provided in his 1720 will that his wife, Loreda, was not to 'dispose of my shallop until all of my debts are paid.'"

sharecropper: See *cropper, etc.*

sharps and shorts: See *bolting, etc.* and see *flour, meal.*

sheep bell: See *cowbell, etc.*

shenanigans: unlike now, early meaning deceit or trickery, e.g., "It was said by early colonials from England, Scotland and Wales that Irishmen were known for shenanigans in business or trade, meaning that they would engage in trickery and deceit in bargaining."

sheriffwicke, sheriffwick: as in *bailiwick* (q.v., *What Did They Mean By That?*), the territory within which a bailiff had authority; ancient term referring to that county or political subdivision within which a sheriff had jurisdiction, e.g., "In the American colonies that traced their law to England, the word sheriffwicke is occasionally found, the oath for which sheriffs in 1652 in part was, '…do right to the poore as to the Rich.:…'"

shinny: homemade whisky. See *corn whisky* in *What Did They Mean By That?*

ship fever: probably typhus or malaria, e.g., "As with so many diseases diagnosed before modern medicine, a log of ship fever is largely not further explainable today."

ships' furniture: everything needed by and on a ship to render it usable and operable at sea, e.g., "The captains (masters) of ships always appointed a man, often called a chandler, to see to the ships' furniture, and to fail at that task was a most serious offense."

shiver, shivers: unlike now, Johnson (1755) citing Woodward defines the term as shattering or splitting into many smaller pieces, e.g., "Just as early seamen exclaimed wonder or surprise by 'shiver my timbers,' the early colonel was said to have 'shivered many lances,' meaning he had defeated many adversaries in battle."

shooting firearms: See *hunting or shooting, prohibitions of.*

short ton: See *long ton, etc.*

shortnin' bread, shortening bread: a universally known and highly favored Southern sweet bread, e.g., "Diane was known widely for her shortnin' bread, made from the more expensive light brown sugar, butter, a tad of cream, and wheat flour, baked and served hot with even more butter and usually some preserves."

shorts: See *flour, meal.*

show cause: See *for cause.*

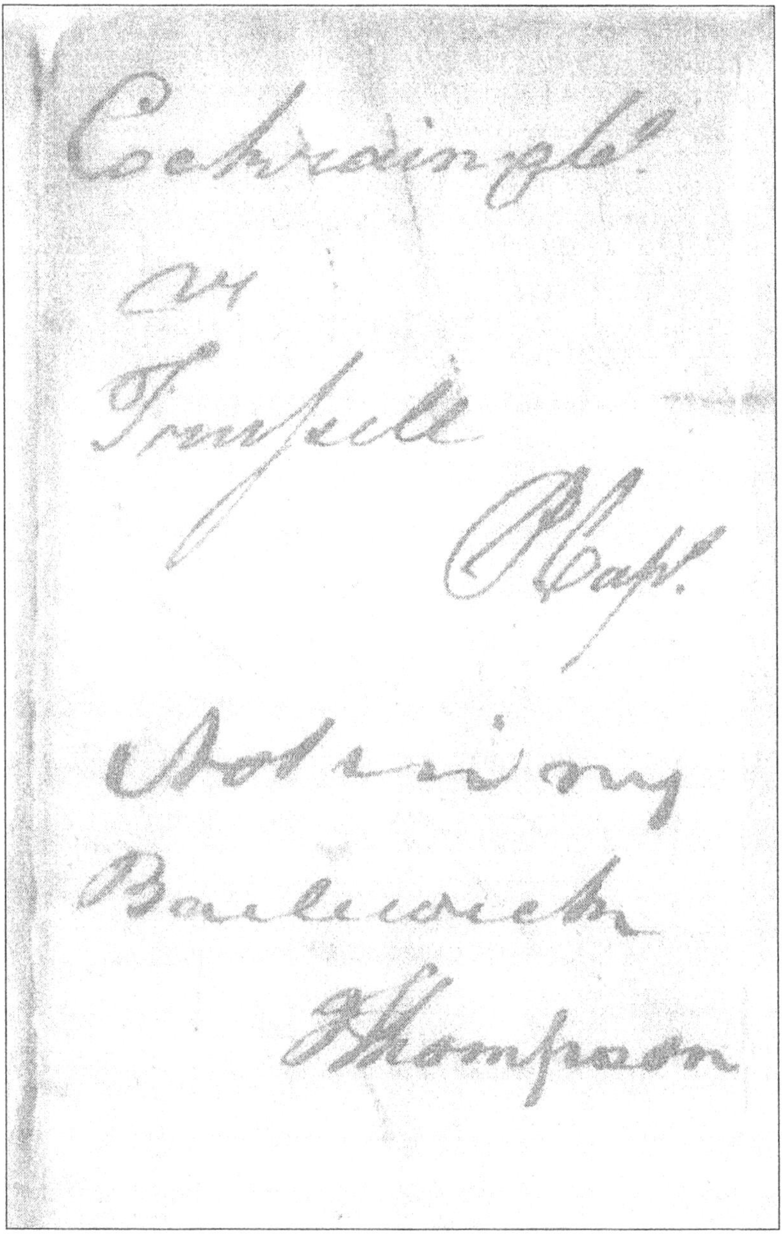

Figure 29. 1870 sheriff endorses an order given him,
"Not in my Bailiwick." See *sheriffwicke*.

Figure 30. Three very pretty girls look out from
a *silver gelatin print* of 1875.

shreeve: sheriff and derived from the ancient term "shire-reeve," meaning that officer who had the duty to see to the enforcement of the courts' orders and the commands of the Crown, e.g., "The Essex County records of 1664 reveal that the term shreeve, as a contraction of shire-reeve, was in use in the Virginia colony at that time." Also see *sheriff* in *What Did They Mean By That?*

shrub, raspberry, etc.: a drink made of vinegar, sugar and berry or other fruit juice, e.g., "The diary of Dr. Drake revealed his recipe for raspberry shrub, which he used for the perceived medicinal value and as a pleasurable drink thought to ward off ailments of many sorts."

signator, signet, signell: very general terms meaning one who has signed a formal document or legal instrument, e.g., "The terms were needed to distinguish those who were mere scriveners from those whose signatures or seals impacted upon the legal effects or intended results of the documents." Also see *signet ring* in *What Did They Mean By That?*

Silent Brigade: See *night riders* and see *Ku Klux Klan* in *What Did They Mean By That?*

silver gelatin print: the photographic prints resulting from the application of compounds of silver to surfaces for exposure and then development, e.g., "The silver gelatin process well known to virtually every photography buff or professional throughout the 125-plus years from 1880 to the advent of our digital processes brought vast fortunes to such as Kodak."

similars, law of: the belief, even to now by some, that plants, fruits, and berries that resembled a part of the body or the symptoms of disease should be administered for the curative value supposedly to be had there, e.g., "The American Indians, in their beliefs in the law of similars used *decoctions* (q.v.) of milkweed were given to mothers having lactation problems, and since walnuts appear as does an exposed brain, walnut meats were administered for lunacy or mental imbalance."

simplins: a laughable, usually ignorant or coarse person, especially a man, whose comical actions and posturing are not those of gentlemen, e.g., "Referring to a scene in Ohio, Nathan, *Dan Emmett and Negro Minstrelsy* (Univ. of Oklahoma Press, 1962), pg. 106) wrote, 'This Simplins was as grotesque as the Ohio wilderness itself: a musician, dancer, self-styled actor...' and public spectacle."

sine die, adjournment: an adjournment, especially of a judicial or legislative body, without setting another date for reconvening; a final meeting of any governmental agency, body, or committee, e.g., "Every term of Congress ends with a declaration and an entry that it was 'adjourned sine die.'"

siriasis: probably sunstroke or heatstroke and little understood, e.g., "Dr. Mason noted that Mikaila's siriasis likely was a result of an inflammation of her brain caused by the sun."

sisters, inheriting: See *parceners, co-parceners.*

skull-cap: A plant thought to have medicinal value. See *nervines.*

slander and libel: in torts, words, pictures, photographs, depictions, music, signs or writings that belittle, humiliate, embarrass, or in some way harm the reputation of another person, to both of which truth is a defense, e.g., "Spoken words are slander, while written or graphically portrayed words or depictions that are equally harmful to reputation are libel."

sleeping sickness: encephalitis; very often mistaken for fatigue, an inflammation of the brain, for which there was no known cure, e.g., "When Beth observed that Ryan was sleeping ten to twelve hours a night, she presumed sleeping sickness."

slice: a spatula, usually with a wooden handle, used to turn food in a cooking utensil, e.g., "Betty had several slices of various sizes." Also see *slice* in *What Did They Mean By That?*

slip: as now; early, to unleash a dog, e.g., "From the context of the court's minutes, it is apparent that the 1728 reference that someone 'did let his dog slip' meant that a dog had gotten loose or slipped out of its collar and injured a child."

slipshod: a horse, mule or other draft animal not shod for the conditions upon which it will need to walk or work; very early, shoes for people that had no support or containing space above the actual heel, e.g., "An early New England writing speaks of being slipshod; 'my shoes were not pulled up at the heels,' and many early references may be found that lament the fact that a horse had fallen because it was slipshod."

sloe, sloeberries: the fruit of the blackthorn tree, like small, black, wild plums, known for centuries as a wine base to which alcohol or gin is added, e.g., "Not only has sloe gin been a favorite drink for centuries, but the wood from blackthorn trees has made fine walking sticks for such as Presidents Ronald Reagan and Bill Clinton, and Speaker 'Tip' O'Neill."

sloos, bulies and*:* See *bulies, sloos.*

slop bowl: a bowl placed on a dining table usually by more affluent families, and in which bones, gristle, and scraps from the plates were placed, e.g., "The 1822 Deborah Kokes inventory revealed a 'creamboat, slop bowl and sugar tongs.'" Also see *cream boat.*

slumgullion: a stew made from whatever meats, fish and vegetables were available; a very early term, probably arising from early comparisons with waste from the killing of whales and the foul materials in the bilge of a ship, e.g., "Whaler captain Paul wrote that by the end of the voyage the crew were fed slumgullion almost every day."

smicket, smiket: obsolete and now likely forgotten; a very early undergarment or a smock for a woman, e.g., "The word was said to have occasionally appeared in early New England, and Johnson defines the term as 'an undergarment worn by women.'"

smoke bay: See *smoke loft.*

smokeloft, smoke bay: as to the former, Johnson said, "the highest floor"; a room above others and used to smoke such as hams, bacon and beef; as to smoke bay, a doored compartment built into a fireplace, it also used to smoke bacon, beef, hams, and other meats, e.g., "As early as 1635, American inventories were revealing the presence of flitches (slabs, uncut) of bacon and hams in smokelofts and smokebays."

social agency: that agency or department of a state that administers the adoption laws of that state. Also see *adoption, system, etc.*

social worker: a person appointed by a social agency, a state or a court to supervise and report the conditions surrounding problems in adoption methods and placements. Also see *adoption, system, etc.*

sod, soden: obsolete, food cooked by boiling, and a common expression yet in 1755 when defined by Johnson, e.g., "Most of the food of our early settler ancestors was sodden, that is, cooked in an open fire, in a fireplace, or by boiling."

softening of the brain: paresis, progressive paralysis, often leading to a loss of faculties early listed as a cause of insanity, e.g., "Though we can not be sure at this distance, it is thought from the notation that in 1819 John Carner had succumbed to 'softening of the brain,' he probably had paresis."

soho: the term describing the early sound used to summon or call someone from a long distance, e.g., "The shouted sound, 'soho-oooooooo' can be heard for a very long distance."

soldiers, American Revolution, rations for: See *Rations for soldiers, etc.*

Somersett's Case: the 1771 case that for all time abolished slavery in England, Scotland and Wales, e.g., "Somersett's Case abolished slavery in England, and it also ruled that persons who had been so held could not be transported to these colonies or anyplace else where slavery was yet legal."

sororoside: now obsolete, the murder of a sister, e.g., "From long before the sixteenth century and continuing through the eighteenth, sororocide was occasionally charged when a sister had been slain, likely because in addition to the killing of another, the murderer had violated the family."

sorrance: a general term meaning any disease, affliction, sore, or injury to a horse, e.g., "Many early records and letters refer to remedies for various sorrances, and it is suggested that soring a horse may derive from that ancient expression." See *soring, etc.* in *What Did They Mean By That?*

sot, sop: one who is stupefied from alcohol consumption; to steep, soak or marinate in warm brandy, liquor or wine, e.g., "Referring to her practice of steeping beef in wine, Allison smiled and said that her uncle also was an old sot."

sounder, drift, parcel, P:cell or percell or pursel of hogs: origin unknown, a gathering or small group of swine, e.g., "The kids chuckled when old George spoke of 'my sounder of boars' and at other times, 'my drift of pigs'"; "In April of 1671, in the case of Holts v Clark, it was said that a P:cell of hogs was the subject of the case."

soup to nuts: a superlative; complete, broad in content, and a metaphor drawn on a dinner of many courses, starting with the soup course and ending after desserts with small dishes of nuts here and there on or about the dining area, e.g., "When Beth had a grand opening, you could be sure she would do it up right, from soup to nuts."

souse: an early and favorite inexpensive combination of scraps of pork and pickling spices, and still well known and eaten, e.g., "Colleen recalled that '...my Mother made (souse) when I was a child. It was made from scraps of meat when they would butcher hogs...everything but the squeal...and spices. It was cooked on top of the stove (by boiling), then packed in a pan with a weight or brick placed on top to make a loaf (a *cheese*, q.v.), then was eaten like luncheon meat'"; "*Housekeeping in Old Virginia* (1889) noted that 'one head and a dozen ears will make a good-sized cheese.'"

souterkin, sooterkin: an imaginary and bizarre creature, well known and feared for centuries, and supposedly a creature that attended the birth of children of women from Holland, e.g., "Likely an afterbirth or a false pregnancy, and once said to look similar to a wet rat or a weasel, the sooterkin was thought to embody evil and follow the birth of a normal child."

Southern frames: probably now forgotten, perhaps small, decorated wooden containers for general use in the home, e.g., "The 1820 inventory of Cook's Virginia store listed '6 Southern frames' valued at 50 cents each."

spaddle: a small spade, e.g., "Many early inventories list spaddles in association with other tools and implements."

speak in tongues, to, glassolalia: those Pentecostals who, in the belief that the Holy Ghost can and often does speak through the conduit of every person, that speaking taking the form of sounds unlike any language known, e.g., "Thought to be evidence of possession by a higher power, the Pentecostals speak in tongues which ritual they call *glassolalia.*"

specie: any coin placed in circulation, made of silver or gold, and bearing marks that reveal it was authorized and issued by a government, e.g., "The specie of the U.S. has varied in base metals, weight and denomination over the centuries, and gold and silver are no longer used for our coinage."

spermatazoon: See *homunculi.*

spinet: a small harpsichord, e.g., "Spinets were both less expensive and smaller than the often massive harpsichords, and Mikaila thought hers made tinkling sounds." Also see *pianoforte* and see *harpsichord.*

spirit lamp: a small lamp burning alcohol for illumination, e.g., "Little Diane asked Allison why she called the night lamp 'spirit,' and Allison explained because it burned alcohol." Also see *Betty lamp* in *What Did They Mean By That?*

spirits, bottled or *in barrels:* See *liquor, distilled, etc.*

splenic fever: See *anthrax.*

spoken will: See *nuncupative will* in *What Did They Mean By That?*

spoon bread: seasoned meal or flour of any sort moistened to cause it to stick together and placed a spoonful at a time into very hot grease, e.g., "In the colder months Maggie's iron cookstove was very near her kitchen table, and she could make spoon bread and with a sieve-like ladle remove the little cakes, drain those, and pass such directly to the plates of the children." Also see *suppawn.*

spoonmeat: probably obsolete; any food, and not necessarily meat, that is a liquid and eaten with a spoon, e.g., "Shakespeare, as did his contemporaries and the English speaking world in general, referred to spoonmeat down to and including the late nineteenth century."

springtide: having nothing to do with the seasons, a term meaning high tide, and also the tide at the new and the full moon, e.g., "The early *almanacs* (q.v., *What Did They Mean By That?*) frequently spoke of springtides."

spruce beer: a favorite beer of the middle American colonies, e.g., "Bruce's spruce beer recipe was 'three cups molasses, one-half ounce of yeast, one-fourth pound of fresh spruce tips, and a gallon of water; break up the tips and add to the water, simmer for three hours, add a little water when it boils off, skim foam and particles that rise to surface, strain the liquid and add molasses, bring to a boil again, simmer for twenty-five to thirty minutes, cool till it is hot, but not scalding to the touch, stir in the yeast, leave loosely covered for three or so days till yeast quits working, bottle up and cork tightly.'"

sprue: unknown, seemingly a disease frequently diagnosed in the heat of the Deep South, e.g., "Sprue was said to be the cause of intestinal disorders and sore throat."

spurway, spurway trail: a trail for horses, usually those being ridden, e.g., "Cartways and foot paths had their obvious purposes, and spurways were narrow, often cleared paths through the forests and to neighboring properties or remote places on one's own land where carts were not needed, and where people seldom walked." Also see *cart paths.*

spye glass: a small, hand-held telescope, usually retractable or collapsible, e.g., "The inventory of the Patriot Thomas Mason and of Thomas Roberts each revealed the presence of 'one spye glass.'"

square meal: a generous meal served on a usually divided square plate, e.g., "In early times, plates for workers were square in order to conserve space in a kitchen, and so arose the expression, 'he was paid $10.00 a week and three squares a day.'"

St. Stephen's Day: See *Boxing Day.*

St. Anthony's fire: one of several diseases noted as causes of death in New England, e.g., "In addition to St. Anthony's fire, a report listed as causes of death during 1720 *tissick* (q.v.), French pox, fistula, thrush (thrusa), *planet struck* (q.v.), twisting of the guts, pleurisy, and purples." Also see *deaths, causes of, etc.*

Stamp Acts: those English parliamentary acts of the mid-eighteenth century that designated which documents and writings were to bear a stamp revealing that the prescribed duties had been paid on those writings, e.g., "The Stamp Acts greatly aroused the ire of the American colonists and figured prominently in writings of the causes of the American Revolution."

stamp money: See *postage currency.*

staple: quite unlike now, Johnson (1802) citing Dryden says a business established in commerce, a market or emporium, e.g., "There was a staple near the *Old Brick Church* on what is now Virginia Rt. 10."

stare decisis: the fundamental doctrine of American and English law that prevails and tends to powerfully urge all courts to act in keeping with prior decisions in the same subject matters, e.g., "The doctrine of stare decisis is more evident in our lower courts than elsewhere, since judges of lesser authority are so trained, follow the decisions of courts superior to their own, are only occasionally called upon to research the law at great depths, and their decisions are seldom appealed."

state court web sites: not including the Federal Court system, the courts of the States of the U.S. vary in jurisdiction and name to such a degree and can be most confusing. So many are those titles and authorities that we suggest you search the Internet for the words, *State Courts web sites* or for *National Center for State Courts* and at those places investigate the courts in which you need to search the records. Also see *Federal courts, information as to.*

State's Attorney: See *lawsuits, common, procedural steps.*

states of the U.S., names and titles of probate courts in: the probate courts handling estates, as with other courts, often have names that vary from state to state. Following are the names given probate divisions of each states. In the following, NSC means no separate court and so you must ask at the courthouse where the wills estates, guardianships, and/or adoptions records are located. **Alabama**-Probate Court, **Alaska**-NSC, **Arizona**-NSC, **Arkansas**-NSC, **California**-NSC, **Colorado**-NSC, **Connecticut**-NSC, **Delaware**-Court of Chancery, **District of Columbia**-NSC, **Florida**-NSC, **Georgia**-NSC, **Hawaii**-NSC, **Idaho**-Magistrates Division, **Illinois**-NSC, **Indiana**-Trial Court (except St. Joseph Probate Court), **Iowa**-NSC, **Kansas**-NSC, **Kentucky**-NSC, **Louisiana**-NSC, **Maine**-County Register of Probate, **Maryland**-Orphan's Courts, **Massachusetts**-Probate Court, **Michigan**-Probate Court, **Minnesota**-NSC, **Mississippi**-Chancery Court, **Missouri**-NSC, **Montana**-NSC, **Nebraska**-NSC, **Nevada**-NSC, **New Hampshire**-Probate Court, **New Jersey**-NSC, **New Mexico**-NSC, **New York**-Surrogate's Court and Family Court, **North Carolina**-NSC, **North Dakota**-NSC, **Ohio**-Probate Court, **Oklahoma**-NSC, **Oregon**-Family Court and Lane County Probate, **Pennsylvania**-Court of Common Pleas, **Rhode Island**-Municipal Affairs, **South Carolina**-Judicial Department Probate, **Tennessee**-Administrative Office of the Courts plus Probate Court in Davidson and Shelby counties, **Texas**-Probate Judge and Court, **Utah**-NSC, **Vermont**-Probate Court, **Virginia**-NSC, **Washington**-NSC, **West Virginia**-NSC, **Wisconsin**-NSC and **Wyoming**-NSC. There are NO Federal Court probate courts. (**Note, names may vary slightly here and there by reason of custom and local abbreviation; ask in any office in the courthouse.)

stateswoman: interestingly until the mid-twentieth century, Johnson's definition seems to have prevailed, e.g., "Johnson defined a stateswoman as 'a woman who meddles in public affairs.'"

statu liberi: Latin; commonly found in Louisiana antebellum reports and referring to the status of individuals who had been emancipated either by law or by their owners, e.g., "The slave, Johan, was statu liberi as a result of being freed by the will of his master."

statutes at large: though the familiar volumes by Hening bear that title, the term is very general and refers to the laws of a legislature that prevail at a writing at a place designated, e.g., "When Mr. Bater of Maryland referred to the statutes at large, he was speaking of the laws of his colony and not to Hening's fine work."

statutes of limitation: See *limitation, statues of.*

staves: those vertical, curved, wooden sides of a barrel, around which bands of metal were placed to hold the same together and to the top and bottom, e.g., "In 1845 Howe wrote that large quantities of shingles, tar, turpentine and staves were being shipped from Nansemond County down the river in ships of up to 100 tons *burden* (q.v.)."

steen: obsolete, and meaning a fired clay container or vessel, e.g., "The researcher will on occasion find an inventory listing steens, usually accompanied by other items of crockery."

sterling money: a common expression describing and designating the nature and quality of the money that would be acceptable in any exchange, e.g., "In 1667 in New England Abel James agreed that he would pay the sum of '£5L,1S Sterling money of England' for a tract of land." Also see *Sterling* in *What Did They Mean By That?*

stock mark, stock brand, flesh marks, dew lap: those identifying marks and locations by which an animal, usually livestock, is marked, e.g., "Mrs. H states that in colonial North Carolina, as in other colonies, stock marks were cuts on the ears of cattle, hogs, sheep, oxen, horses, goats, etc., stock brands were symbols, letters, etc. burned into the skin of such cattle, usually on the hips or buttocks, and flesh marks were scarring marks placed on the dew lap (a loose fold of skin falling over the throat) of such stock."

stockfish: dried cod, e.g., "Cod being most plentiful, the records of the more northern coastal colonies often mention *stockfish*."

stocking cap: See *Monmouth cap.*

stomatitis: said to be an inflammation of the mouth, e.g., "As with so many of the early diagnoses, what the term stomatatis meant is not now understood."

stone horse, stonehorse: a horse not neutered, stones referring to its testicles, e.g., "Throughout the colonies and the entire English speaking world, for that matter, the expression 'stone horse' was very common." Also see *gelt.*

stone soup: when cooking carrots, onions, potatoes, and turnips, a stone the size of a fist was added for reasons now not remembered, e.g., "Allison's kids laughed whenever she added a stone to the stew, since they were sure no one could eat that."

straymaster, stray master, ranger: that man appointed and paid by a county or town, often in New England but widely in the colonies, to hunt down, gather and return stray animals, whether wild or domesticated that posed danger to a community, e.g., "George Wimberly was appointed straymaster for the year August 1 1779 till July 31 1780, and was to be paid for days worked and needed."

strong hand, vi et armis: early and largely obsolete terms, meaning that physical force was used in committing a crime, and a legal form often attendant in descriptions of trespasses, e.g., "The words of the early Maryland court that Curle had 'with strong hand stolen the silver' of Mrs. Haskins meant that someone resisted his criminal acts as he committed the same"; "The complaint alleged that Weller had committed trespass *vi et armis*, and the fact that it stated nothing more than that he had so trespassed, reveals that the court did not require the lawyer to prove that Weller had used force of arms, though that is the Latin definition of the term."

strumous synavitis: See *white swelling, etc.*

strumpet, rip: an ancient term meaning whore, e.g., "The term strumpet dates to at least the time of Henry I and before 1400." As to Henry I, see *What Did They Mean By That?*, *Regnal years.*

stuffs: See *fabrics and etc.* and also see *stuff* in *What Did They Mean By That?*

stumpage: money or other thing of value paid or traded to a landowner by someone who enters upon his land and takes trees away, whether standing and then cut, or otherwise, e.g., "The term 'stumpage' appears regularly in the records of the early lumber producing states."

subpoena, alius: See *alius dictus.*

subscribing witness: a person who was present and, having seen the signing by the maker or writer, then swore to those facts, e.g., "There may be several witnesses, each as to some element of the events, however the subscribing witness is the person who witnessed and swore to the fact that the principles' signature(s) was placed on the document." Also see *signator, etc.*

succession: when used in the law, meaning the descent of title from an earlier to a later owner, e.g., "The succession of title was Lazarus Drake to Drury Drake to Amos Johnston, to Jacob Johnson."

succotash: probably deriving from the "sukqutta" hash of the American Indians of the Northeast, a staple in the diet of those in the New England colonies, e.g., "From Indian corn, beans, milk and a bit of flour, Loreda made succotash at least once a week."

sudatory: a sweat house, e.g., "Almost forgotten is the fact that the American Indians used the sudatory for quite nearly every failing of health."

sudorific: any of a number or herbs and chemical compounds that induce perspiration, e.g., "Many were the ailments that were thought best treated by bringing about excessive sweating, and for those sudorifics such as horseradish, saffron, sage, snake-root, pleurisy root, mayweed, catnip, and ginger were universally prescribed."

sue and implead: See *implead, sue and.*

sue, to: See *lawsuit, suit, etc.*

suffered to seat themselves (himself): an expression of the law of the colonies of the seventeenth and eighteenth centuries, meaning that for whatever reasons residents had, through inaction, permitted a person or a group of people to take up residence on land to which that group had no rights of occupation, e.g., "On March 10, 1665 the Council of Virginia declared that 500 to 600 'Indians are driven from the mountains and lately are sit down near the falls of the James…(and those should not)…be suffered to seat themselves there or any where near us.'" Also see *seating, etc.* in *What Did They Mean By That?*

suffrage: the act of voting or having the privilege to do so, e.g., "Women did not have suffrage in the U.S. until 1922."

Sugar Act: 1764, a reviled tax placed by Britain on all sugar and "Indigo, coffee, wines (except French wine), all wrought silks, bengals, and stuffs…, silk or herbs from Persia, China, or East India, and all callico painted, dyed, printed, or stained there, and upon all foreign linen…known as Cambrick and French Lawns," e.g., "The preamble to the Sugar Act recites its purposes as being for the '…expences of defending, protecting, and securing…' the citizenry of 'the colonies.'"

sugar box: wooden container to store blocks of and occasionally granulated sugar, e.g., "Mikaila had two maple sugar boxes in her kitchen, one holding two five-pound blocks, and the other, only one block."

sugar chest: as the title reveals, a chest usually about four feet high, three feet wide and fourteen to eighteen inches wide, used to store blocks or bags of sugar, and kept in the pantry, e.g., "Colleen's cherry sugar chest was made by her husband and was beautiful."

suit: See *lawsuit, suit, etc.*

summons, alius: See *alius dictus.*

superannuated, superannuate: Johnson, 1802, uses the term for those "impaired or disqualified by age or length of life," e.g., "Margaret noted that in 1860 in Virginia, John Villon, then 73 years old, was spoken of as a superannuate."

superfoetation, superfetation: impregnation of a woman already pregnant; well-known for centuries and discussed in reports here as early as 1702, e.g., "In 1714 Dr. Parsons of Charleston wrote of a mother giving birth to a white child and then to a black paternal twin a few hours later, the latter said to be the result of a rape."

Superior Courts: See *state court web sites.*

supersedeas, supersedeas bond: an order by a higher court directing that a lower court cease a legal proceeding, e.g., "When a supersedeas is requested, courts often require that the person so requesting must post a supersedeas bond, lest the person whose process was ceased suffer undeserved damages as a result of the order." Also see *bonds, surety, etc.* and see *probate bonds, etc.*

suppawn: a very early staple in the northern colonies, made of boiled cornmeal and milk, also used for spoon bread, e.g., "Suppawn was very inexpensive, and yet it provided a satisfying meal for even those men who did heavy physical labor in the cold." Also see *spoon bread.*

supplies for wagon migration: See *migration west; supplies suggested.*

Supreme Courts: See *state court web sites.*

surety: an ancient noun describing a person who voluntarily agrees to do some act or pay some money or thing of value on a specific date if another named person does not so, both parties usually executing the agreement to pay, e.g., "A surety is a principal debtor and must pay a debt when the assured person does not do so, and the creditor has no duty to first attempt to collect from that assured first debtor." Also see *guarantor* and see *co-signer.*

surnames, See *occupations* and *What Did They Mean By That?,* generally.

surprisal, surprisall: early term meaning a state of surprise, and usually referring to a community or neighborhood, e.g., "A Surry proclamation of July 1696 ordered the preparation of the militia against attack and stated that the purpose of the notice was 'Putting this country in readiness and Preventing surprisal.'"

Surrogates' Courts: See *state court web sites.*

surveyor: See *poleman* and see *pole.*

swab: noun and verb; a mop; to clean with a mop, e.g., "While people of the medical professions routinely use the word swab to reveal a cleansing or sampling of some part of the body, for centuries the word swab meant to mop or to clean with a large cleaning tool especially aboard ship." Also see *swabby*.

swabby: an enlisted or low ranking sailor, so known for the requirement that men of low rank wash and mop decks and floors of ships, e.g., "Very few are the newly enlisted Navy personnel who have not been called swabbies and have not swabbed the decks or floors of their bases." Also see *swab*.

swag: a peddler's bundle, typically carried by hoboes or itinerant salesmen of the early days, e.g., "The stereotypical picture of a hobo or poor peddler usually reveals his swag on the end of a stick or over his shoulder."

swamp sickness, damps fever (see *What Did They Mean By That?*, *damps*), e.g., "Though the early symptoms of *malaria, typhoid fever,* and *yellow fever* (all q.v., *What Did They Mean By That?*) were much the same, before the Civil War Dr. Drake often diagnosed those symptoms as Swamp Sickness or Damps Fever."

swapt, swap, swapt, swop: seen occasionally in the seventeenth-century colonial records, and quite unlike these words seem to suggest, the words mean "hastily," e.g., "Johnson (1802) says 'with hasty violence,' although the word 'swap' now has come to mean a trade."

sweeps: See *hoes, etc.*

sweet grass, Gullah grass: that ever more scarce swamp-like plant from which, when dried, the Gullah people of coastal South Carolina weave the well known "Gullah baskets," e.g., "Beth commented that knowledge of the plants needed and the technique of weaving what are known as Gullah baskets was brought to the Southern colonies, particularly South Carolina, in the memories of early slaves."

Swem Index: See *Henings Statutes At Large.*

syllabus, syllabi (pl.): a summary of the contents of a writing, and in the law usually a summary of the parties, legal issues, order of proceeding, and the decision, e.g., "All researchers should read the syllabi of cases wherein their ancestors were parties, yet must remember that the syllabus of a case is neither the law nor is it the decision, those conclusions being found in the body of the decision."

synovitas: See *white swelling, etc.*

T

tabour: a small drum, e.g., "Inventories occasionally list tabours, often revealing someone in the family was associated with the militia, home guards, of other groups of citizens who marched."

Tadodaho: See *wizard.*

taffy, taffie, taffy pull: See *candy pull* in *What Did They Mean By That?*

take charge of powder, fixt to: See *fixt to take, etc.*

tamarind: See *honey tamarind.*

tan pitt: perhaps now forgotten; a pit was defined as a "hole in the ground," and perhaps those were improvised in a way that avoided the need for the very expensive (then) crockery containers used for salting and soaking the skins in tanning fluid, e.g., "The Surry Courts' Orders for 1669 refer to several records of 'tanning pits.'"

tangible assets, tangible property: usually not including real property, assets that are revealed to our senses and may be touched, weighed, seen, and sometimes smelled, and have worth by virtue of the physical value of such objects, e.g., "One's horse, tractor, wagon, stove, pots and pans, spinning wheels, books, mementos, and all many of other objects that have physical existence are one's tangible assets." Also see *intangible assets, etc.*

tansy cotton root: See *emmenagogues* and see *black cohosh.*

tapers: small diameter, rather long, usually finer candles, e.g., "Marly placed new tapers on the beautifully set dining table."

tax lien: See *lien, mechanics tax, etc.*

Tea Act: 1773; a principle cause to which the American Revolution was ascribed, e.g., "The British government had the power to legislate levies for the colonies, and the American colonists had refused to buy tea because of the taxes so levied against it – 3d per lb., that tax being exacted at the source of the tea, thereby allowing the shippers to sell here to whoever they chose, and thereby creating monopolies and raising the prices to colonists, all bringing much anger of our merchants."

tea board: a serving tray for cups of tea and accompanying sugar and milk, and seldom found in other than inventories of wealthy colonials, e.g., "The Richard Lee estate inventory revealed the presence of several tea boards."

terrify: unlike now, to irritate or mildly aggravate, as with an itch from an insect bite; obsolete except in areas of west Tennessee and northern Alabama and Mississippi, and lines 176-179 of Milton's *Paradise Regained* (1665-1667) seem to so employ the term, e.g., "West Tennessean Frank told that his little daughter had been 'terrified from them jiggers,' meaning she had been irritated by chigger bites."

testacy, intestacy: dying with a will; dying without a will, e.g., "Very common expressions used to describe what law was applicable to the proceedings in the estate of one who has died, e.g., "He apparently thought that testacy was no more desirable than to die intestate, and wrote no will." Also see ***intestate*** and see ***testate*** in *What Did They Mean By That?*

testament: the disposition of one's personal property as in a will, e.g., "Though in the earliest times the word testament was precisely defined and did not include real property, American law did not so distinguish, and so the expression 'last will and testament' has since been construed as ordering who should get what at the death of that testator."

thible, thibble: a slice, spatula, or a skimmer, e.g., "Many early inventories list slices and thibbles in association with other cooking utensils and objects." Also see ***peel*** in *What Did They Mean By That?*

thick neck: goiter, e.g., "Though not at all understood, Dr. Pierce seemed to know that iodine had something to do with this crippling scourge and suggested that it might be a circulatory problem. He wrote that it should be treated with 'electrolysis' and with 'Iodine one drachm, Iodide of potassium 4 drachms and 3 oz. of water mixed and applied on the surface of the enlargement twice a day with a feather or hair pencil.'"

thrumcloth: obsolete, it seems; cloth with tassels or loose ends left on the edges in the loom when woven; a decorative coverlet or what we know as a lightweight bedspread, e.g., "A few early New York inventories list thrumcloth."

tick fever: probably infection or Rocky Mountain Spotted Fever, e.g., "The appearance of a tick on the skin usually was of little concern, however occasionally the reddening of the area, followed by notes as to nausea, high fever, and some measure of delirium probably reveals what now we know as Rocky Mountain Spotted Fever."

tike: colonial to now, a common name for a little dog and often for a small child, usually a boy, e.g., "Shakespeare speaks of a dog named Tike."

timber cruiser: an experienced lumberman who could walk through a selected section of forest and assess the quantity and value of the timber to be recovered from that tract, e.g., "It was said that Darlene's husband was the best timber cruiser in Ohio."

timber, rive cut: See **rive, rive cut timber**.

timbrel, tabret: an ancient musical instrument, occasionally listed in colonial inventories, and well known in the Bible at, among other references, *Genesis*, 31:27; *Exodus*, 15:20; and *Judges*, 11:34, e.g., "At least three references to timbrels have been found in early Southern inventories."

tinder: wood shavings and very small thin pieces of wood used to start new, or build up almost dead fires, e.g., "Bethany's husband spent time every week or so creating shavings from small dry oak logs kept in the shed."

tinderbox: a small, usually wood or tin, sometimes lidded container for storing tinder, e.g., "Allison's wooden tinder box was kept under the steps to the cellar in order to keep the tinder dry."

tippet: a neck scarf early worn by the affluent of both sexes, usually by men, but by the nineteenth century, seemingly usually worn by women, e.g., "In Foxe's *Book of Martyrs*, and as also appears in several inventories of the early South, it was said that when he went to the scaffold Ridley wore '...a *tippet* of velvet furred likewise about his neck....'"

tipsy parson: See *trifle, etc.*

tipsy squire: See *trifle, etc.*

tissick: a painful and severe cough of which 455 people of 25,450 died in 1720; usually, consumption, see *What Did They Mean By That?*, *tuberculosis*, e.g., "Henry VII is said to have died in 1509 from '...great fits and labours of the tissick." See Bacon, *History of the reign of Henry VII*, p. 237. Also see ***death, causes of etc.***

tissue: Johnson, 1775, says "to interweave," e.g., "In 1802 the word tissue was used in an inventory as meaning a fabric interwoven with 'gold, silver or figured colors.'"

tite (tight) hogshead: a barrel capable of holding fluid, e.g., "There are numerous early inventory references to tite hogsheads, revealing that those were to be used for purposes of transporting and storing liquids such as rum, turpentine, and oils."

titles, charges and dowry troubles: an expression often found in early deeds and as a part of the warranties provided as to good title to the land conveyed, e.g., "In 1669 Miss Bethany agreed that her husband George Watkins might convey a tract of his land with a guarantee that the buyer would experience 'no dowry troubles.'"

tobacco bill: See ***bill, due bill***.

tobacco cask: See ***tobacco roller, etc.***

tobacco roller, tobacco cask: not a trade or occupation; a term used in describing the labor needed to move casks of tobacco to and from wharves, towns, plantations, warehouses, etc., e.g., "Tobacco being the most frequently traded raw material in the early old South, was transported in casks, usually weighing 550 pounds." Also see *cask* in *What Did They Mean By That?*

tobacco, seconds: See *clear from ground leaves or seconds.*

tooth rash: See *eczema.*

Tory: in America, the label given those citizens who favored the policies and reign of the sovereigns and opposed the Revolutionary War; those in opposition to the colonists who sought independence. See *Tories* in *What Did They Mean By That?*

touichole: probably corrupted French, and meaning "touchhole", e.g., A term found in seventeenth-century Massachusetts records referring to that small hole drilled into the breech of early guns or cannons, and into which gunpowder was poured, then a fire was touched to that powder, as found on ***matchlocks*** (q.v., in *What Did They Mean By That?*,), the powder ignited and the charge forced the projectile out of the barrel."

town and village courts: See *state court web sites.*

town-mark, town brand: a brand symbol; cattle usually displayed both the individual brands and the mark of the town from which cattle might escape, e.g., "Many New England towns had town-marks well known to neighboring communities, those having been necessary because cows and other cattle were scarcely fenced till the middle of the nineteenth century, and as frequently as were private brands in other colonies, so too were these recorded."

Townshend Duties: 1767 and following; some of the principle causes of the American Revolution, e.g., "These duties were *'external' taxes* (q.v.), and as was the ***Sugar Act*** (q.v.), the Townshend Duties were designed to raise revenue from our colonies through taxes at the point of departure of ships bound for here carrying products or raw materials such as tea, lead, paint, glass, or paper, all of which were vital to life and work here." Also see ***external taxes, internal taxes.***

townsman, town-born: meaning born in that community, e.g., "The term townsman was quite common in New England, even very early, but hardly heard in the Southern colonies."

Trade Winds: Barbados and the islands became a haven for early entrepreneurs and traders in water, sugar, and slaves, but also in ships' stores, pitch and repairs, sail material, rope and hemp, hardwoods, including such as mahogany, sugar, plants and herbs thought to have medicinal value, indentured servants, etc., e.g., "But for the Trade Winds travel to and fro and the advance of civilization in Europe, Britain, and the Americas would have proceeded much more slowly."

traffic courts: See ***state court web sites.***

trammel: a shackle for a horse; more often, a device with links or indents at varying heights for hanging pothooks and pots in a fireplace, e.g., "Changing the position of the pothooks on the trammel was the method by which the temperature of a pot or kettle was regulated."

travail, in: quite unlike now, that state of a woman during the period between the commencement of labor pains and the birth of the child, e.g., "Many early writings, including those of Ms. Haskins, spoke of women being in their travail."

trebucket: See ***cucking stool, tumbrel, etc.***

triad, adoption: See ***adoption, system, etc.***

Tribunal of Well-born men: See ***Well-born men, Tribunal of.***

trifle, tipsy parson, tipsy squire: a highly favored aperitif, especially in Virginia and the early South, made with eggs, milk, sugar and thick strawberry or cherry preserves, mixed with custard and sherry, e.g., "By reason of the high price of sherry and similar wines and alcoholic fruit drinks, only the more affluent of colonial Virginians served trifles on a regular basis."

trimmer: a ***yard locomotive*** (q.v.) specially used to operate in ***railroad yards*** (q.v.) and to add to or remove train cars from made up trains, e.g., "In March of 1944 the magazine *Trains* (p. 31) told of an emergency change of wheels on a troop train, that change requiring the use of a trimmer to cut the train." Also see ***locomotive.***

true act and deed: See ***reale act and deed.***

true bill: the signature of a Grand Jury, usually made by the foreman in its behalf and written or printed on an indictment, revealing that the decision of that jury is that the indictment should be considered true and the matter should proceed to trial, e.g., "Early indictments bearing the notation 'a true bill' usually were so endorsed with care and in a clear hand."

truncheon: sometimes, a club, but more often a staff or decorative light cudgeon representing a position of command or authority, e.g., "An early New England newspaper described an inscribed baton as a 'truncheon of the superintendent' of police."

tuberculosis, knee: See ***white swelling, etc.***

tumbrel: a dung cart, e.g., "Porter loaded his tumbrel every morning, went four miles to the city, and there sold the dung as fertilizer for gardens of rich families."

turn the road, turn a path: a frequent order of courts when roads were mere cart paths or bridle trails, and a landowner had permitted such to remain on his property, and now wished to till or otherwise use his land over which that path or road existed, e.g., "The Edgecombe County Court permitted Jesse Drake to turn that part of the *Meeting House Road* that passed over his pasture by moving it sixteen poles to the middle of his land and so laying it out that it rejoined the old path at his west property line."

tutor, tutrix, under-tutor: as now; in Louisiana, a person appointed by the court who has responsibility for a minor very much like a guardian; a 'tutrix' is an appointed female tutor; 'under-tutors' are persons appointed by a court under the statute and having authority to act in behalf of a child, should the child's interest conflict with that of the 'tutor,' e.g., "For genealogical purposes tutors in Louisiana may be considered the same as a child's guardian in other states."

twenty-four hour fever: See *diary fever*.

typhoid fever: See *typhus*.

typhus, typhoid fever, jail fever, pernicious fever, malignant fever, enteric fever: "In 1882 Dr. Walker believed that these diseases were all related, branded such simply as 'fevers,' and prescribed massive doses of quinine, tincture of aconite, alkaline sponge-baths, and a *concoction* (q.v., *What Did They Mean By That?*) of 'quinine sulfate, sulfuric acid, water and starch'!!"

U

unborn child: See *in ventre sa mere*.

***uncertainty of currency*;** especially following the American Revolution, many courts' orders and contractual arrangements carried this expression revealing the uncertainty of the future value of the currency to be used as the bargained or then current medium of settlement, e.g., "In February of 1780 John Stewart was ordered to pay Rebecca ____ for the care of his illegitimate son borne of her, '...the sum of £200 per year, that amount...for the current year and remain to further order therein as required by uncertainty of currency.'"

underbed: believed to be what we would call a mattress or bed pad, e.g., "The 1824 inventory of a Cole family reveals an underbed, yet also lists *ticking bags* (q.v., *What Did They Mean By That?*), indicating that the two were to be distinguished."

undivided interest: joint ownership of two or more people resulting from deeds, lawsuits, or estates by which one becomes an owner with others in land or other assets, and if created by other than the law of intestate estates, then quite usually granted or given over by virtue of the same document/instrument, e.g., "When Donna's widower father died intestate owning the 125 acre tract, she and her two brothers became owners, each of an undivided interest in that tract; they were joint tenants"; "When Evan died he devised to his 'surviving children' sixty-six acres of land, thereby creating for them undivided ownership by each in the whole tract."

unseated land: from Pennsylvania and other states, individually owned land that has not been, as Black's Law Dictionary says, tilled, cultivated, settled or made a place of residence, e.g., "Unseated land is considered as 'seated' when it is occupied by anyone who intends to use it as a residence." Also see *seated, etc.* in *What Did They Mean By That?*

uremia: See *nephritis*, etc., and see *Bright's disease* in *What Did They Mean By That?*

utter, uttering: as commonly used; in the law, meaning to offer up, send, or affect a trade or transfer of a check, note or negotiable instrument that is worthless or nearly so, e.g., "After passing many checks with insufficient funds in the bank, Jack was charged with "uttering a check in the amount of $260.00."

V

veil over her face, death veil, death pall: a term probably describing the pall that comes over a person at the point of imminent death, e.g., "Nurse Frances, though not having seen the effect, often heard those who had been at the bedside of the dying describe the appearance of those dying as 'there was a veil over her face.'" Also see *death rattle.*

vellum: calfskin prepared and shaved for writing as with paper, e.g., "While the differences have been largely ignored, in early times vellum was distinguished from parchment, the latter being of lamb, sheep, or goat."

venal: usually a purchase or sale of illegal or otherwise base or corrupt personal property, e.g., "The Alabama court commented that his possession of pornographic materials resulted from 'evil motives and venal trading.'"

vendable: any personal property that might legally be sold, e.g., "In 1695 a Virginia defendant named Shelley was said to have church items that were not vendable."

venditionas exponas: Latin, an often written order to a sheriff by a court directing that the sheriff offer for sale some specific property, e.g., "In 1858 the Bledsoe court issued a writ venditionas exponas that Sheriff Haskins sell Lamb's personal property to satisfy a debt."

venire facias de novo: an order by a court to a sheriff that he bring or cause to be brought a new venire of "good and lawful," qualified citizens in order, as in a venire facias, that they might be examined to the end that they serve on a jury, e.g., "In early times, the sheriff frequently questioned those on his venire in order to save time and efforts in bringing them to the court, determining their eligibility, and expediting the work of the court." Also see *venire, etc.* in *What Did They Mean By That?*

vested estate: an interest, usually in land, that carries with it the right of the owner to sell or transfer the same as and when he or she chooses, e.g., "At the death of her mother who had enjoyed a life estate on the farm, Gloria's remainder vested in her, and thereafter she was able to sell the land to whomever and whenever she chose." Also see *vest, vested, etc.* in *What Did They Mean By That?*

vestry, parish: in the American colonies, the seventeenth and eighteenth-century panel or board of men who controlled the business and financial activities and usually selected or rejected priests appointed to the parish of an Anglican Church, e.g., "Almost without exception, the parish vestries in the American colonies were made up of twelve leaders who were men of respect and some prominence within the parish."

vi et armis: Latin; by force of arms. See *strong hand, etc.*

vicar: early, one who acts as a substitute; now, an incumbent to an ecclesiastical office or position of benefit, e.g., "A vicar of Albemarle Parish was said to stand in line to be deacon."

victuallar, victuals: obsolete; rare, one who maintains a café that also serves alcoholic beverages, e.g., "An early twentieth-century Massachusetts case referred to the owner of a 'Dining Hall' as a victuallar and to the foods he served as victuals."

Village Courts: See *state court web sites.*

vinegar plant: small, usually one-family vinegar manufacturing facility, e.g., "A considerable number of early settlers maintained apple trees and a small vinegar plant, from which they could manufacture vinegar for pickling or for sale."

violent carbuncles: See *anthrax.*

virgate: an ancient and now obsolete term meaning twenty-five acres of land, e.g., "Many early English deed descriptions refer to virgates, however the term fell into disuse on this continent, since land was typically transferred in smaller or larger tracts." Also see **hide.**

Virginia Company, __ of London, __ of Plymouth: Not commonly known, yet important to all genealogical researchers of the seventeenth-century colonies, e.g., "During the first thirty years of settlement, citizens referred to what we know as New England as 'Plymouth Company' (*Virginia Company of Plymouth*) and they referred to what we know as the Virginia, North and South Carolina as 'London Company' (*Virginia Company of London*)."

vittles, vittals: slang for victuals. See *victuallar, victuals.*

viz.: abbreviation for the Latin, videlicit, meaning "namely," "in other words," or "is meant to say," e.g., "The grand jury returned a *true bill* (q.v.) in the matter of the charges against him, viz., a trial or other disposition will ensue."

voir dire: an examination of a juror by the court and the lawyers in a lawsuit, touching upon the juror's qualifications to be seated, e.g., "Upon voir dire it came to light that the prospective juror was very much prejudiced against Native Americans, so he was dismissed."

voiture, voiture et eight: a train carriage or a train car; the phrase adopted by the American Legion after World War I, referring to French train cars used during that war and capable of carrying eight horses and twenty soldiers in each, e.g., "In many American cities even to now, the Legion Posts have designed floats or vehicles inscribed 'voiture et eight' to be used in parades and ceremonies."

voltaic battery: See *galvanic battery, etc.*

voluntary respite: see *respite, etc.*

voting, early: voting varied among the colonies until the twenty-first century. Quite usually, ownership of the land of one's residence was required, and only men had the franchise. There was a religious component in every colony. Careful researchers will search the Internet under "voting" followed by the name of the colony or state in which the ancestor lived, e.g., "Generally, in early Virginia, white male citizens, twenty-one or over, owning or formally leasing at least twenty-five acres of land with a house measuring twelve feet square or more, and with some portion of the land broken to the plow, owning fifty acres of unimproved land, or having a town lot and house, were eligible to vote in the county where their home or land was situated." Also see *colonial government.*

vs., v.: abbreviation for the Latin "versus"; against and in opposition to, and found in virtually all lawsuit headings and citations of authority in writings, e.g., "Marbury vs. Madison, with its opinion written by the great Chief Justice John Marshal, is one of the most well known cases ever decided by the U.S. Supreme Court."

W

waft, wafting: to float anything on water, almost obsolete by the early eighteenth century; usually found in talk of transporting animals or people by raft, e.g., "The Surry reports of 1668 reveal that a man drowned as he was 'wafting a horse across Gray's Creek.'"

waif, waifs: personal property found that is claimed by no one after some period of time, and to be distinguished from *bona fugitiva* which are items of personal property belonging to or stolen and dropped or left behind by a fugitive from justice, e.g., "Early cases from Mississippi, New Jersey and New York were careful to distinguish between waifs and bona fugitiva."

wain scott, wainscot, wainscott chair: a chair so shaped that the top back touches the wall at wainscot height, e.g., "The 1664 Surry County, Virginia inventory of James Sowersby listed a 'wain scott chair' and 'one *tite hogshead* (q.v.).'"

waiter: aside from those who served others, waiters were saucers such as used under a cup of liquid, e.g., "William Cook's estate inventory listed *japanned* (q.v.) waiters."

waiver of administration: See *no asset administration.*

walk-ins: quite unlike now, the taking possession of the body of an infant at death by a separate and different soul, e.g., "Dr. Drake told of anecdotes wherein mothers could look into the eyes of a child thought dead at birth and know that the 'being that looked back at them was not the same soul.'"

wallplate, wall-plate tobacco house: a timber along the top of a wall to support the ends of joists, etc., and distribute the load; a building constructed with wallplates, e.g., "After the 'Great Gust' of 1667, an inventory of the loss on the Colledge (Coolidge) property in Surry revealed '3 Sixty foote wallplate tobb. Houses' and many other buildings that had been severely damaged or destroyed."

war dead of the U.S.: Not including the several Indian Wars of the latter half of the nineteenth century and the Mid-East and Iraq wars of the period 1990-2005, our dead in the major wars have been, American Revolution, 6,188; War of 1812, 4,505; Mexican War, 4,152; Civil War, 618,000+-; Spanish-American War, 2,446; World War I, 116,516; World War II, 405,399; Korea, 54,256; Vietnam, 58,167; Desert Storm, 293; approximate total, 1,250,000.

War of Canadian Independence of 1837: See *Patriot War of 1837.*

warped and wept, weft: warp and woof, or warp and weft; warp are the yarns that run lengthwise (up and down, or front to back) in the loom and are held taut during the weaving, and weft, wept or woof (commonly called weft) is that yarn that is woven across the warp threads to finish the cloth (stuff, fabric), e.g., "In 1845 a Philadelphia weaver advertised that he did 'warp and wept of cotton, silk, wool, zari (metal thread of gold or silver) or any other fiber yarn.'"

warping bars, warp bars: part of a loom over which ***bouts*** (q.v.) of thread or yarn are wrapped, e.g., "The 1862 Sarah Bradshaw inventory listed '2 warp bars' and a 'bundle of *bouts.'"

warrant of distress: See **distress, levy of, etc.**

warrant, alius: See ***alius dictus.***

warrant: of which there are many ordering various acts; generally a writing from one having authority over some other person or institution and directing that some action be taken or be forborne, e.g., "Just as an arrest warrant is an order to a sheriff by a court that someone be taken into custody, arrested or otherwise be required to act, a common bank check is a warrant directing that a bank pay money to a person named in the check as a payee."

waste: destruction or damage done to the property (usually land) of another by one who is legally on the property, e.g., "When Paul's lease tenant girdled and thereby killed the walnut trees that Paul had reserved, the court found the tenant to have committed waste and awarded damages in the reasonable value of the trees." Also see ***ameliorate, etc.***

water closet: usually a lavatory; commode; flushable toilet water reservoir, derived from the early placement in a closed space of the water bowl for the commode, e.g., "Since now we have no need for supplies of water in a lavatory other than through the plumbing system, the term water closet is almost forgotten."

water courts: See ***state court web sites.***

wax, sealing: See ***sealing wax*** and also see ***seal*** in *What Did They Mean By That?*

weft: See ***warped and weft.***

well laid on: a common expression of the early colonies and often found in courts' orders directing punishment; meant that the person assigned to administer punishment should not refrain from causing the intended pain, e.g., "In early Surry the sheriff was ordered to give James Ely '10 lashes well laid on' for having broken into 'into a chest of Thos. Clarys.'"

Well-Born Men, Tribunal of: a panel, first of twelve and then of nine men who in the seventeenth century had authority in New Amsterdam, first in such as criminal matters, and later also as to churches, schools, fortifications, and taxes, e.g., "For those of ancestry from Holland, yet in existence are many records of the Well-Born Men."

wept: See ***warped and weft.***

westward migration, supplies for: See ***migration west; supplies suggested.***

wheel lock or ***wheel-lock:*** See ***flintlock*** and ***matchlock*** in *What Did They Mean By That?*

wheel of cheese: a circular shaped block of cheese, early often weighing upwards of two to as many as six hundred pounds per wheel, e.g., "Gorgonzola cheese (quite similar in all ways to Bleu cheese) dates to the year 869 and is now made in wheels of eighteen to twenty-six pounds."

wheelage: those tolls collected for the use of a bridge, road, or right of way by men, animals and vehicles, e.g., "Since the earliest days, we have had toll roads and bridges, the majority of which were privately owned or maintained and the wheelage was intended to offset those costs."

wheezing conniption: usually laughter so intense that one gasps for breath; occasionally a reaction to sickness, emotions or sadness so intense as to bring the same effect, e.g., "Jane described her asthma attack as bringing her nearly to a wheezing conniption."

wherry: a light boat used for light hauling or transport of people on rivers in the early colonies, e.g., "There are many references to wherries in the early records, those used to ferry folks short distances up and down the rivers and bays of the east."

whip saw: early, a very common saw with a blade in a frame, similar to what we now know as a hack saw, usually having a blade for cutting wood, e.g., "A whipsaw was among those items thought most necessary for a family traveling to the frontier by wagon." See ***migration west, etc.***

whipping boy: though the appearance of such is extremely rare and the reports perhaps more often spurious than not, to have a boy for that purpose is said to have occurred, e.g., "It is written that Negro boys of similar age to a son of a white family were whipped for the mischief of the white youngster, those Blacks being known as the whipping boys."

the 26 1759

State I have taken the Body of

and Comitted him to his Majesties

Sam'l Chipman and D'o Sheriff

Servus Cappus 6/8

...t he has jailed a person by order of a court. See *warrant*.

white leg: probably loss of circulation in the legs and resulting from temporary loss of circulation by reason of blood clots or other circulatory blockage and apparently once common in women immediately after childbirth, e.g., "During the Civil War years Dr. Drake prescribed an imaginative mixture of one-half ounce each of blue flag root, prince's-pine, tag alder, burdock, and yellow dock root, one quart of 'good whisky,' one quart of cold water, and one pound of sugar, that blend to be administered one tablespoonful twenty minutes before each meal."

white man's flies: See *honeybees.*

white mule: See **corn whisky** in *What Did They Mean By That?*

white swelling, hydrathras, synovitis, strumous synavitis, knee tuberculosis: swelling of the flesh around large joints such as shoulders, elbows, and especially the knee joints that appears almost white and has no characteristic pink or flesh coloring; some have suggested blood clots, e.g., "It is likely that the 'white swelling' Dr. Drake diagnosed, and for which he prescribed warmth and various mixtures applied locally was a loss of blood circulation at the knee joint."

White-caps, Tillman's White-caps, White-capping: white men who rode and raided at night in many areas of the South from the years 1885-1900, were identifiable by their white caps, and who terrorized Black farmers, recently freed Blacks, and tobacco growers in Kentucky, e.g., "Tennessee, Alabama, North Carolina, and Mississippi all well knew the White-caps, those being states where the raids were the most prevalent."

whites: See *leucorrea, etc.*

Whitsunday: See *perambulation, etc.*

Whitsuntide: the "feast" (celebration) of the Pentecost, e.g., "While several English celebrations were present in Virginia and other colonies, that of Whitsuntide seems not to appear in the records after the beginning of the American Revolution."

whortleberries, hurtle berries: common blackberries, e.g., "Many early recipes of the Northeast refer to a dessert or sweet dish as requiring whortleberries."

Winchester measure: a very early measure from Winchester, England and found in Virginia and North Carolina, among other colonies, and being eight gallons equal to one bushel, e.g., "An early court report from North Carolina speaks of forty gallons as equal to five bushels."

wind colic: See *appendicitis.*

winding sheet: a long sheet or several sewed together, usually of bleached cloth and used to wind around a body in mummy style, e.g.,

"An early North Carolina estate inventory listed a winding sheet, perhaps indicating that some member of the household was near death or had survived near death."

winnoclothe, winnowcloth: apparently now unknown, e.g., "A fabric or cover found in at least two seventeenth-century New England inventories in association with bedroom furniture and with *thrumcloth* (q.v.)."

winter fever, January fever: any of the several severe congestive afflictions of the lungs or chest that were and remain common, e.g., "Though her daughter stated that Margo's sister had choked and died of winter fever, the cause probably would now likely be labeled pneumonia."

wire nails: See *cut nails, square nails.*

Witch of Wall Street: See *Hetty Green, etc.*

with prejudice, settled: meaning prejudiced against asserting or bringing the same claim again, e.g., "When a lawsuit is settled or otherwise ended and the conclusion extinguishes the claim, or the claimant agrees that in exchange for a settlement he will not again have the right to sue, the case is said to be settled with prejudice."

withe: a willow switch, e.g., "Several early colonial writings have been found revealing mothers and school masters who punished children by the administration of a 'heavy withe.'"

wizard, hedge wizard: Johnson (1802) says, "an enchanter, a he witch, a conjuror"; a man who practiced witchcraft; "hedge wizards" were those who practiced witchcraft with no training in the "black arts," e.g., "Indians of the Onondaga tribes of the North believed their campaigns to defeat their Iroquois enemies were continually blocked by the evil wizard, *Tadodaho*, an Onondaga who ruled through fear of his wrath."

woods colt: an illegitimate child; derived from the reference to colts born of a mare that wandered off and was bred by an unknown stallion, e.g., "Carolyn and Veronica recalled that illegitimate boys were regularly called woods colts."

woods goat: See *woods girl.*

Woods girl, woods goat: a young woman supposedly promiscuous and of low morals as revealed by her willingness to have sexual encounters anywhere, including in a woods, e.g., "Audra was widely known as a woods girl and was snubbed by the women of the town."

woof: See *warped and weft.*

wool sorters' disease: See *anthrax.*

wool, a pack: See *pack of wool.*

wool, grease: See *grease wool.*

wool, loden: See *loden.*

woompompeak: See *peake, woompompeak, and Roanoke.*

work clothes: as now; the apparel of days when one was working in the farm fields or away from home, e.g., "His work clothes for winter days consisted of a wool coat and *jersey* (q.v.) gloves, *long johns* (q.v., *What Did They Mean By That?*), pants of *oznaburg* (q.v.), wool socks, and a shirt of wool flannel."

Workers' Compensation Courts: See *state court web sites.*

wrangle, wrangler: unlike now, to be peevish or quarrelsome, defined in 1755 by Johnson as "disputative," e.g., "Though Don's cattle drovers now are known as wranglers, for centuries that term had different meanings."

writ ne exeat: See *ne exeat, etc.*

writ, alius: See *alius dictus.*

writ: an order of a court, or other body having power to so issue, directing that some action be taken, ended or prevented, e.g., "The 1765 Sussex County writ directed that John Hines be taken into custody, however the sheriff noted on the back of the writ, 'He would not be taken.'" It is interesting that throughout the period 1600 even to now, writs were and are not to be served on Sundays."

writs of assistance, Revolutionary War: those most hated orders from courts and royal governors that permitted officers of the Crown to enter houses and businesses to search for whatever might be found, rendering the ancient proposition that "a man's home is his castle" only empty words, e.g., "Unlike the law to which they had been accustomed for centuries, commencing in 1771 it was not required that writs of assistance state the objects of the search nor at what place in the house or business such objects were supposed to be located."

wyne: wine; See *bulies, sloos.*

Y

yard locomotive: a *locomotive* (q.v.) used to move cars to and fro in an area of a railroad facility where trains are made up, e.g., "Carl often was called to work as an engineer of the yard locomotives at Marion." Also see *locomotive* and see *trimmer.*

yellow fever, American plague: See *calenture* in *What Did They Mean By That?*

yprocras: See *hippocras.*

yspareunia: See *anaphrodisia.*

Z

zari: See *warped and weft.*